Applied Cross-Cultural Data Analysis
for Social Work

POCKET GUIDES TO
SOCIAL WORK RESEARCH METHODS

Series Editor
Tony Tripodi, DSW
Professor Emeritus, Ohio State University

Applied Cross-Cultural
Data Analysis
for Social Work

Thanh V. Tran

and

Keith T. Chan

OXFORD
UNIVERSITY PRESS

OXFORD
UNIVERSITY PRESS

Oxford University Press is a department of the University of Oxford. It furthers
the University's objective of excellence in research, scholarship, and education
by publishing worldwide. Oxford is a registered trade mark of Oxford University
Press in the UK and certain other countries.

Published in the United States of America by Oxford University Press
198 Madison Avenue, New York, NY 10016, United States of America.

© Oxford University Press 2021

Library of Congress Cataloging-in-Publication Data
Names: Tran, Thanh V., author. | Chan, Keith T., author.
Title: Applied cross-cultural data analysis for social work /
Thanh V. Tran, Keith T. Chan.
Description: New York, NY : Oxford University Press, 2021. |
Series: Pocket guides to social work research methods |
Includes bibliographical references and index. |
Identifiers: LCCN 2021003188 (print) | LCCN 2021003189 (ebook) |
ISBN 9780190888510 (paperback) | ISBN 9780190888541 (epub) |
ISBN 9780190888527 (digital-online)
Subjects: LCSH: Social work with minorities—United States—Methodology. |
Cultural awareness—United States—Methodology. |
Social service—Research—Methodology. | Quantitative research—Methodology.
Classification: LCC HV3176 .T7138 2021 (print) | LCC HV3176 (ebook) |
DDC 361.3072/7—dc23
LC record available at https://lccn.loc.gov/2021003188
LC ebook record available at https://lccn.loc.gov/2021003189

DOI: 10.1093/oso/9780190888510.001.0001

1 3 5 7 9 8 6 4 2

Printed by Marquis, Canada

*To my family: Uyen-Sa D. T. Nguyen, Minh-Y. T. Tran, and
Dai-Chi T. Tran.*

—Thanh V. Tran

*To my family by blood and by fate, who are too many to name. We are
connected through our resolve to keep learning, keep listening, and
passing on what we know to help make the world a better place.*

—Keith T. Chan

Contents

Acknowledgments

The writing of this book was a labor of love, supported by many people and organizations that made this possible.

* * *

Thanks to Dean Gautam Yamada of Boston College School of Social Work for his support and thanks to Boston College for granting me a sabbatical leave to work on this project. I also acknowledge the former students of my cross-cultural measurement class who inspire me to learn and to continue to search for better approaches to study cross-cultural issues in social work.

Thanh V. Tran

* * *

Thanks to Dean Mary Cavanaugh, the Silberman School of Social Work at Hunter College and my funders for supporting my research, the Health and Aging Policy Fellows Program, the NIH National Institute of Minority Health and Health Disparities Loan Repayment Program, the Rutgers University Asian Resource Centers for Minority Aging Research Center (under NIH/NIA Grant P30-AG0059304), the John A. Hartford Foundation, and the Council on Social Work Education Minority Fellowship Program.

Keith T. Chan

1

Introduction to Applied Cross-Cultural Data Analysis

Applied cross-cultural data analysis comprises theoretical orientations, frameworks, and techniques for examining and interpreting
data for cultural group comparisons. This book aims to provide practical
strategies for cross-cultural data analysis for students and researchers
from social work and other human service disciplines. Culture is a complex concept that encompasses human and societal dimensions; it has
been defined by the United Nations Educational, Scientific and Cultural
Organization (**UNESCO**) as "the set of distinctive spiritual, material,
intellectual and emotional features of society or a social group, and that
it encompasses, in addition to art and literature, lifestyles, ways of living
together, value systems, traditions and beliefs" (http://unesdoc.unesco.
org/images/0012/001271/127162e.pdf). Cross-cultural analysis requires
a systematic approach to compare common aspects of human life such
as economic, educational, health, psychological, and social phenomena.
Researchers from sociology and anthropology have examined cultural
differences through various lenses, such as the East–West dichotomy

Applied Cross-Cultural Data Analysis for Social Work. Thanh V. Tran and Keith T. Chan,
Oxford University Press. © Oxford University Press 2021. DOI: 10.1093/oso/9780190888510.003.0001

(Ojalehto & Medin, 2015), the cultural values framework (Schwartz & Sagiv, 1995), individualism and collectivism (Hofstede, 2001), and other cross-cultural models (Minkov & Hofstede, 2013). Within the discipline of cross-cultural psychology, there is an emphasis on examining etic and emic approaches to study cultures. An *etic view* of a culture can be described as the perspective of an outsider looking in. An example may be social work researchers who study the acculturation of an immigrant community in the United States, though they are not a member of that community. An example of an *emic view* of culture would be when a social work researcher is a member of a cultural and/or ethnic community and studying the acculturation of their own community into the American mainstream (Morris Leung, Ames, & Lickel, 1999).

We concur with the view held by the American Anthropology Association (AAA) on culture, which asserts that:

> Human cultural behavior is learned, conditioned into infants beginning at birth, and always subject to modification. No human is born with a built-in culture or language. Our temperaments, dispositions, and personalities, regardless of genetic propensities, are developed within sets of meanings and values that we call culture. Studies of infant and early childhood learning and behavior attest to the reality of our cultures in forming who we are. (AAA, 1998)

Building on this, we argue that persons born into various identified social groups (e.g., those belonging to race, national origin, gender, class, or religion) may learn different cultural behaviors specific to their social groups. Moreover, persons from different identified social groups within a society may interpret and react differently to a common social behavior or cultural norm.

In this book we approach cross-cultural analysis by drawing from key demographic variables such as countries of origin, race, ethnicity, language, sex, religion, and related cultural identifications. The assumption is that people who share the same cultural identification also share similar values and behaviors. This is important for social workers and human service professionals in understanding individuals' life experiences and the circumstances that influence their well-being. Cross-cultural analyses and comparisons "can range from those on a global scale (e.g., East–West); to cross-national analyses; to within-nation cultural contrasts; or even to within-culture differences linked to socio-economic class, religious affiliation, age, or gender . . . and that significant cultural differences also distinguish groups within nations and societies" (Ojaleho & Medin, 2015, p. 252; Stephens et al., 2014). Cross-cultural comparisons also can be done within a small community in a confined geographical area based on important cultural markers that are relevant to outcomes of health and psychological well-being (Ojalehto & Medin, 2015). It is also important to identify certain aspects of culture that may be universal for most if not all groups of human beings. For instance, past evidence has found that in cross-national research, some universality of value meanings persisted even though unique cultural variations were apparent in almost all nations (Schwartz & Bilsky, 1990; Schwartz & Sagiv, 1995).

Altogether, frameworks from multiple disciplines and theoretical perspectives have provided useful tools for cross-cultural research development. From the perspective of cross-cultural psychology, Triandis (1996) developed a conceptual framework to address cultural similarities and differences for blended social systems where patterns of shared attitudes, beliefs, categorizations, self-definitions, norms, role differences, and values are organized in themes that can be identified among those who speak different languages. Through a different lens, McCrae (2004) emphasized that human nature and culture relate to the individual within a society through personality and cultural interpretations in cross-cultural research. Schwartz and Bilsky (1990) focused on human values and specific types of value contents or motivational domains (e.g., achievement, enjoyment, maturity, prosocial, restrictive conformity, security, and self-direction). Hofstede and Soeters (2002) homed in on work-related values to conceptualize and categorize cross-cultural similarities and differences across nations. "Power Distance" labeled as the first dimension, is defined as the degree of inequality among people which the population of a country considers to be normal. "Uncertainty Avoidance" is defined as the degree to which people in a country prefer structured (clear rules on how one should behave) over unstructured situations (flexibility in how one behaves; Hofstede & Soeters, 2002). Some cross-cultural researchers emphasized the dichotomy of "Individualism vs. Collectivism" as the guide to examining cross-cultural differences. Others looked at the dichotomy of "Masculinity vs. Femininity" to study social roles across cultural groups. Recent theory development has begun to integrate multiple perspectives and markers for examining culture in research. The "cultural mosaic" framework conceptualizes how demographic (age, gender, race), geographic (climate, temperature, regional/country), and associative features (family, religion, profession) relate to culture (Chao & Moon, 2005).

In this book we focus on the application of a number of statistical approaches that can be used to perform cross-cultural comparisons. Thus, we emphasize the utilization of these statistical approaches, rather than their statistical theories or technical aspects of statistical computations. Our position is that variables that can be used as proxies of cultural identification such as race, ethnicity, sex, religion, and so forth, should be viewed as independent variables or moderator variables and not as confounding nor controlling variables. It is through this lens that we present the contents of the book for applied cross-cultural data analysis.

The book is organized into six key chapters as follows.

Chapter 1 addresses the concepts of culture and how culture and the implications of culture can be integrated into social work practice and research.

Chapter 2 discusses the evolution of cross-cultural research in the twentieth century.

Chapter 3 demonstrates and illustrates the application of Stata statistical software for descriptive statistics for the purposes of cross-cultural comparisons.

Chapter 4 demonstrates and illustrates the use of ordinary least squares (OLS) regression in cross-cultural analysis. We begin with examples using simple regression, and explain the key statistical concepts and assumptions of regression analysis. For our examples in the application of multiple regression analysis, we emphasize the use of interaction analysis for cross-cultural comparisons. We demonstrate the use of techniques from seemingly unrelated estimation to compare regression coefficients across cross-cultural models. We demonstrate a brief application of mediation analysis in cross-cultural analysis. In addition to these approaches, we introduce the use of Zellner's Seemingly Unrelated Regression (SUR) to handle analyses with two and three dependent variables or to examine two regression models with the same dependent variable but different independent variables.

Chapter 5 demonstrates and illustrates the use of logistic regression analysis for the purposes of cross-cultural analysis. This chapter demonstrates how to estimate the odds and odds ratio to further explain the meanings of these important concepts in logistic regression. In addition, we illustrate the application of multiplicative and additive interaction in cross-cultural research. With respect to additive interaction or biological interaction, we believe that this topic has not been adequately explored in social work research.

Chapter 6 demonstrates and illustrates the use of Structural Equation Modeling (SEM) to compare path models across two or more cultural groups. SEM can be used to test the goodness of fit of a causal model, as well as testing equivalence of causal relationships among variables of interests across different cultural groups. We demonstrate the use SEM through the use of Stata for these purposes with data from the Children of Immigrants Longitudinal Study (CHILS).

Chapter 7 demonstrates and illustrates the application of HLM in cross-cultural research. This method of analysis has not been sufficiently explored in social work research, but it can be a highly useful and appropriate statistical approach for making cross-cultural comparisons. We demonstrate the use of HLM by examining race, geography, disability, and income using data from New York City.

Chapter 8 discusses some of the aims we wanted to address, along with limitations and future directions.

REFERENCES

AAA. (1998). Statement on race. Retrieved from http://www.americananthro.org/ConnectWithAAA/Content.aspx?ItemNumber=2583

Chao, G. T., & Moon, H. (2005). The cultural mosaic: A metatheory for understanding the complexity of culture. *Journal of Applied Psychology, 90*(6), 1128–1140.

Hofstede, G. (2001). *Culture's consequences: Comparing values, behaviors, and organizations across nations* (2nd ed.). Thousand Oaks, CA: Sage Publications.

Hofstede, G. H., & Soeters, J. (2002). Consensus societies with their own character: National cultures in Japan and the Netherlands. *Comparative Sociology, 1*(1), 1–16.McCrae, R. R. (2004). Human nature and culture: A trait perspective. *Journal of Research on Personality, 38*, 3–14.

Minkov, M., & Hofstede, G. H. (2013). *Cross-cultural analysis: The science and art of comparing the world's modern societies and their cultures*. Los Angeles, CA: Sage.

Morris, M. W., Leung, K., Ames, D., & Lickel, B. (1999). Views from inside and outside: Integrating emic and etic insights about culture and justice judgment. *Academy of Management Review, 24*(4), 781–796.

Ojalehto, B. L., & Medin, D. L. (2015). Perspectives on culture and concepts. *Annual Review of Psychology, 66*, 249–275.

Schwartz, S. H., & Bilsky, W. (1990). Toward a theory of the universal content and structure of values: Extensions and cross-cultural replications. *Journal of Personality and Social Psychology, 58*(5), 878–891.

Schwartz, S. H., & Sagiv, L. (1995). Identifying culture specifics in the content and structure of values. *Journal of Cross-Cultural Psychology, 26*(1), 92–116.

Stephens, N. M., Markus, H. R., & Phillips, L. T. (2014). Social class culture cycles: how three gateway contexts shape selves and fuel inequality. *Annual Review of Psychology, 65*, 611–634.

Triandis, H. C. (1996). The psychological measurement of cultural syndromes. *American Psychologist, 51*(4), 407–4150.

2

Culture and Social Work

*Alejandra Pallamar & Sanjee Dahal**

In this chapter, we investigate the concepts of culture and explore the role that culture plays in contemporary social work practice. This chapter highlights the historical construction of the concept of culture from 1990 to 2000 and contemporary understanding of culture across disciplines. We explore the idea of culture in anthropological research, in sociological research, and in the fields of psychology and communication. Considering the expansion of market in all spheres of life, the chapter will examine how social work intersects with other disciplines to look at culture and consider cross-cultural issues. We link the importance of the role of culture in the field of social work.

*Alejandra Pallamar & Sanjeev Dahal, PhD Students, School of Social Work, Boston College. This chapter is the product of the authors' work from Professor Thanh V. Tran's Cross-Cultural Measurement Course

Applied Cross-Cultural Data Analysis for Social Work. Thanh V. Tran and Keith T. Chan, Oxford University Press. © Oxford University Press 2021. DOI: 10.1093/oso/9780190888510.003.0002

GENERAL CONCEPT OF CULTURE

The concept of culture is central to contemporary social sciences and has become prevalent and integrated into everyday language. This centrality and prevalence add to the complexity of culture due to its broad scope, multiplicity of definitions, and the controversies that has accompanied its development.

Kroeber and Kluckhohn found 164 different variables related to culture as early as 1952. After more than a century of efforts by anthropologists to define culture, it remains a polemic concept (Spencer-Oatey, 2012). Lang (1997) states that attempts to define culture unequivocally and definitively are useless and unattainable. Some have said that it is a useless concept (Barber, 2008), others have argued that it is not only useless, but negative, because it is a way to simplify and classify human life forms: "the concept of culture retains some of the tendencies to freeze the difference that concepts such as race have" (Abu-Lughod, 1991, p. 144). On the contrary, authors such as Brumann (1999) advocate the use of the term culture. Jahoda (2012) and Sewell (2005) propose that it is a fundamental and indispensable concept. They call, however, for respecting the complexity of the concept and for using it in a contextualized manner, that is, explaining the specific way in which it is used and being aware of the impossibility of addressing it completely.

A practical approach in defining culture was proposed by Minkov (2013), wherein "culture can be pragmatically defined by the contents and boundaries of the interests of the scholars who study it . . . . Defining the contents and boundaries of culture may also be necessary for the purposes of clarity and avoidance of confusing statements" (p. 10). Although it is fundamental to create clear boundaries and explicit definitions of culture, we should be aware of both the impossibility of a comprehensive picture of the concept and of the relevant implications in selecting one or another theory for definition or operationalization (Minkov, 2013; Jahoda, 2012).

In the multiplicity of the concept we can recognize differences in epistemological, theoretical, and methodological approaches. Some classifications of these various approaches are: Culture as Subjective (mind, mental) versus Objective culture (institution, artifact); Culture as a System of Behaviors versus culture as a Set of Meanings; Culture as Independently Existing Phenomenon versus Subjective Human Construct (Minkov, 2013).

Debates around the concept of culture can express legitimate conceptual differences, though this has contributed to a lack of clarity in various uses of the word and its meaning. Two broad yet distinctive definitions of the term have been found, ranging from abstract to concrete (Sewell, 2005). The former is the notion of culture as an abstract aspect of social life, different from other social concepts such as society, economy, art, or politics. The discussion at this more general level concerns the understanding of a conceptual object when we study culture as an aspect of social life, and what should be included or excluded in its definition and when conducting observations. The latter notion refers to a specific, concrete, and more or less identifiable group or community that has meaning from the present or the past. In this lens, we are interested in understanding beliefs and practices of people bounded in space (real or virtual) and in time. The emphasis is on the particularities, differences, or similarities in beliefs and practices of a specific subpopulation set, for example, older adults who are retired and living alone in the United States, African American educators working in K–12 public schools, the emerging middle-class of young and middle-aged adults in Ethiopia, migrant workers from various countries in South America, or indigenous persons from rural communities in Alaska.

History of Culture as an Academic Concept

In this section, we discuss the history of culture as an academic concept, with focus on developments in the twentieth century. We identify key concepts and ways of understanding culture in across various decades from 1900 to 2000.

1900–1920: Culture as General Evolution or Particularism

Although culture has been studied and examined since antiquity, most academic exploration into the definitions of culture appeared in the nineteenth century. These definitions emphasized the idea of cultivation through education. Initial definitions of culture were conceived from an elitist perspective, wherein culture was associated with "high culture" such as artistic and intellectual achievements (Arnolds, 1867). This is aligned with the perspective of Greco-Roman classical culture, which also was highlighted in periods of the Western Renaissance (Spencer-Oatey, 2012). Edward Burnett Tylor (1871) provided the first anthropological definition of culture, where "Culture or Civilization, taken in its wide ethnographic sense, is that complex whole which includes knowledge, belief, art, morals, custom, and any other capabilities and habits acquired by man as a member of society."

Franz Boas's theory of historical particularism (1920), which emphasized cultural relativism contrasted with the evolutionist position of high culture. He posited that nonculture has value beyond high culture, and that it is impossible to classify cultural aspects as "humane nature." He further asserted that cultural aspects can assume meaning within the context of interrelated elements internal to a specific culture, and that behaviors are not biologically based but are acquired through learning. For Boas, each culture represents a particular form of being human, which deserves respect and protection if threatened (Cuché, 1966). Boas's theories of culture strongly influence the work of many of his students, which include noted anthropologists such as Margaret Mead, Ruth Benedict, and Alfred Kroeber (Moore, 2012).

1930–1940: Culture as Patterns, Functionality, and Social Structures

Ruth Benedict (1934) built on theories of culture from Boas and introduced the concept of "cultural pattern." Each culture has a singular configuration of elements, such as a style or model, with a coherent gestalt configuration that shapes beliefs and actions. Benedict posited that these wide patterns were inclusive though limiting, and the work of cultural anthropologists is to provide nuanced and contextualized descriptions for all possible types of cultural patterns (Cuche, 1966). Benedict observed that there was consistency in culture and cultural patterns existed "as bounded wholes" (McGee & Warms, 2013). Margaret Mead (1935) in her investigation of culture emphasized how culture is transmitted among individuals and how they are incorporated into culture as domains. Her research highlighted the process of socialization and transmission through the influence of educational institutions on personality development.

During this decade, functionalist theory dominated the conceptual landscape of culture. Bronislaw Malinowski (1944) posited that culture was a complex system created through the functional fulfillment of biological, psychological, and social needs (Moore, 2012). Malinowski saw institutions as the central element of culture, which represented a collective solution to satisfy the individual's needs in society. For Malinowski, the focus in anthropological scholarship was placed in the study of the relations between the needs of an individual and the satisfaction of those needs through cultural and social frameworks (Barnard, 2000). Furthermore, each social institution can be understood by the function it performs as part of the whole, thereby all integrated units cannot be understood as isolated elements. The centrality of universal human needs (nutrition, reproduction, bodily comforts, safety, relaxation, movement, and growth) as part of how culture should be understood was hotly debated among anthropological scholars (McGee & Warms, 2013; Stanlaw, 2006).

Critical of functionalist frameworks, Radcliffe-Brown developed a structural-functionalist perspective through inspiration from the seminal sociological scholarship of Durkheim. While Malinowski's functionalism emphasizes the primacy of individual needs as the origin of social institutions, Radcliffe-Brown gives supremacy to institutions over individuals, and emphasized the importance of social structure (McGee & Warms, 2013). Through a structural-functionalist lens, culture is viewed as comprising social structures that are regularized and observable in their social forms, with repeated patterns of relations between individuals (Kupfer, 2015). Structural-functionalism focused on the observation of *real structures* (daily life, role, status, positions) and formal structures (norms, rules, and customs; Gaona, 2007). Whereas functionalism is concerned with individual action and needs (Eriksen & Nielsen, 2013; Barnard, 2000), the primary concern of structural-functionalism is the place of individuals within a social order and the coadaptation of institutions to maintain society as a coherent system.

1950–1960: Cultures as Environmental Adaptation, Regularities, Norms, and Values

As a continuation of functionalist theory, Leslie White (1959) and Julian Steward (1972) presented the neoevolutionary framework for examining culture. In contrast to Malinowsky, White argued that culture was suprabiological. Although initially rooted in the biology of humans needs, culture was external to the body and comprises technological, sociological, and ideological elements. Their scholarship examined the functions of culture to fulfill the environmental needs of the society rather than the needs of individuals (Moberg, 2012).

Neoevolutionist scholars were highly interested in how human groups adjusted to their environments through technology, food, and energy production. From this perspective, social systems and cultural patterns arise out of resource exploitation and technological adaptation of a cultural group to its natural environment (McGee & Warms, 2013). They examined the impact of this adaptation in regard to similarities and differences in long-term historical trajectories (Moberg, 2012; Moore, 2012). White viewed culture as a pattern of evolution related to the efficiency of adaptations and adjustment, wherein a culture becomes increasingly advanced and complex through technological breakthroughs. An example of this would be the advent of the Industrial Revolution, which led to upheavals in culture and the development of culture. It is important to note that despite an assertion of evolution and progress, neoevolutionist scholars rejected that there was one singular and universal pattern of development across cultures. Specifically, Steward bridged neoevolutionism and Boas's historical particularism by "dismissing the idea that all cultures progress through the same stages of evolution—opting instead for a multilinear evolutionary perspective—while criticizing historical particularism for ignoring the linkage between culture and environment" (Moore, 2012, p. 174). This framework laid the foundations of "Cultural Ecology," which emphasized the relationships between society and the environmental context, asserting that the strategies used by societies in their adaptations to the environment will strongly influence culture (Sutton & Anderson, 2010).

Claude Lévy Strauss (1963) examined culture in research through yet another lens. He did not emphasize particularism, instead focusing on the universal meaning of human culture. Rather than examining what made cultural groups different, he honed in on what made them similar. In other words, the emphasis was on cultural invariance rather than cultural variance. Such a perspective, with a focus on cultural invariance, can be described as cultural structuralism (Cuche, 1966). Claude Lévy-Strauss argued that the human mind was an invariant structure in organizing knowledge, as seen in the regularities of language structure, a structuring that operates similarly throughout human culture (Kuper, 1999).

During this decade, conceptualizations of culture based in unitary, homogeneous, as well as discrete characteristics were challenged and counterchallenged. The position of Lévy Strauss and his adherents is that cultural units are not isolated units and the interaction of human groups is evident across different scales (Fernández de Rota, 2009). In addition, Edmund Leach posited that social and cultural reality can never form a coherent whole, and it is fragmentary and inconsistent by nature (Fernández de Rota, 2009).

By 1958, Kroeber and Parsons differentiated the concepts of culture and society, and thus formalized a delimitation on the objects of study of anthropology and sociology (Gable & Handler, 2008; Turk, 1962). Culture was then defined as "transmitted and created content and patterns of values, ideas, and other symbolic-meaningful systems as factors in the shaping of human behavior" (Kroeber & Parsons, 1958, p. 583). From this perspective, the focus of sociology became centered on the relationship between culture and society. Society was defined as patterns of social interaction, patterns of behaviors, and institutions. Culture was instead understood as the system of meaning containing abstractions of values, ideas, beliefs, and norms, and from these abstractions came more concrete patterns of action and interaction. Values guide and drive action, whereby cultural context (values consensus) determines (or strongly influences) social life, social interaction, and social relationships (Gable & Handler, 2008).

1960–1970: Culture as a Text

From mid-1960 to the mid-1970s, the discussion on culture was shaped by "symbolic and interpretive anthropology." This framework can be viewed as an opposition to materialist, positivist, and objective approaches on the study of culture (McGee & Warms, 2013).

One of the most influential exponents of the American interpretative approach was Clifford Geertz (1973), who was influenced by semiotic, interpretative, and hermeneutic philosophy. His main focus of interest comprised meaning, significance, symbols, signs, and cognition (Beldo, 2010; Eriksen & Nielsen, 2013). He viewed culture as a cognitive symbolic system, where "complex webs of significance and meanings (were) constructed through the interaction with and creation of meanings and signs" (Sewell, 2005, p. 239).

Geertz approached culture as being "semiotic but not structuralist" (Barker, 2004). He described cultural studies as the investigation of the role of ideas in human practice. The main questions are concerned with how people create meaning and interpret themselves and their own experiences within their culture, rather than how meanings create subjects (McGee & Warms, 2013). Given that meanings are polysemic and ambiguous (many interpretations are possible), the role of the researcher is not to explain culture but to read or interpret it, similar to a text, and the interpretation of culture is the interpretation of narrative rather than experimentation through the scientific method. This should be done methodologically by "thick descriptions," which provide rich, detailed descriptions in the observation of cultures through social life (Birx, 2010; Barker, 2004; McGee & Warms, 2013).

Geertz as a predecessor of postmodernist stance asserted that a researcher's interpretation of culture does not reveal a complete truth because it is impossible to be fully immersed and observant as a nonmember of a culture. He challenged the authoritative point of view of the researcher, which is limited because it is foreign and external. His theories allowed for considerations of reflexivity and the consciousness of the role of the researcher in the process (Birx, 2010; Trias i Valls & Roula, 2009).

Critics of the relativist perspectives have challenged the notion that investigations of culture should be viewed as interpretations of narrative, and assert that this view ignores history, social structures, conflict, action, and issues of power in the process of meaning construction (Austin, 1979; David, 2010; Ross, 2004). Despite these criticisms, postmodernist frameworks have influenced contemporary conceptualizations of culture and its development within many social science disciplines (Beldo, 2010; Sewell, 2005). Other influential scholars of this period include David Schneider (1968), who defines culture as "definitions, premises, postulates, presumptions, propositions, and perceptions about the nature of the universe and man's place in it" (p. 202), which reflects these frameworks.

1980–1990: Culture as Struggle and Resistance

During this decade, the study of culture grew exponentially within multiple academic fields and disciplines (e.g., literature, history, sociology, art, political science) and was described as a "kind of academic culture mania" (Sewell, 2005, p. 36). Cultural studies became a consolidated approach in this period. Originally developed in the 1960s in England (Birmingham Center for Contemporary Cultural Studies), a blossoming of cultural studies was extended to many other countries during the 1980s (Walton, 2013).

Scholars such as Richard Hoggart and Stuart Hall understood culture in the context of a theory of social dominance, hegemony, and reproduction. Culture is seen as a place of struggle, between dominant values and resistant values, such that "cultural forms served either to further social domination, or to enable people to resist and struggle against domination" (Kellner, 2001, p. 396). The framework embraced a radical antielitist approach with respect to culture, focusing on the effects of oppression, which permeated through subcultures, popular practices, everyday life, sociocultural hierarchies, and institutional dominance (Rowe, 2017).

Three French Poststructuralist scholars in particular had a transdisciplinary impact on this trend: Lacan, Derrida, and Foucault. Poststructuralists do not seek to categorize human culture through the identification of atemporal and general regularities. They view culture as complex, changing, and contradictory phenomena, and their focus of interest is on specific and local resistance (Markus, 2011). Poststructuralists also emphasize the importance of language as well as structuralism, and that language constitutes but does not reflect reality and has no fixed or immutable meaning (Andrews, 2000).

For Derrida (1982) meaning is transient rather than stable and is open to constant and continuing change. Foucault (1980) focused on power and how it operates in daily social relations and micropractices through discursive contexts (Fawcett, 2008). Lacan (1978) problematizes the idea of human identity as unitary, intelligible, and defined, and views meaning as elusive, incomplete, relational, and contextualized in a complex social network (Leader & Groves, 1996). In research on culture, poststructuralist scholars interrogated social practices and situations in order to analyze how they are created, deconstructing the façade of fixed and stable reality to unearth the mechanisms that contribute to their dominance at a particular context and time (Fawcett, 2008; Andrews, 2000).

1990–2000: Expanded and Critical Approach

Out of the French critical deconstructionist tradition, Pierre Bourdieu became one of the most important influencers of this decade (1990). His scholarship identified concepts such as distinction, habitus, cultural capital, cultural reproduction, and cultural field, which have been used to examine research in culture (Bennett & Frow, 2008). His *structuralist constructivism* approach integrates objective and subjective aspects of cultural life (mental, social, and economic structures). Furthermore, Bourdieu's work involved the integration of empirical research, historical perspective, and theory development in understanding cultural issues using multiple methodologies from various disciplinary fields (Ainsworth, 2013).

Three major concepts (habitus, field, and capital) have been extensively used by culture researchers. Bourdieu defined habitus as socially conditioned sensibilities through which individuals both perceive and generate social practices. Fields, which are closely tied to the definition of habitus, are a network or configuration of objective relations between positions. He further asserts that "each field has its own logic . . . and dynamics of fields cannot be understood without the critical role played by economic, social, cultural, and symbolic capitals" (Ainsworth, 2013, p. 80). As a whole for Bourdie (1993), cultural practices consist of a way by which a (dominant) system reproduces and legitimizes itself.

This decade saw an explosive growth in various methods of dealing with the contemporary realities of a globalized culture. This immense expansion spurred dialogue on different research approaches, social points of view, competing methodologies, and intersecting disciplines. There was a paradigm shift to more empirically oriented research and a greater appreciation for time and history (diachronic perspective) as well as attention to cross-cultural comparative studies (Bryant & Peck, 2007). The concluding decade of the twentieth century was also a period of varied discourse and charged debates regarding "culture." Critics debated from diametrically opposed theoretical orientations and positions on methodologies, which reflected the struggle in conceptualization of culture. At the beginning of the 1990s, Lila Abu-Lughods presented the seminal work, "Writing against Culture" (1991), and at the end of this decade Christoph Brumann countered with "Writing for Culture: Why a Successful Concept Should Not Be Discarded" (1997). The historical context and evolution of the concept of culture informs an understanding of its complexity and the theoretical and operational use of culture in research.

Contemporary Definitions and Criticisms of Culture

In reviewing culture and its conceptualization, Brumann (1999) examined criticisms of the conceptualization of culture, which can be distinguished into three main themes (Ross, 2004). The first theme concerns the overgeneralization of cultural meaning and the arbitrary homogenization of people and groups into unitary entities that may not reflect the difference and fragmentation between groups (Abu-Lughod, 1991). The second theme highlights the paucity of understanding in the historical construction of culture in time and space, and the resulting power struggles that permeate this process. Culture "is not a fixed unit . . . meaning is always negotiated and created in processes that should be studied" (Ross, 2004, p. 42). The third theme that emerged emphasizes the need to use culture as a latent variable, which too often is viewed erroneously as an independent variable that explains similarities and differences in a tautological form (DiMaggio, 1997).

Other postmodern critiques involved the semiotic definition of culture, and the view that research on culture has become mainly a hermeneutic and interpretive project rather than observational research (Boggs, 2004). Critiques of culture also have been raised from within postmodern anthropology (postcultural, poststructural), where from this perspective, researchers interpret or (create) culture from a situated, particular, and dominant point of view. As a consequence, studies on culture may reflect stereotypes, false dichotomies, and false uniformed entities, reflecting the point of view of the researcher more than the culture itself. This can be a problematic situation that raises questions regarding the conceptualization of culture as an analytical tool (Beldo, 2010). It is important to note that this position is not a rejection of the concept of culture. Rather, it serves as a call for a *reflexive stance* from the researcher as a necessary methodological component.

Reflexivity has been highlighted as a strategy within postmodern epistemology (Nordentoft & Olesen, 2018). Increasing self-awareness and practicing critical examination of a researcher's own biases can be useful tools for the translational process of knowledge (Archer, 2012; Alley, Jackson, & Shakya, 2015; Caetano, 2015). Despite the complexity and controversies involved in examining the concept of culture (Hall, 1976), there is value in examining culture as a phenomenon that is shared among groups of people. Culture ultimately is not innate but learned, and comprises a system of interconnected assumptions, expectations, connections, and practices, which can exist outside of one's conscious awareness in intercultural communication (Condon & LaBrack, 2015).

Culture and Social Sciences

Culture and Psychology

Psychology as a social science has made significant contributions to the concept of culture. Culture has been incorporated into psychological theories, research and practice, this has furthered the understanding of culture in scholarship as it relates to intercultural communication and competence (Bennett, 2015).

Cultural psychology operates within a theoretical framework that emphasizes "the formative power of culture at two levels: first, as a process of selection which exerts pressure that shaped humans as a species; second, as a diverse set of socially transmitted operating instructions that fundamentally shape human psychological functioning" (Morlin & Masuda, 2012, p. 429). From a methodological point of view, cultural psychologists focus attention on the process of mutual constitution, which can be understood as the ways in which culture shapes people and how people produce culture and use preferably mixed methods that integrate quantitative approaches with qualitative and descriptive tools to inform cross-cultural research processes within the field of psychology (Morlin & Masuda, 2012).

Cross-cultural psychology emphasizes the examination of what are universally applicable psychological dimensions versus those that are culture-specific. Cross-cultural psychology is intertwined with research methodology because it was developed in the context of culture-comparative studies, and researchers search for similarities or differences in the variable of interest across cultural groups (Fiske & Macrae, 2012). Cross-cultural psychology has made important contributions in measurement methodology, and researchers from this perspective have interest in "using equivalent methods of measurement to determine the limits within which general psychological theories do hold, and the kind of modification of these theories needed to make them universal" (Triandis, Malpass, & Davidson, 1973, p. 1).

Culture as a concept receives significant attention within the field of psychological and behavioral studies. Kitayama and Uskul (2011) explore the relationship between culture and the ways culture affects the human brain and psyche. They highlight that "culture is best conceptualized as a collective-level phenomenon that is composed of both socially shared meanings such as ideas and beliefs and associated scripted behavioral patterns called practices, tasks, and conventions" (p. 422). For Kitayama and Uskul (2011), culture consists of at least two parts: one is the value and the other is the practice or behavior that reflects these values. They argue that while values get transmitted vertically, it is through horizontal imitation that practices and behaviors are copied and transmitted. Any individual at any given time, however, always has a pool of practices from which to choose. This choice of practices and behaviors by an individual and its repetition forms the cultural identity of a given individual. Once practices are repeated over time, "sustained engagement in cultural tasks, relevant brain pathways will undergo substantial rewiring . . . revealing a hitherto unexpected degree of neuroplasticity" (p. 442). As a result, because the brain has been wired according to codes of cultural values, it can automatically and seamlessly produce appropriate cultural codes of behavior and practices.

Culture, Marketing, and Communication

Many other fields also have shown considerable interest in understanding culture. Two such fields are communication and marketing, which have expanded to include international and global dynamics. Businesses have expanded beyond national boundaries of geography and culture. Cross-cultural communication is an integral part of international business and marketing strategies.

As markets expand on an international scale, companies are increasingly finding the need to understand culture at various levels—national, micro, macro, and global—in order to strengthen their marketing strategies and relationships. Owing to this necessity, research on the role of culture in marketing (international marketing in particular) has increased in scale. For instance, Steenkamp (2001) has identified cultural models to understand and analyze culture at various levels, including local and global, to understand what constitutes a national culture and its composition. Steenkamp focuses on four dimensions, autonomy versus collectivism, egalitarianism versus hierarchy, mastery versus nurturance, and uncertainty avoidance. Other prominent models examine dimensions in communication across various cultures such as individualism/collectivism, power distance, masculinity/femininity, and risk avoidance. Engelen and Brettel (2011) note that there is a growth in cross-cultural marketing research to understand consumer behavior and marketing attitudes with respect to culture. They stress that this field of research has been dominated by the researchers from North America and Canada, which highlights the need for new models of culture in communication. Similarly, Huang (2010) noted that cultural variables impact cross-cultural communication and business negotiations. These variables include greetings, negotiation styles (which involves further cultural variables such as gender, status and role, religion, individualism and collectivism, and style of self-expression), attitudes to time, the meanings attached to numbers, gift giving and receiving customs, and significance of gestures. Cultural variables can be complex; knowing and respecting the culture of the other party is a necessity for avoiding blunders and failures in cross-cultural business relations.

Culture and Social Work

Within the field of social work, focus is placed on understanding the cultural diversity of human groups and communities rather than theoretical conceptualization. Research studies in culture within social work are limited in size and scope compared to other disciplines such as anthropology, sociology, psychology, and communication. The majority of studies are dedicated to cultural competency, cultural diversity, and cross-cultural studies in social work. Questions of culture focus on social practices related to "intercultural competence" with less attention on the theoretical development of culture.

Intercultural competence refers to knowledge, skills, and attitudes necessary for successful (effective and appropriate) management of human interactions across different cultural groups (Deardorff, 2015; Yoshida & Fisher-Yoshida, 2015). The field of social work has implemented numerous cultural competency models in its practice and education (Alvarez-Hernandez & Choi, 2017). Tran, Nguyen, and Chan (2017) noted that social work as a professional field has long recognized "the importance of cultural influences on human behaviors and social work practices" (p. 8).

Existing professional and educational organizations such as the National Association of Social Workers (NASW) and the Council on Social Work Education (CSWE) have formulated guidelines and standards to address cultural competence in the practice and education of social work. Since 1973, CSWE explicitly states that the social work curriculum should address knowledge on diversity, ethnicity, and race. In 1976, women's studies was incorporated into social work education. In the 1980s, broader categories of special populations and topics were included to address the needs of vulnerable populations, "such as sexism, heterosexuality, ageism, ableism, cultural and social diversity, different language, ethnic minorities of color, age, religion, and sexual orientation" (Alvarez-Hernandez & Choi, 2017, p. 386).

In 2001, the NASW Standards for Cultural Competence in Social Work Practice were published, and indicators of competence were identified for these standards in 2007 (NASW, 2007). Since 2008, CSWE has emphasized that students should learn how to apply their knowledge and skills related to diversity on assessments, interventions, and research (Alvarez-Hernandez & Choi, 2017; Jani et al., 2011). NASW includes ten cultural competence standards for its members, namely, ethics and values, self-awareness, cross-cultural knowledge, cross-cultural skills, service delivery, empowerment and advocacy, diverse workforce, professional education, language diversity, and cross-cultural leadership; (Tran, Nguyen, & Chan, 2017; NASW, 2015). In 2015, NASW (through the National Committee on Racial and Ethnic Diversity) revised the definition of culture and cultural competence and introduced new developments that built on previous competencies (NASW, 2015).

The revised standards expand the concept of culture as being inclusive but not restricted to ethnicity; sexual orientation, gender identity or expression, and religious identity or spirituality were included as essential components of culture. This is reinforced in the application of the standards at all levels of practice, namely, micro, mezzo, and macro levels, as well as in assessment, intervention, or evaluation (NASW, 2015). Two new concepts were included in the definition of the competencies: "cultural humility" and "intersectionality." Cultural humility refers to the need for self-evaluation and self-critique, as well as the need to understand imbalance of power and to develop a nonpaternalistic approach to advocacy with populations. Intersectionality offers a perspective that integrates various forms of inequality and injustice that may compound the effects of oppression (NASW, 2015). A deeper understanding of self-reflection was added for managing "language and communication" issues, which is necessary for linguistic cultural competence. Finally, the need for leadership to advance cultural competence was further highlighted, with a focus on expanding understanding of structural and institutional oppression (NASW, 2015). It is with these considerations that the cross-cultural approaches of data analysis demonstrated and illustrated in this book will assist social work researchers to analyze data relevant for social work practice.

REFERENCES

Abu-Lughod, L. (1991). Writing against culture. In Fox, R. G. (Ed.). *Recapturing anthropology: Working in the present* (pp. 137–162). Santa Fe, NM: School of American Research Press.

Ainsworth, J. (2013). *Sociology of Education: An A-to-Z Guide.* Thousand Oaks, CA. SAGE Publications.

Alvarez-Hernandez, L. R., & Choi, Y. J. (2017). Reconceptualizing culture in social work practice and education: A dialectic and uniqueness awareness approach. *Journal of Social Work Education, 53*(3), 384–398.

Andrews, D. L. (2000). Posting up: French post-structuralism and the critical analysis of contemporary sporting culture. In Coakley, J., & Dunning, E. (Eds.). *Handbook of sports studies* (pp. 106–137). London: Sage Publications.

Archer, M. S. (2012). *The reflexive imperative in late modernity.* Cambridge: Cambridge University Press.

Austin, D. J. (1979). Symbols and culture: Some philosophical assumptions in the work of Clifford Geertz. *Social Analysis, 3,* 45–59.

Barber, N. (2008). *The myth of culture: Why we need a genuine natural science of societies.* Newcastle-Upon-Tyne, UK: Cambridge Scholars Press.

Barnard, A. (2000). *History and theory in anthropology.* Cambridge: Cambridge University Press.

Barker, C. (2004). *The SAGE dictionary of cultural studies.* London: Sage Publications.

Beldo, L. (2010). Concept of culture. In Birx, H. J. (Ed.). *21st century anthropology: A reference handbook* (Vol. 1; pp. 144–152). Thousand Oaks, CA: Sage Publications.

Bennett, J. M. (2015). *The SAGE Encyclopedia of Intercultural Competence.* Thousand Oaks, CA: SAGE Publications.

Birx, H. J. (Ed.). (2010). *21st century anthropology: A reference handbook.* Thousand Oaks, CA: Sage.

Boggs, J. (2004). The culture concept as theory, in context. *Current Anthropology,* 45(2), 187–209.

Bourdieu, P. (1993). *The field of cultural production: Essays on art and literature.* New York: Columbia University Press.

Brumann, C. (1999). Writing for culture: Why a successful concept should not be discarded. *Current Anthropology,* 40(S1), S1–S27.

Bryant, C. D., & Peck, D. L. (2007). *21st century sociology: A reference handbook.* Thousand Oaks, CA: SAGE Publications.

Caetano, A. (2015). Personal reflexivity and biography: Methodological challenges and strategies. *International Journal of Social Research Methodology,* 18(2), 227–242.Condon, J., & LaBrack, B. (2015). Culture, the definition of. In Bennett, J. M. (Ed.). *The SAGE encyclopedia of intercultural competence* (pp. 192–195). Los Angeles: Sage Publications.

Cuché, D. [(1966) 2002]. Cultura e Identidad. En La noción de Cultura en las Ciencias Sociales. Capítulo VI (pp. 106–113). Buenos Aires. Nueva Visión.

David, M. (Ed.). (2010). *SAGE benchmarks in social research methods: Methods of interpretive sociology* (Vols. 1–4). London: Sage Publications.

Deardorff, D. K. (2015). Definitions: Knowledge, skills, attitudes. In Bennett, J. M. (Ed.). *The SAGE encyclopedia of intercultural competence* (pp. 217–220). Los Angeles: Sage Publications.

Derrida, J. (1982). *Margins of philosophy.* Chicago: University of Chicago Press.

DiMaggio, P. (1997). Culture and Cognition. *Annual Review of Sociology, 23,* 263–287.

Engelen, A., & Brettel, M. (2011). Assessing cross-cultural marketing theory and research. *Journal of Business Research,* 64(5), 516–523.

Eriksen, T., & Nielsen, F. (2013). *Small places—Large issues* (2nd ed.). London: Pluto Press.

Fawcett, B. (2008). Poststructuralism. In L. M. Given (Ed.). *The Sage encyclopedia of qualitative research methods* (Vols. 1 & 2, pp. 659–669). Los Angeles, Calif: Sage Publications.

Fernández de Rota, J. A. (2009). El concepto de Cultura en Antropologia Contemporanea. Seminario interdisciplinar o(s) sentido(s) da(s) cultura(s). Consello da Cultura Galela. España-Galicia.

Fiske, S. T., & Macrae, C. N. (2012). *The SAGE handbook of social cognition.* London: SAGE.

Foucault, M. (1980). *Power/knowledge: Selected interviews and other writings, 1972–1977.* Gordon, C. (Ed.). New York: Pantheon Books.

Gable, E., & Handler, R. (2008). Anthropology and culture. In Bennett, T., & Frow, J. (Eds.). *The Sage handbook of cultural analysis* (pp. 25–46). Thousand Oaks, CA: Sage Publications.

Gaona, T. H. (2007). Radcliffe-Brown, A. R. (1881–1955). In Clark, D. S. (Ed.). *Encyclopedia of law and society: American and global perspectives* (pp. 1264–1265). Los Angeles: Sage Publications.

Geertz, C. (1973). *The interpretation of cultures* (Vol. 5019). New York: Basic Books.

Hall, E. T. (1976). *Beyond culture*. New York: Doubleday.

Huang, L. (2010). Cross-cultural communication in business negotiations. *International Journal of Economics and Finance, 2*(2), 196–199.

Jahoda, G. (2012). Critical reflections on some recent definitions of "culture." *Culture & Psychology, 18*(3), 289–303. https://doi.org/10.1177/1354067X12446229

Jani, J., Pierce, D., Ortiz, L., & Sowbel, L. (2011). Access to intersectionality, content to competence: Deconstructing social work education diversity standards. *Journal of Social Work Education, 47*, 283–301.

Kellner, D. (2001). Cultural studies and social theory: A critical intervention. In Ritzer, G., & Smart, B. (Eds.). *Handbook of social theory* (pp. 395–409). London: Sage Publications.

Kitayama, S., & Uskul, A. K. (2011). Culture, mind, and the brain: Current evidence and future directions. *Annual Review of Psychology, 62*, 419–449.

Kroeber, A. L., & Parsons, T. (1958). The concepts of culture and of social system. *American Sociological Review, 23*(5), 582–583.

Kuper, A. (1999). *Culture: the anthropologists' account.* Cambridge, Mass: Harvard University Press.

Lacan, J. (1978). *The four fundamental concepts of psychoanalysis. Book XI.* Miller, J.A. (Ed.). New York: Norton.

Leader, D., & Groves, J. (1996). Introducing Lacan. Edited by Richard Appignanesi, Introducing Series. New York: Totem Books.

Lévi-Strauss, C. (1963). *Structural Anthropology.* Harmondsworth: Penguin Books.

Markus, G. (2011). *Culture: The making and the make-up of a concept. An essay in historical semantics.* Leiden, The Netherlands: Brill. doi:https://doi.org/10.1163/ej.9789004202405.i-666

Margaret, M. (1935). *Sex and temperament in three primitive societies.* London: Routledge.

McGee, R. J., & Warms, R. L. (Eds.). (2013). *Theory in social and cultural anthropology: An encyclopedia.* Thousand Oaks, CA, USA: Sage Publications.

Minkov, M. (2013). *Cross-cultural analysis: The science and art of comparing the world's modern societies and their cultures.* Thousand Oaks, CA: Sage Publications.

Moberg, M. (2012). *Engaging Anthropological Theory: A Social and Political History* (1st ed.). Routledge. https://doi.org/10.4324/9780203097991

Moore, J. D. (2012). *Visions of Culture: An Introduction to Anthropological Theories and Theorists*. Lanham, MD: AltaMira Press.

Morlin, B., & Masuda T. (2012). Social cognition in real worlds: Cultural psychology and social cognition. In S. T. Fiske & C. N. Macrae (Eds.). *The SAGE handbook of social cognition* (Chapter 22). London: SAGE.

National Association of Social Workers. (2015). Standards and indicators for cultural competence in social work practice.

Nordentoft, H. M., & Olesen, B. R. (2018). A critical reflexive perspective on othering in collaborative knowledge production. *Qualitative Research Journal, 18*(1), 55–66.

Ross, N. (2004). *Culture and cognition: Implications for theory and method.* Thousand Oaks, Calif.: Sage Publications.

Rowe, D. (2017). *The Wiley-Blackwell Encyclopedia of Social Theory.* Birmingham Centre for Contemporary Cultural Studies.

Schneider, D. (1968). *American kinship.* Chicago: University of Chicago Press.

Spencer-Oatey, H. (2012). What is culture? A compilation of quotations. GlobalPeople Core Concept Compilations. Available at www.warwick.ac.uk/globalknowledge

Sewell, W. H., Jr. (2005). *Logics of History: Social Theory and Social Transformation.* University of Chicago Press.

Stanlaw, J. (2006). Malinowski, Bronislaw (1884–1942). In Birx, H. J. (Ed.). *Encyclopedia of anthropology* (Vol. 1; pp. 1520–1521). Thousand Oaks, CA: Sage Publications.

Steenkamp, J. B. E. (2001). The role of national culture in international marketing research. *International Marketing Review, 18*(1), 30–44.

Steward, J. H. (1972). *Theory of culture change: The methodology of multilinear evolution.* Urbana and Chicago: University of Illinois Press.

Sutton, M., & Anderson, N. (2010). *Introduction to cultural ecology* (2nd ed.). Walnut Creek, CA: Altamira Press.

Tran, T., Nguyen, T., & Chan, K. (2017). *Developing cross-cultural measurement in social work research and evaluation.* New York, NY: Oxford University Press.

Trias i Valls, A., & Roula, P. (2009). Geertz and Postmodernism. The later years. Exploring Religions and Cultures. Document. https://csapoer.pbworks.com/f/PowerPoint++Geertz_and_Postmodernism+2R.pdf

Triandis, H. C., Malpass, R. S., & Davidson, A. R. (1973). Psychology and culture. *Annual Review of Psychology, 355–378.

Turk, A. T. (1962). An examination of the Kroeber-Parsons Distinction between "Culture" and "Society." *The Sociological Quarterly, 3*(2), 135–140.

Walton, D. (2013). Cultural studies. In Kaldis, B. (Ed.). *Encyclopedia of philosophy and the social sciences* (Vol. 1, pp. 144–147). Thousand Oaks, California: Sage Publications.

White, L. A. (1959). The concept of culture. *American Anthropologist, 61*(2), 227–251.

Yoshida, R., & Fisher-Yoshida, B. (2015). Disciplinary approaches to culture: An overview. In Bennett, J. M. (Ed.). *The SAGE encyclopedia of intercultural competence* (pp. 243–255). Thousand Oaks, California: Sage Publications.

3

Data Management and Cross-Cultural Descriptive Analysis

Quantitative cross-cultural analysis requires the application of statistics to study the variability of a phenomenon (variables) across cultural groups. Noted American statistician John Tukey (1915–2000) defined statistics as "a science, not a branch of mathematics, but uses mathematical models as essential tools" (http://www.amstat.org/asa/what-is-statistics.aspx?hkey=4f800e15-a03d-45fd-a21c-5a2f68cd2389). The Department of Statistics at the University of California, Irvine succinctly defined statistics as " the science concerned with developing and studying methods for collecting, analyzing, interpreting and presenting empirical data" (https://www.stat.uci.edu/what-is-statistics/). In cross-cultural analysis, we use statistical tools to compare variables (phenomena) of interest across cultures. We study the uncertainty of outcomes across cultural groups and examine the variation of the outcomes caused by multiple sources such as the measurement of the variables and methods of data collection.

Applied Cross-Cultural Data Analysis for Social Work. Thanh V. Tran and Keith T. Chan,
Oxford University Press. © Oxford University Press 2021. DOI: 10.1093/oso/9780190888510.003.0003

This chapter aims to provide practical applications of descriptive statistics to describe the variables used in a cross-cultural research/ evaluation project. We use statistical methods to describe the variables of interest and to test the hypotheses derived from theories. More specifically, we want to know whether our hypotheses are supported by the data across different cultural groups. In order to describe and to test hypotheses, we need first to know how the variables of interest are measured. Michell (1986) discussed the challenges of measurement theories in psychological research. In this book, we follow the measurement theory presented by Stevens (1946), which defines measurement as the process of assigning numerical values to represent different attributes of variables. It is important to know that different measurement levels require different types of statistics. Steven's representational theory of measurement encompasses four basic levels of measurement as described in Table 3.1.

Table 3.1. Levels of Measurement and Descriptive Statistics

Levels	Definition	Examples	Statistics	Special Case
Nominal	Categories of attributes, characteristics	Sex, marital status, occupations	Percent Mode	Coded as dummy variable with 0 and 1 values. The mean equals % of the group coded as 1.
Ordinal	Ordered categories of attributes or characteristics	Grade levels, Likert scale Depression Self-esteem Life satisfaction		Coded with numerical values (e.g. 1,2,3,4 and 5). Can compute the mean and other descriptive statistics.
Interval	Variable with relative zero value	Temperature,	Median Mean SD[a] Skewness Kurtosis	
Ratio	Variable with absolute zero value	age, weight, height	Median Mean SD[a] Skewness Kurtosis	

DATA MANAGEMENT

After storing the data, analysts need to retrieve the data and ensure that the variables were coded and stored properly before any attempt to conduct analysis.

Examine the Codebook. The codebook is the dictionary of a data set. A good codebook contains all relevant information on the variables in the data set. The aptly named Stata command *codebook* provides information for each variable, a list of variables, or the whole data set. Once the desired variables for analysis are identified from the data set, analysts can use *codebook* to review the variables of interest. We use the 2014 Behavioral Risk Factor Surveillance System Codebook Report and its data set as examples in this book. It is recommended that analysts become familiar with the printed version of the codebook of the data sets. The data set was prepared for SAS statistical software, but can be easily converted to other statistical software such as SPSS and Stata.

The use of secondary data sets requires researchers to know the data set well before performing any statistical analyses. The following are a few Stata commands that could be used to review the data and the selected variables for specific research purposes. In the following example, the variable of interest is general health status.

```
. codebook GENHLTH
```

```
GENHLTH                                                          GENERAL HEALTH

              type:  numeric (byte)

             range:  [1,9]                        units:  1
     unique values:  7                        missing .:  4/464,664

        tabulation:  Freq.  Value
                     82,044  1
                    151,711  2
                    142,506  3
                     61,880  4
                     24,831  5
                        827  7
                        861  9
                          4  .
```

Note: "codebook" is a STATA command

Oftentimes, the printed version of the codebook from the data archive provides more detailed information on the selected variable. The

Centers for Disease Control and Prevention (CDC) data include detailed codebooks for the Behavioral Risk Factor Surveillance System (BRFSS) data sets. For example, for the General Health variable (GENHLTH) it contains the following information.

General Health

						Type: Num
Section:	1.1	Health Status				
Column:	80					SAS Variable Name: GENHLTH

Prologue:

Description: Would you say that in general your health is:

Value	Value Label	Frequency	Percentage	Weighted Percentage
1	Excellent	82,044	17.66	19.03
2	Very good	151,711	32.65	31.58
3	Good	142,506	30.67	31.01
4	Fair	61,880	13.32	13.13
5	Poor	24,831	5.34	4.81
7	Don't know/Not Sure	827	0.18	0.17
9	Refused	861	0.19	0.27
BLANK	Not asked or Missing	4		

The *describe* command produces summary information on the whole data set or a selected variable.

```
. describe

Contains data from /Users/thanh/Desktop/RESEARCH PROJECTS/BRFSS 2014/BRFSS2014.DTA
  obs:       464,664
  vars:          333                          24 Nov 2017 05:56
  size:  207,704,808

              storage   display    value
variable name   type    format     label      variable label

_STATE         byte     %8.0g                  STATE FIPS CODE
FMONTH         byte     %8.0g                  FILE MONTH
IDATE          str8     %8s                    INTERVIEW DATE
IMONTH         str2     %2s                    INTERVIEW MONTH
IDAY           str2     %2s                    INTERVIEW DAY
```

The *describe* command produces outputs that include the sample size (obs) and number of variables in the data set (vars). The size (size of the data set in megabyte) and display format can be useful for understanding how to best store the data, but they are not specifically of interest for cross-cultural research. The variable label column provides a detailed description from the label of the variable. For example, if we look at the variable IDAY, we can only determine that the variable contains information on the day of the interview during a given month through examining its variable label.

You can use the Stata command *inspect* to view the general distribution of a variable's data.

```
. inspect GENHLTH

GENHLTH:   GENERAL HEALTH                              Number of Observations

                                        Total      Integers    Nonintegers
  #                      Negative         -            -            -
  #    #                 Zero             -            -            -
  #    #                 Positive      464,660      464,660         -
  #    #
  #    #                 Total         464,660      464,660         -
  #    #   .   .   .     Missing             4
 ─
 1                9                    464,664
```

For more information on the distribution of a variable, you may wish to use the *histogram* command, which provides a graphical display of its kernel distribution.

histogram GENHLTH

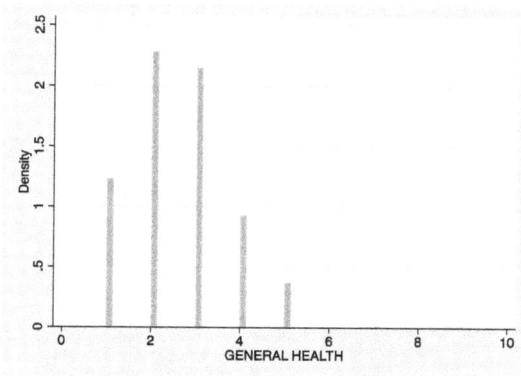

We also can examine the distribution of the variable GHNHTL (general health) to determine whether the variable approximates a normal distribution curve.

```
histogram GENHLTH,normal
```

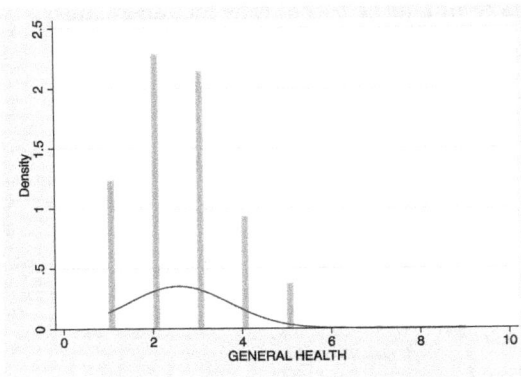

The Stata command *tabulate* (tab) can be used to generate frequencies distribution of this variable.

. **tab GENHLTH**

GENERAL HEALTH	Freq.	Percent	Cum.
1	82,044	17.66	17.66
2	151,711	32.65	50.31
3	142,506	30.67	80.98
4	61,880	13.32	94.29
5	24,831	5.34	99.64
7	827	0.18	99.81
9	861	0.19	100.00
Total	464,660	100.00	

Currently, the variable has no value label. We can assign the value label by using the following procedures.

1. Users can define the label for the selected variable and store information in the file.

label define k (k contains all the labels you assign to the categories).
label define k 1 "excellent" 2 "very good" 3 "good" 4 "fair" 5 "poor" ///
7 "don't know/not sure" 9 "refused"
Note: if the line is too long you can use /// to continue into the
next line.

2. Once the labels are defined, you can assign them to the selected
   variable.
   label value GENHLTH k
   Note: In the label value command, you assign all values labels
   stored in k to the selected variable.

SYNTAX AND RESULTS

```
. label define k 1 "excellent" 2 "very good" 3 "good" 4 "fair" 5 "poor" 7 "don't know/not sure" 9 "refused"

. label value  GENHLTH k

. tab  GENHLTH
```

GENERAL HEALTH	Freq.	Percent	Cum.
excellent	82,044	17.66	17.66
very good	151,711	32.65	50.31
good	142,506	30.67	80.98
fair	61,880	13.32	94.29
poor	24,831	5.34	99.64
don't know/not sure	827	0.18	99.81
refused	861	0.19	100.00
Total	464,660	100.00	

If the user wishes to assign the categories "don't know/not sure"
and "refused" as missing data, the variable can be recoded into a new
variable.

```
. recode GENHLTH (1=1 "excellent") (2=2 "very good") (3=3 "good") (4=4 "fair") (5=5 "poor") (9 7=.),gen (srhealth)
(1688 differences between GENHLTH and srhealth)

. tab srhealth
```

RECODE of GENHLTH (GENERAL HEALTH)	Freq.	Percent	Cum.
excellent	82,044	17.72	17.72
very good	151,711	32.77	50.49
good	142,506	30.78	81.27
fair	61,880	13.37	94.64
poor	24,831	5.36	100.00
Total	462,972	100.00	

We can now compare the frequencies of the five value categories of variable "GENHLTH" and the newly recoded variable "srhealth" by using the *tabulate* command for both variables. We find that the frequencies of these categories did not change. The total sample of the variable "srhealth" is 462,977 compared to 464,660 of the "GENHLTH" variable. The "srhealth" excluded the categories 7 and 9. We can examine the number of missing cases with the following syntax.

`. tab srhealth,m`

self rated health	Freq.	Percent	Cum.
excellent	82,044	17.66	17.66
very good	151,711	32.65	50.31
good	142,506	30.67	80.97
fair	61,880	13.32	94.29
poor	24,831	5.34	99.64
.	1,692	0.36	100.00
Total	464,664	100.00	

Note: the "." refers to the total number of cases with missing values or cases, which were reassigned for the categories 7 and 9. To run the one-way frequencies for two or more variables you can use "tab1" instead of "tab."

. **tabl srhealth resex**

-> **tabulation of srhealth**

self rated health	Freq.	Percent	Cum.
excellent	82,044	17.72	17.72
very good	151,711	32.77	50.49
good	142,506	30.78	81.27
fair	61,880	13.37	94.64
poor	24,831	5.36	100.00
Total	462,972	100.00	

-> **tabulation of resex**

sex	Freq.	Percent	Cum.
Female	271,694	58.47	58.47
Male	192,970	41.53	100.00
Total	464,664	100.00	

.

Changing the label of an existing variable can make it easier for presentation and coding purposes. The label of the variable "dayspoor-health" in the Stata output below may be too long.

```
. tab dayspoorhealth
```

RECODE of POORHLTH (POOR PHYSICAL OR MENTAL HEALTH)	Freq.	Percent	Cum.
1	11,511	11.71	11.71
2	12,419	12.63	24.34
3	7,868	8.00	32.34

You can use the *label* syntax to change a variable's old label or a long label to a cleaner label as follows:

```
. label variable dayspoorhealth "days with poor health"
```

```
. tab dayspoorhealth
```

days with poor health	Freq.	Percent	Cum.
1	11,511	11.71	11.71
2	12,419	12.63	24.34
3	7,868	8.00	32.34

The variable "dayspoorhealth" now has a shorter and cleaner label than before by using the *label variable* command.

We also can use the *summary* (sum) command to find how the variables were measured or coded.

```
. sum age race sex daypoorhealth
```

Variable	Obs	Mean	Std. Dev.	Min	Max
age	464,664	55.49154	16.85709	18	80
race	464,664	1.527796	1.112479	1	5
sex	464,664	.4152893	.4927724	0	1
daypoorhea~h	98,328	12.23165	10.97622	1	30

The *sum* command produces output that shows the number of observations (respondents), the mean, standard deviation (Std. Dev. Or SD), and the range values from the lowest (Min) to the highest (Max).

Note. The mean (or average) is most meaningful for continuous variables such as "age" and "daypoorhealth." For the variable "race," the mean cannot be meaningfully interpreted because it is a nominal variable with five distinct categories or groups (racial groups). The range values (Min & Max) inform how many categories were coded for each variable. In the case of the age variable, we see that respondents' age ranged from 18 to 80. For dummy variables or binary variables with values of 0 or 1, the mean can be interpreted as the percentage of the category coded as 1. In the following example from the sex variable, male was coded as 1 and female as 0. In this case, a mean or average of .4152893 produced by the *sum* syntax is the percent of male in the data, which is identical to the output below from the *tab* command.

```
. tab sex
```

sex	Freq.	Percent	Cum.
Female	271,694	58.47	58.47
Male	192,970	41.53	100.00
Total	464,664	100.00	

DESCRIPTIVE STATISTICS FOR CROSS-CULTURAL COMPARISON

We will use the data from the "Children of Immigrants Longitudinal Study (CILS), 1991–2006 data set" (Potes & Rumbaut, 2006) to illustrate the use of descriptive statistics in cross-cultural comparison for the following examples. We created a new variable representing three ethnic groups: Mexican, Filipino, and Indochinese from the variable v432 in the data set.

```
v433                                                    Race/ethnic identification

                type:  numeric (long)
                label:  V433, but 8 nonmissing values are not labeled

                range:  [0,99]                    units:  1
        unique values:  70                      missing .:  2,001/5,262

             examples:  10    Mexican-American
                        23    Filipino-American
                        68
                         .
```

We use the *recode* command to create the ethnic variable with three
ethnic groups from the variable v433.

```
recode v433 (9 10=1 "Mexican") (22/23=2 "Filipino")
(25/30=3 "Indochinese") ///
   (else=.), gen(Ethnic _ 3)
```

Notes: The values 9 and 10 refer to Mexicans and Mexican Americans;
22 and 23 refer to Filipino and Filipino Americans, and 25 to 30 refer to
all groups that originated from Cambodia, Laos, and Vietnam.

```
. tab Ethnic_3
```

Ethnic Groups	Freq.	Percent	Cum.
Mexican	265	27.72	27.72
Filipino	501	52.41	80.13
Indochinese	190	19.87	100.00
Total	956	100.00	

We can now examine descriptive statistics of the variables, such as
central tendency (mean, median, mode) and dispersion (standard deviation, coefficient covariance, minimum, maximum).

Measures of central tendency. These descriptive statistics describe
the location of the data by the summary numerical values such as the
arithmetic average or the mean, the median, and the mode. The mean
and the median are useful for continuous variables (e.g., age, income)
and discrete variables (e.g. self-esteem measured on a scale from 10 to 40).

DESCRIBE THE MEAN AND MEDIAN IN CROSS-CULTURAL COMPARISONS

Let us look at the mean and median of self-esteem as measured by ten items of the Rosenberg Self-Esteem Scale across three ethnic groups of children of immigrants in the United States.

```
. des v101-v110

                 storage    display     value
variable name    type       format      label      variable label

v101             long       %18.0g      V101       I am a person of worth
v102             long       %18.0g      V102       I have a number of good qualities
v103             long       %18.0g      V103       I'm inclined to feel I'm a failure
v104             long       %18.0g      V104       I do things as well as other people
v105             long       %18.0g      V105       I do not have much to be proud of
v106             long       %18.0g      V106       I take a positive attitude toward myself
v107             long       %18.0g      V107       I am satisfied with myself
v108             long       %18.0g      V108       I wish I had more respect for myself
v109             long       %18.0g      V109       I certainly feel useless at times
v110             long       %18.0g      V110       At times I think I am no good at all
```

Note that this ten-item self-esteem scale has five positive items and five negative items. Let us look at how the positive items and negative items were coded before creating a summative index.

```
. codebook v101 v103

v101                                                             I am a person of worth

               type:  numeric (long)
              label:  V101

              range:  [1,4]                     units:  1
      unique values:  4                      missing .:  87/5,262

         tabulation:  Freq.   Numeric  Label
                      3,311         1  Agrees a lot
                      1,439         2  Agrees a little
                        294         3  Disagrees a little
                        131         4  Disagrees a lot
                         87         .

v103                                                      I'm inclined to feel I'm a failure

               type:  numeric (long)
              label:  V103

              range:  [1,4]                     units:  1
      unique values:  4                      missing .:  65/5,262

         tabulation:  Freq.   Numeric  Label
                        173         1  Agrees a lot
                        558         2  Agrees a little
                        988         3  Disagrees a little
                      3,478         4  Disagrees a lot
                         65         .
```

-> tabulation of v101

I am a person of worth	Freq.	Percent	Cum.
Agrees a lot	3,311	63.98	63.98
Agrees a little	1,439	27.81	91.79
Disagrees a little	294	5.68	97.47
Disagrees a lot	131	2.53	100.00
Total	5,175	100.00	

-> tabulation of v103

I'm inclined to feel I'm a failure	Freq.	Percent	Cum.
Agrees a lot	173	3.33	3.33
Agrees a little	558	10.74	14.07
Disagrees a little	988	19.01	33.08
Disagrees a lot	3,478	66.92	100.00
Total	5,197	100.00	

The positive and negative items were coded in the same direction. We need to reverse the values of the positive items to reflect scores that range from low to high self-esteem.

```
. recode v101 v102 v104 v106 v107 /// /* Space before anf after /// */
>   (1=4 "Agrees a lot") (2=3 "Agrees a little") ///
>   (3=2 "Disagrees a little")  (4=1 "Disagrees a lot") ///
>   (else =.), gen (v101re v102re v104re v106re v107re) ///
>   label(vlabel)
```

Note that we changed the values so that a score of 4 refers to "Agree a lot" and 1 refers to "Disagree a lot." We only changed the value labels and not the number of respondents. Let us compare the original variable and the recoded variable.

```
-> tabulation of v101
```

I am a person of worth	Freq.	Percent	Cum.
Agrees a lot	3,311	63.98	63.98
Agrees a little	1,439	27.81	91.79
Disagrees a little	294	5.68	97.47
Disagrees a lot	131	2.53	100.00
Total	5,175	100.00	

```
. tab v101re
```

RECODE of v101 (I am a person of worth)	Freq.	Percent	Cum.
Disagrees a lot	131	2.53	2.53
Disagrees a little	294	5.68	8.21
Agrees a little	1,439	27.81	36.02
Agrees a lot	3,311	63.98	100.00
Total	5,175	100.00	

MEASUREMENTS OF ABSTRACT CONSTRUCTS IN CROSS-CULTURAL COMPARISONS

It is important to always review the content of the measurement items to ensure that they are coded properly before conducting any data analysis. For multi-item measures (scales) of a single construct such as self-esteem, we can sum up the items into a single score representing a range of values that encompass the degrees or levels of a selected construct. It is easier to interpret the analysis if the scores of a scale capture its meaning. By that we mean one would expect that a measure of self-esteem should have higher scores to reflect higher self-esteem not vice versa. The item, "I am a person of worth" has scores ranging from 1 to 4. Conceptually, one would expect that the response, "Agree a lot," must have a score greater than the response, "Disagree a lot." In this data set, however, the response, "Agree a lot," was assigned a numerical value of 1 and a numerical value of 4 was assigned for the response, "Disagree a lot." If one creates a summative score for these ten items of self-esteem and ignores the content and the coding of the items, the outcome will be misleading and incorrect. Let us compare the values of the self-esteem scale using the original items without recoding and the one with proper recoding of the positive items.

```
gen selfest_o=v101+v102+v103+v104+v105+v106+v107+v108+v109+v110
```

The command line above creates a summative score scale (selfest_o) for the ten items of the Rosenberg Self-Esteem Scale without any recoding.

```
gen selfest_r=v101r+v102r+v103+v104r+v105+v106r+v107r+v108+v109+v110
```

This command line creates a summative score scale (selfest_r) for the ten items of the Rosenberg Self-Esteem Scale with the recoding of the five positive items.

The summary descriptive statistics here show the mean and the standard deviation of the two scales are substantively different.

```
. sum selfest_o selfest_r
```

Variable	Obs	Mean	Std. Dev.	Min	Max
selfest_o	5,006	22.9149	3.09483	10	40
selfest_r	5,006	33.03795	5.218517	10	40

MEASURES OF CENTRAL TENDENCY

The summary (*sum*) gives the mean and its standard deviation but not descriptive statistics, such as the median, coefficient of variance, range, skewness, and kurtosis. We can estimate the mean (arithmetic average) and the median (the median represents the midpoint of the distribution, which shows 50% of observations on either side of the median value) of the correct measure of self-esteem using the syntax we employ here. The Stata symbol of median is "p50." The results shown here reveal that 50% of respondents had a self-esteem score under 34 and 50% above 34. The mode is a measure of location of the data where a given value occurs most frequently. We did not include this statistic for our example because it is not useful for our purposes of cross-cultural comparisons.

```
. tabstat selfest_r,stat (mean median n)
```

variable	mean	p50	N
selfest_r	**33.03795**	**34**	**5006**

We can create a table of mean and standard deviation for self-esteem using the following:

```
. table  v18 Bornmainland ,contents(mean selfest_r sd selfest_r ) by (Ethnic_3)
```

Ethnicity and Sex	Mainlandborn	
	OutsideUS Born	US Mainland Born
Mexican		
Male	31.28889	33.45454
	5.336931	5.215898
Female	32.09615	32.70238
	4.979407	5.772347
Filipino		
Male	32.96907	33.63971
	5.14266	4.823819
Female	31.93578	31.84
	4.447794	4.945447
Indochinese		
Male	30.5375	33.83333
	5.053997	3.250641
Female	30.58025	33.46667
	4.824065	4.206571

The results show that the mean or average of self-esteem (as measured by the Rosenberg Scale) for US-born Mexicans was 33.45 compared to 31.28 of those who were born outside the United States.

MEASURES OF VARIANCE OR DISPERSION OF THE DATA

When conducting cross-cultural research, respondents or the participants of a study will most likely have different scores with regard to variables of interest. Variance is the degree to which individual scores differ from the group's mean. Variance is measured by the square of the difference between the individual score and the group's mean and is an important statistic for estimations. By itself, however, the variance does not allow for meaningful comparisons. The square root of the variance or the standard deviation (SD) is more useful for comparisons of the dispersion of the data within a sample or a group. The coefficient of variation (CV) is expressed as the ratio of the standard deviation to the mean (CV = SD/Mean). It can be used to compare the variability of a variable when the measurement units in an analysis are different. We also can use the coefficient of variance to compare the variability of a variable across various cultural groups or samples. The Stata command for the measure of dispersion is shown here. You can spell out the full statistic notation when using Stata or just use the first letter or first few letters. For example, s is for standard deviation, v is for variance, cv is for coefficient of variance, min is for minimum, max is for maximum, and range can be r.

```
. bysort Ethnic_3: tabstat selfest_r dad_age mom_age if
>     s(sd v cv min max range n) format(%8.2f) long
```

```
-> Ethnic_3 = Mexican
```

stats	selfes~r	dad_age	mom_age
sd	5.41	7.36	5.84
variance	29.23	54.15	34.14
cv	0.17	0.18	0.15
min	15.00	21.00	28.00
max	40.00	69.00	59.00
range	25.00	48.00	31.00
N	247.00	191.00	220.00

```
-> Ethnic_3 = Filipino
```

stats	selfes~r	dad_age	mom_age
sd	4.89	6.80	5.62
variance	23.94	46.19	31.61
cv	0.15	0.16	0.13
min	14.00	20.00	32.00
max	40.00	76.00	70.00
range	26.00	56.00	38.00
N	492.00	365.00	352.00

```
-> Ethnic_3 = Indochinese
```

stats	selfes~r	dad_age	mom_age
sd	4.90	8.48	7.77
variance	24.03	71.96	60.31
cv	0.16	0.18	0.18
min	18.00	33.00	25.00
max	40.00	79.00	66.00
range	22.00	46.00	41.00
N	182.00	83.00	89.00

```
-> Ethnic_3 = .
no observations
```

Note that the commands that produced these results have a number of specifications that are useful for data analysis. The *bysort* command prefix tells Stata to sort the results according to the categories of the Ethnic_3 variable. The *if* qualifier tells Stata not to include cases assigned as ".". The *format(%8.2f)* option tells Stata to report two decimals, or 1/100th, for the numerical values of the results. The *long* option tells Stata to list the statistics in rows and the variables in columns.

If you wish for Stata to report the statistics in columns and variables in rows you can use the command *col(stat)* instead of *long*.

```
.
. bysort Ethnic_3: tabstat selfest_r dad_age if Ethnic_3 <. , ///
>     s(sd v cv min max range n) format(%8.2f) col(stat)
```

```
-> Ethnic_3 = Mexican
```

variable	sd	variance	cv	min	max	range	N
selfest_r	5.41	29.23	0.17	15.00	40.00	25.00	247.00
dad_age	7.36	54.15	0.18	21.00	69.00	48.00	191.00

We can use the *table* command to create complex table as below.

```
. table  v18 Bornmainland ,contents(mean selfest_r sd selfest_r ) by (Ethnic_3) format (%8.2f)
```

Ethnicicty and Sex	Mainlandborn	
	OutsideUS Born	US Mainland Born
Mexican		
Male	31.29	33.45
	5.34	5.22
Female	32.10	32.70
	4.98	5.77
Filipino		
Male	32.97	33.64
	5.14	4.82
Female	31.94	31.84
	4.45	4.95
Indochinese		
Male	30.54	33.83
	5.05	3.25
Female	30.58	33.47
	4.82	4.21

These Stata results show the estimates of the mean of self-esteem for ethnic groups based on sex between US-born adolescents vs. those born outside the United States. If we wish to compare the estimated means of self-esteem based on place of birth and sex across three ethnic groups, we can organize the results as shown here. Our comparative variable is ethnic groups instead of birthplace.

. table v18 Ethnic_3 ,contents(mean selfest_r sd selfest_r) by (Bornmainland) format (%8.2f)

Mainlandborn and Sex	Mexican	Filipino	Indochinese
		Ethnicicty	
OutsideUS Born			
Male	31.29	32.97	30.54
	5.34	5.14	5.05
Female	32.10	31.94	30.58
	4.98	4.45	4.82
US Mainland Born			
Male	33.45	33.64	33.83
	5.22	4.82	3.25
Female	32.70	31.84	33.47
	5.77	4.95	4.21

. table v18 Ethnic_3 ,contents(mean selfest_r sd selfest_r) by (Bornmainland) format (%8.2f)

Mainlandborn and Sex	Mexican	Filipino	Indochinese
		Ethnicicty	
OutsideUS Born			
Male	31.29	32.97	30.54
	5.34	5.14	5.05
Female	32.10	31.94	30.58
	4.98	4.45	4.82
US Mainland Born			
Male	33.45	33.64	33.83
	5.22	4.82	3.25
Female	32.70	31.84	33.47
	5.77	4.95	4.21

MEASURES OF THE SHAPE OF A DATA DISTRIBUTION

The measures of central tendency (mean, median, mode) are used to describe the normality in the values of a variable, while measures of variance or dispersion are used to examine the spread of the data of a variable or its variation around a central value. A variable may have the same mean and median between two groups but different levels of variability or vice versa. Besides examining the location and variability of the data of a variable, we also need to examine its distribution shape or the measures of skewness and kurtosis.

Skewness measures symmetry or the lack of symmetry in the distribution of the data of a variable. A distribution of the data of a variable is symmetric if the left and right sides of its center point (mean) are the same. A normal distribution has a skewness of 0. Negative skewness indicates data that are skewed to the left (-) and positive skewness indicates data that are skewed to the right (+). Data sets with low kurtosis tend to have light tails, or a lack of outliers. Kurtosis describes the peak of the frequency distribution with a given variable. Statistical software packages use different formulas to estimate the value of kurtosis, though they will produce values that can be used to interpret the same concept (UCLA Statistical Consultant Group, 2018). Stata uses the formula that produces a value of 3 for a perfect normal distribution (Bock, 1975), but SAS and SPSS use the formula that produces the value of 0 for the normal distribution (Snedecor & Cochran, 1967).

The *tabstat* with the prefix *bysort* command can be used to estimate the skewness or kurtosis of a variable across cultural groups as illustrated below.

```
. bysort Ethnic_3: tabstat selfesteem if Ethnic_3 <., ///
>     s(sk k n) format(%8.2f) col(stat)


-> Ethnic_3 = Mexican

    variable |  skewness  kurtosis         N

  selfesteem |     -0.42      2.48    247.00


-> Ethnic_3 = Filipino

    variable |  skewness  kurtosis         N

  selfesteem |     -0.47      2.78    492.00


-> Ethnic_3 = Indochinese

    variable |  skewness  kurtosis         N

  selfesteem |     -0.17      2.32    182.00
```

Both skewness and kurtosis can be illustrated by a histogram. In cross-cultural comparisons, we want the data of the comparative variables to have a similar distribution and shape among cultural groups of interest.

. **histogram selfesteem, discrete by(Ethnic_3) normal**

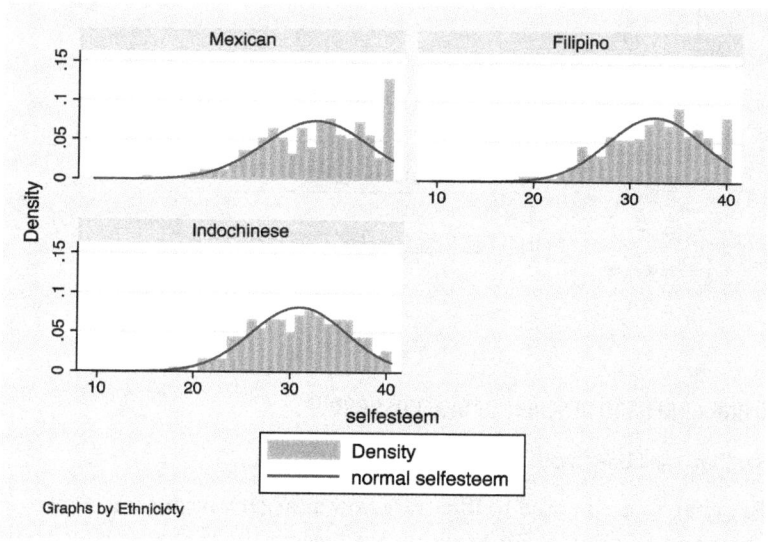

Graphs by Ethnicity

The histograms shown earlier reveal negative skewness for self-esteem across three ethnic groups. The histograms shown here reveal positive skewness of depression for all three ethnic groups.

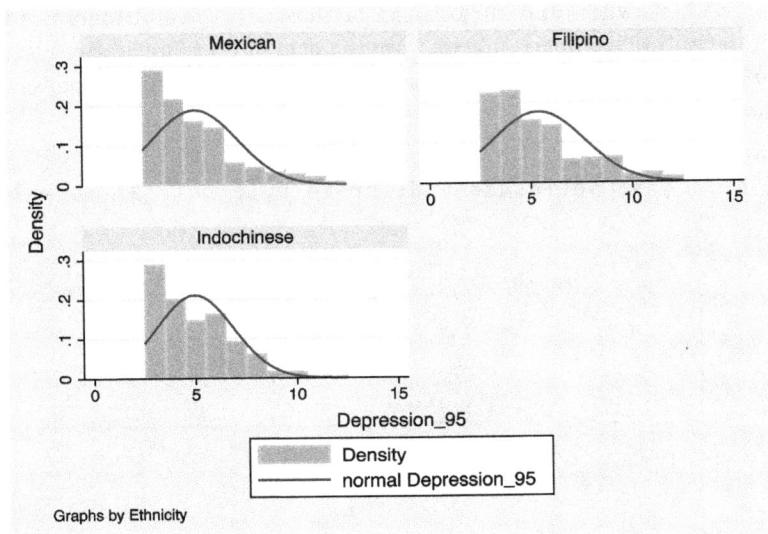

Graphs by Ethnicity

USING GRAPHS TO DESCRIBE DATA ACROSS GROUPS

Bar Charts and Line Charts

Bar charts can be used to illustrate how a target variable varies across comparative groups. For example, we present the mean of self-esteem measured in 1992 between males and females, US-born vs. non-US-born, and across three ethnic groups (Mexican, Filipino, and Indochinese).

The command syntax here produces the desired graph. Note that the option "*bargap(10)*" separates the bars from each other. The option "*intensity(60)*" changes the colors of the bar. We can vary the intensity number in the parentheses to find the best color solutions. We can only have up to three *over()s* options when one *yvar* is specified.

```
graph bar (mean) Selfesteem _ 92, over(sex)
over(Birthplace) over(Ethnic _ 3) ///
  bargap(10) intensity(60) ///
  title("Self-esteem 1992 ") ///
  subtitle("by Sex, Birth Place, and Ethnic
Groups") ///
  note("Source: Children of Immigrants Longitudinal
Study (CILS), 1991-2006 (ICPSR 2052")
```

Stata output:

```
. graph bar (mean) Selfesteem_92, over(sex) over(Birthplace) over(Ethnic_3) ///
>    bargap(10) intensity(60) ///
>    title("Self-esteem 1992 ") ///
>    subtitle("by Sex, Birth Place, and Ethnic Groups") ///
>    note("Source:  Children of Immigrants Longitudinal Study (CILS), 1991-2006 (ICPSR 2052")
```

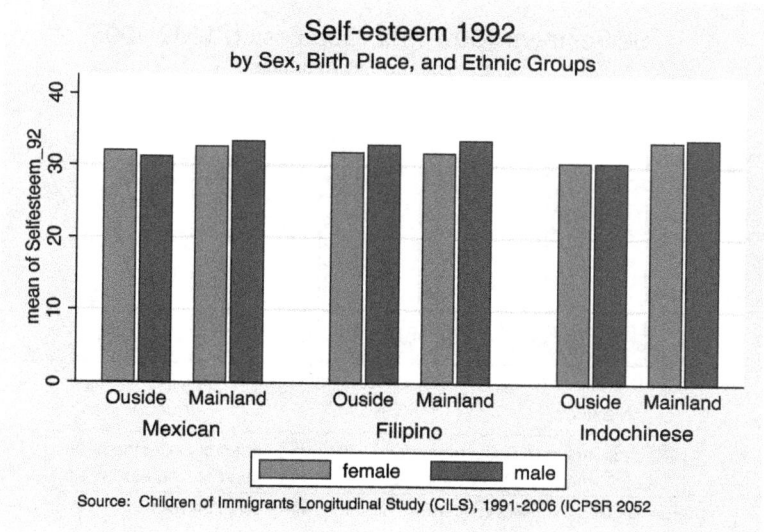

Source: Children of Immigrants Longitudinal Study (CILS), 1991-2006 (ICPSR 2052

Bar Graph with Multiple *Y* Variables

We can produce graphs for multiple target variables, but it is important not to include too much information for a single graph. The command syntax below produces a bar graph with four target variables. When multiple target variables are specified, no more than two *over()* options may be specified.

```
graph bar  (mean) Self-esteem _ 92 Self-esteem _ 95
Depression _ 92 Depression _ 95, ///
  over(sex) over(Ethnic _ 3) bargap(10)
intensity(60) ///
  title("Self-esteem 1992-1995 Depression 1992-
1995") ///
  subtitle("by Sex and Ethnic groups") ///
  note("Source:Children of Immigrants Longitudinal
Study(CILS),1991-2006(ICPSR 2052")
```

Stata output:

```
. graph bar (mean) Selfesteem_92 Selfesteem_95 Depression_92 Depression_95, ///
>    over(sex) over(Ethnic_3) bargap(10) intensity(60) ///
>    title("Self-esteem 1992-1995 Depression 1992-1995") ///
>    subtitle("by Sex and Ethnic groups") ///
>    note("Source:Children of Immigrants Longitudinal Study(CILS),1991-2006(ICPSR 2052")
```

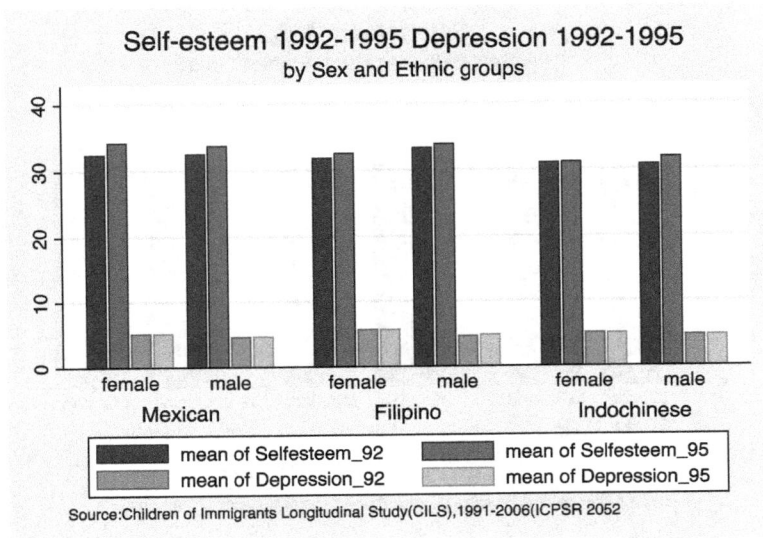

Self-esteem 1992-1995 Depression 1992-1995
by Sex and Ethnic groups

Source:Children of Immigrants Longitudinal Study(CILS),1991-2006(ICPSR 2052

Line Graph

The following line graph presents the association between depression measured in 1995 and self-esteem measured in 1992 for three selected ethnic groups.

```
. preserve

. collapse (mean) selfesteem1, by(depressw2 Ethnic_3)

. twoway line selfesteem1 depressw2 if Ethnic_3==1, sort || ///
>    line selfesteem1 depressw2  if Ethnic_3==2, lp(dash) sort || ///
>    line selfesteem1 depressw2  if Ethnic_3==3, lp(longdash) sort ||, ///
>    legend(order (1 "Mexican" 2 "Filipino" 3 "Indochinese")) ||, ///
>    xtitle(Self-esteem 1992) ///
>    ytitle(Depression 1995) ///
>    title("Depression in 1995 and Self-Esteem Measured 1992") ///
>    subtitle("by Three Ethic Groups") ///
>    note("Source:  Children of Immigrants Longitudinal Study (CILS), 1991-2006 (ICPSR 20520)")

. restore
```

The commands above produce the graph below. The syntax *"preserve"* and *"restore"* inform Stata to return to the original user's data after changes are made to produce the desired results.

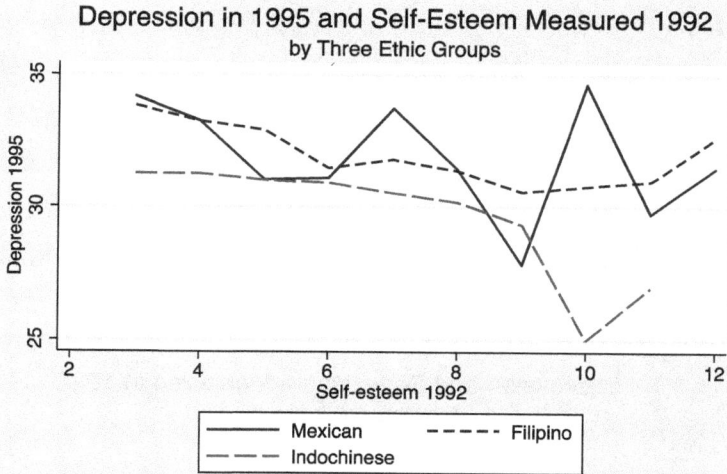

Depression in 1995 and Self-Esteem Measured 1992
by Three Ethic Groups

Source: Children of Immigrants Longitudinal Study (CILS), 1991-2006 (ICPSR 20520)

We can produce smoother lines by using the *"lowess"* command syntax instead of *"line."*

```
preserve
  collapse (mean) self-esteem1, by(depressw1
Ethnic _ 3)
  twoway lowess self-esteem1 depressw1 if Ethnic _
3==1, sort || ///
  lowess self-esteem1 depressw1 if Ethnic _ 3==2,
lp(dash) sort || ///
  lowess self-esteem1 depressw1 if Ethnic _ 3==3, lp
(longdash) sort ||, ///
  legend(order (1 "Mexican" 2 "Filipino" 3
"Indochinese")) ||, ///
  xtitle(Depression) ///
  ytitle(Self-esteem) ///
  title("Depression and Self-Esteem Measured in
1992") ///
  subtitle("by three ethic groups") ///
```

```
    note("Source: Children of Immigrants Longitudinal
Study (CILS), 1991-2006 (ICPSR 20520)")
    restore
```

Stata output:

```
. preserve

.
. collapse (mean) selfesteem1, by(depressw1 Ethnic_3)

.
. twoway lowess selfesteem1 depressw1 if Ethnic_3==1, sort || ///
>    lowess selfesteem1 depressw1  if Ethnic_3==2, lp(dash) sort || ///
>    lowess selfesteem1 depressw1  if Ethnic_3==3, lp(longdash) sort ||, ///
>    legend(order (1 "Mexican" 2 "Filipino" 3 "Indochinese")) ||, ///
>    xtitle(Depression) ///
>    ytitle(Self-esteem) ///
>    title("Depression and Self-Esteem Measured in 1992") ///
>        subtitle("by three ethic groups") ///
>        note("Source:  Children of Immigrants Longitudinal Study (CILS), 1991-2006 (ICPSR 20520)")

. restore
```

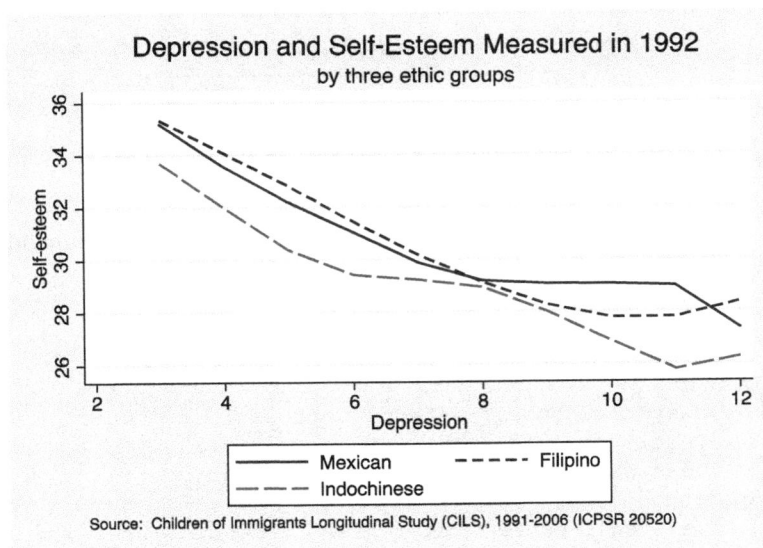

Source: Children of Immigrants Longitudinal Study (CILS), 1991-2006 (ICPSR 20520)

In this chapter, we demonstrated and illustrated basic tasks that are useful to prepare data for cross-cultural analysis. We provided examples of the use of graphics to present descriptive statistics across cultural-comparison groups. For example, the last graph in this chapter showed how the correlation between self-esteem and depression can be illus-trated across three ethnic groups. The lines that crossed one another suggested that there may be ethnic differences in the association between self-esteem and depression. These differences can be further examined in multiple regression analysis.

USEFUL STATA COMMANDS FOR CROSS-CULTURAL DATA ANALYSIS

Descriptive Statistics

```
codebook varname
  summarize varname
  tabulate varname
  bysort groupname: tabulate varname
  bysort groupname: summarize varname
```

These commands are very useful for displaying various summary (mean, median, mode, standard error, standard deviation, skewness, kurtosis) and tabulation/*chi*-square statistics across groups.

For example, the command bysort race: tabulate gender, *chi2* will display the percentages in gender difference for different race groups along with *chi*-square values for determining statistical significance (i.e. χ^2, p-value). The command bysort race: summarize income, detail will display the means, standard deviations, skewness, and kurtosis for different race groups.

Bivariate Analysis

```
ttest varname, by (groupvar)
  oneway varname groupvar, bonferroni tabulate
```

These commands will display tests of significant differences in means. The command ttest income, by (*gender*) will display average incomes for gender, defined as male or female, along with the difference in the means, t-values, standard errors, and p-values. The command oneway income race, bonferroni tabulate will display the results of the F-ANOVA test for statistical differences in average incomes for different race groups. In addition, the bonferroni as an "option" in the command will display comparisons for each group (i.e., White vs. Black, White vs. Asian, White vs. Hispanic, Black vs. Asian, Black vs. Hispanic, Asian vs. Hispanic).

REFERENCES

Bock, R. D. (1975). *Multivariate statistical methods in behavioral research.* New York: McGraw-Hill.

Michell, J. (1986). Measurement scales and statistics: A clash of paradigms. *Psychological Bulletin, 100,* 398–407.

Portes, A., & Rumbaut, R. G. (2006). *Children of immigrants longitudinal study (CILS), 1991–2006.* Ann Arbor, MI: Inter-university Consortium for Political and Social Research.

Snedecor, G. W., & Cochran, W. G. (1967). *Statistical methods* (6th ed.). Ames: Iowa State University Press.

Stevens, S. S. (1946). On the theory of scales of measurement. *Science, 103,* 667–680.

UCLA: Statistical Consulting Group. FAQ: What's with the different formulas for kurtosis? From https://stats.idre.ucla.edu/sas/modules/sas-learning-moduleintroduction-to-the-features-of-sas/ (accessed October 20, 2018).

4

Applied Multiple Regression Analysis in Cross-Cultural Comparisons

This chapter focuses on the application of multiple regression analysis in cross-cultural comparisons using the Stata statistical package. As discussed earlier, comparisons of cultures on their own (i.e., Chinese born in China vs. Chinese American, African American vs. Caribbean American, cisgender vs. nonbinary gender) are insufficient. Our position is that it is almost impossible to measure culture as a variable on its own for the sake of comparisons. We can compare cultures indirectly, however, using cultural markers such as age, sex, gender, ethnicity, or race. Individuals who inherited a cultural marker such as race, sex, gender, and ethnicity are assumed to share similarities in many cultural aspects or characteristics. Individuals who acquired a cultural marker such as immigrant status are also assumed to share cultural similarities with others who belong to the same immigrant group.

Applied Cross-Cultural Data Analysis for Social Work. Thanh V. Tran and Keith T. Chan,
Oxford University Press. © Oxford University Press 2021. DOI: 10.1093/oso/9780190888510.003.0004

The key question that remains to be addressed is whether cultural markers should be viewed as independent (predictor) variables, moderator variables, or covariates? Our position is that we should not view cultural markers as covariates in cross-cultural comparisons, but only as independent (predictor) variables or as moderator variables.

BASIC CONCEPTS

Multiple Regression Analysis refers to the statistical techniques that can be used to examine the linear or straight-line relationships of one dependent variable (outcome) with a number of independent variables (predictors). For example, we examine the linear relationships of life satisfaction with age, sex, income, or education. Thus, our dependent variable is life satisfaction and independent variables are age, sex, income, and education. We can be more specific by declaring age is the independent variable and sex, income, and education are covariates or controlling variables. Multiple regression analysis is illustrated in the equation shown here.

$$y = \beta_0 + \beta_1 x_1 + \beta_2 x_2 + \beta_k x_k + \varepsilon$$

y = the dependent variable

β_0 = the intercept or constant (the expected mean value of the dependent variable y when all independent variables in the equation have a value of zero)

β_1 = the regression coefficient or regression slope (the coefficient represents the average (mean) change in the dependent variable given a one unit change in the independent (predictor) variables. A positive coefficient refers to the same direction of change in both dependent and dependent variables. A negative coefficient refers to the inverse change meaning as the values on one variable increase, the values of the other variable decrease)

ε = the errors or unexplained variances.

Assumptions

The key assumptions of multiple regression include (Daniel, 2005):

1. The independent variables X's are nonrandom or fixed variables. This assumption indicates that inferences arrived at from the sample data can only apply to a specific set of independent variables X's, not other collection of the X's.
2. The dependent variable Y values that correspond to a select set of the independent variables X's values are normally distributed.
3. The variances of the dependent variable are assumed to be equal. This is the assumption of homoscedasticity.
4. The values of the dependent variable are independent from each other. This is the assumption of independent errors.
5. The independent variables X's are not highly correlated. The problem of high correlation among the X's variables is called multicollinearity.
6. The errors in the regression equation are normally distributed.
7. The dependent variable Y must be a continuous variable.
8. The independent variables X can be either continuous or categorical (factor) variables.

Evaluate Variables Before Analysis

1. Run a frequency for categorical variables and descriptive statistics for continuous dependent and independent variables.
2. For the composite scale or composite index variables (i.e., life satisfaction scale, self-esteem scale, and the like), check their internal consistency reliability or the Cronbach's Alpha coefficient.

Transforming Variables: Reasons for Using Transformations

There are many reasons for transformation. The following list, though not exhaustive, outlines some of the most important considerations for cross-cultural data analysis.

1. Convenience
2. Reducing skewness

3. Equal spreads
4. Linear relationships
5. Additive relationships

1. **Convenience.** A transformed scale may be as natural as the original scale and more convenient for a specific purpose (e.g., percentages rather than original data, sines rather than degrees). We can use the standardized scores of the variables instead of the raw score. Most commonly a **standard score** is calculated using the mean and standard deviation (SD) of a variable:

$$z = \frac{Mean\ of\ X}{Standard\ deviation\ of\ X}$$

Standard deviation does not change the shape of a distribution.

2. **Reducing skewness.** A transformation may be used to reduce skewness of the variables. We take roots or logarithms or reciprocals (roots are the least preferable) to reduce skewness to the right. This is the most common problem when managing non-normality in a variable's distribution. Transformations using squares (x^2), cubes (x^3) or higher powers (x^k) can potentially reduce skewness to the left.

3. **Equal spreads.** To meet the condition of **homoscedasticity** we can use transformation to produce approximately equal spreads.

4. **Linear relationships.** This assumption is important in linear regression.

5. **Additive relationships.** The relationships are estimated as additive in a regression equation: y = a + bx.

Transformation of variables does not guarantee that we will meet all the assumptions.

Example

This illustrated regression analysis uses the data from the Children of Immigrants (Portes & Rumbaut, 2007). The extracted data consists of the following variables: depress PSES NEES COO sex SE95.

The variable "depress" is a composite measure of depression based on four items drawn from the Center for Epidemiology Depression (CESD) scale (Skriner, Chu, & Reynolds, 2014) (see Table 4.1).

Table 4.1. Variables Used in the Regression Analysis Examples

Variable: Depression	Label	1 = Rarely	2 = Some of the time	3 = Occasionally	4 = Most of the time
V114	Felt sad past week				
V115	Could not get going past week				
V116	Did not feel like eating past week				
V117	I felt depressed past week				
Positive Self- Image: PSI*		4 = Agree a lot	3 = Agree a little	2 = Disagree a little	1 = Disagree a lot
v101r	Being a person of worth				
v102r	Have good qualities				
v104r	Do things well				
v106r	Positive attitudes				
v107r	Satisfied with self				
Negative Self-Image: NSI*		4 = Agree a lot	3 = Agree a little	2 = Disagree a little	1 = Disagree a lot
v103r	Felt like a failure				
v105r	Do not have much to be proud of				
v108r	Wish had more self-respect				
v109r	Feel useless				
v110r	No good at all				
Country of Origin: COO**	Cuba	Mexico	Philippines	Vietnam	
Sex***	Female	Male			

*These items making up the PSE and NImage scales were recoded such that higher scores refer to higher positive self-image and higher negative self-image.
**Country of origin was created from v21 in the data set.
***Sex was recoded from v18 in the data set. Full description of the items in the Table can be found in the codebook of the data set.

Checking the Data

The *describe* command can be written as *des* or *d*, and it provides basic information of the variables that are used in the analysis. The information includes variable name, value label, and variable label. Other information labeled as "storage type" and "display format" can be ignored.

Stata Output:

```
. des v114-v117 v101-v110 COO sex

                  storage   display    value
variable name     type      format     label     variable label
------------------------------------------------------------------------
v114              double    %12.0g     v114      Felt sad past week
v115              double    %12.0g     v115      Could not get going past week
v116              double    %12.0g     v116      Did not feel like eating past week
v117              double    %12.0g     v117      I felt depressed past week
v101              double    %12.0g     v101      I am a person of worth
v102              double    %12.0g     v102      I have a number of good qualities
v103              double    %12.0g     v103      I'm inclined to feel I'm a failure
v104              double    %12.0g     v104      I do things as well as other people
v105              double    %12.0g     v105      I do not have much to be proud of
v106              double    %12.0g     v106      I take a positive attitude toward myself
v107              double    %12.0g     v107      I am satisfied with myself
v108              double    %12.0g     v108      I wish I had more respect for myself
v109              double    %12.0g     v109      I certainly feel useless at times
v110              double    %12.0g     v110      At times I think I am no good at all
COO               double    %12.0g     COO       COUNTRY OF ORIGIN
sex               double    %12.0g     sex       sex
```

We now can look at some basic distribution statistics of these variables by using the *summarize* or *sum* command. This procedure provides the sample size, the mean, the standard deviation, the minimum and maximum values of each variable. The outputs of this procedure are useful for the investigators to verify the coding of the variables. For example, we can see that all the responses of the items that measure depression, positive self-image, and negative self-image have values ranging from 1 to 4.

`. sum v114-v117 v101-v110 COO sex`

Variable	Obs	Mean	Std. Dev.	Min	Max
v114	5,217	1.685068	.8307232	1	4
v115	5,195	1.675842	.8211347	1	4
v116	5,194	1.572199	.8401427	1	4
v117	5,199	1.684362	.9087915	1	4
v101	5,175	1.467633	.7173277	1	4
v102	5,215	1.38466	.612235	1	4
v103	5,197	3.495286	.815215	1	4
v104	5,216	1.447469	.690659	1	4
v105	5,192	3.399653	.9256423	1	4
v106	5,191	1.575226	.7638729	1	4
v107	5,192	1.598806	.7853053	1	4
v108	5,186	2.629001	1.143865	1	4
v109	5,195	2.838114	1.017261	1	4
v110	5,214	3.085347	1.055802	1	4
COO	3,170	2.105047	1.049428	1	4
sex	5,262	.4893577	.4999342	0	1

To find out more information on the categorical variables, such as COO (country of origin) and sex, we can use the *tabulate* command. The *tabulate* or *tab* command is good for a single variable. To generate the frequencies of multiple categorical variables we use the "tab1" command.

```
. tab1 COO sex

-> tabulation of COO
```

COUNTRY OF ORIGIN	Freq.	Percent	Cum.
Cuba	1,226	38.68	38.68
Mexico	755	23.82	62.49
Philippines	819	25.84	88.33
Vietnam	370	11.67	100.00
Total	3,170	100.00	

```
-> tabulation of sex
```

sex	Freq.	Percent	Cum.
female	2,687	51.06	51.06
male	2,575	48.94	100.00
Total	5,262	100.00	

If you want to know how the categorical variables were coded, you can use the *codebook* command as following:

```
. codebook sex
------------------------------------------------------------
sex                                                       sex
------------------------------------------------------------
type:            numeric (double)
label:           sex
range:           [0,1]                    units:    1
unique values:   2                        missing:  0/5,262
tabulation:      Freq. Numeric  Label
                 2,687       0  female
                 2,575       1  male
```

Based on the information provided by the *codebook* command, the variable sex was coded 1 for male and 0 for female. The coding values of the categorical variables in regression analysis help the investigators to interpret the results. By default, Stata will use the category with the value of 0 or the lowest values of a variable as the reference or base group. This information is important for the interpretation of the regression coefficient. As coded, the interpretation of the "sex" variable will be the comparison between male and female.

Creating and Evaluating Scales

Scales are variables that are made up by a set of items or questions used to measure abstract constructs such as depression and self-esteem (Rosenberg, 1965). In this analysis we have three scales: depression, positive self-image, and negative self-image.

As listed in Table 4.1, depression is measured by four items with scores ranging from 1 to 4 or low to high depression. We always should study the codebook of the data before generating scales. The codebook indicates that these variables were coded such that 1 refers to low and 4 refers to high depression. We can add these four items to generate a depression scale for our analysis.

generate DEPRESS=v114+v115+v116+v117

After summing the four items to generate the depression scale, "DEPRESS," we should check the distribution of the scale to make sure the scores are corrected.

```
. sum DEPRESS
```

Variable	Obs	Mean	Std. Dev.	Min	Max
DEPRESS	5,163	6.616889	2.540192	4	16

The minimum (Min) and maximum (Max) indicate that the scores of the depression scale are correct, given that we have four items with score values ranging from 1 to 4. If a respondent checked 1 for all four items, the total score is 4. On the other hand, if the respondent checked 4 to all four items, the score must be 16.

Check for the Scale's Reliability

Assuming that the items we used to measure the variables of interest are meaningful and valid based on previous research or our own clinical and research experience, we should always check for the internal consistency reliability or the Cronbach's Alpha coefficient of reliability.

```
. alpha v114-v117,item
```

Test scale = mean(unstandardized items)

Item	Obs	Sign	item–test correlation	item–rest correlation	average interitem covariance	alpha
v114	5217	+	0.7937	0.6059	.2634984	0.6262
v115	5195	+	0.7007	0.4649	.3301048	0.7070
v116	5194	+	0.6645	0.4067	.3545346	0.7391
v117	5199	+	0.8216	0.6299	.2348842	0.6075
Test scale					.2957814	0.7342

```
. alpha v114-v117,item  label
```

Test scale = mean(unstandardized items)

Items	S	it-cor	ir-cor	ii-cov	alpha	label
v114	+	0.794	0.606	.2635	0.626	Felt sad past week
v115	+	0.701	0.465	.3301	0.707	Could not get going past week
v116	+	0.665	0.407	.35453	0.739	Did not feel like eating past week
v117	+	0.822	0.630	.23488	0.608	I felt depressed past week
Test scale				.29578	0.734	mean(unstandardized items)

Reading the Outputs

alpha v114-v117,item: list the 4 items of the scale with the option "item."

alpha v114-v117,item std: std refers to standardized scores

the std option produces the correlations. If the std option is not declared, the outputs are based on the covariances.

Test scale = mean(unstandardized items): Use the items' original scores.

Test scale = mean(standardized items): Use the standardized scores.

Item: "item specifies that item-test and item-rest correlations and the effects of removing an item from the scale be displayed" (See Stata Reference Manual).

The results above show useful information about the reliability properties of the scale items and the scale itself. For each item, the results show the sample size of the number of observations. The + sign indicates that all items are positively correlated. This is important because the items that are designed to measure a construct must always be positively correlated. If they are not, we need to recode their values such that all items are measured in the same manner. The "item-rest correlation" refers to the correlation between an item and the entire scale. The "interitem covariance" refers to the correlation between an item and the remaining items of the scale. For example, the correlation of .263 is the correlation between v114 and the sum of v115, v116, and v117. The last column "alpha" shows what the alpha coefficient would be if we removed the item from the scale. For example, if we removed item v114 we would have the total alpha of .6262, which is actually lower than .7342 or the alpha coefficient of the entire scale. We only consider removing an item from a scale if the scale's alpha coefficient increases higher than the current total alpha coefficient. The last row of the table shows the average correlation among the scale's items and the alpha coefficient for the entire scale. Using a simple rule of thumb, we could say the four items of depression have an acceptable level of reliability.

CHECKING RELIABILITY ACROSS CULTURAL GROUPS

It should be noted that in cross-cultural analysis we also should assess the reliability of a scale across the cultural groups.

```
bysort COO:alpha v114-v117 if COO<.,item
```

Note:
bysort COO tells Stata to perform the analysis for all groups but separately.

The country of origin, COO, variable was created by extracting four groups from the original variable v21. Groups that were not selected were coded as (".").

If COO< tells Stata to use data for the groups not coded as (".").

```
. bysort COO:alpha v114-v117 if COO<.,item
```

```
-> COO = Cuba
```

Test scale = mean(unstandardized items)

Item	Obs	Sign	item-test correlation	item-rest correlation	average interitem covariance	alpha
v114	1219	+	0.7986	0.6186	.2450533	0.6261
v115	1216	+	0.6911	0.4641	.3163944	0.7130
v116	1218	+	0.6729	0.4022	.3271577	0.7511
v117	1219	+	0.8293	0.6485	.2169276	0.6034
Test scale					.2764121	0.7375

```
-> COO = Mexico
```

Test scale = mean(unstandardized items)

Item	Obs	Sign	item-test correlation	item-rest correlation	average interitem covariance	alpha
v114	751	+	0.7806	0.5886	.2752518	0.6209
v115	748	+	0.6831	0.4339	.3432186	0.7076
v116	748	+	0.6881	0.4272	.3385262	0.7124
v117	746	+	0.8089	0.6090	.2439461	0.6014
Test scale					.3002293	0.7247

```
-> COO = Philippines
```

Test scale = mean(unstandardized items)

Item	Obs	Sign	item-test correlation	item-rest correlation	average interitem covariance	alpha
v114	814	+	0.8240	0.6506	.2492036	0.6250
v115	815	+	0.6983	0.4630	.3406148	0.7312
v116	812	+	0.6273	0.3911	.3895099	0.7638
v117	812	+	0.8507	0.6766	.22007	0.6050
Test scale					.2998566	0.7480

```
-> COO = Vietnam
```

Test scale = mean(unstandardized items)

Item	Obs	Sign	item-test correlation	item-rest correlation	average interitem covariance	alpha
v114	365	+	0.7846	0.6030	.3014447	0.6716
v115	365	+	0.8137	0.6344	.2791227	0.6547
v116	363	+	0.6319	0.3939	.4112896	0.7752
v117	363	+	0.8100	0.6007	.2664248	0.6692
Test scale					.3145655	0.7546

The alpha coefficients of the depression scale with four items have similar values across the four comparison groups indicating that it is acceptable to use this scale for cross-cultural comparison among the four selected cultural groups based on country of origin (Skriner, Chu, & Reynolds, 2014). We should check the reliability for all scale variables before performing regression analysis or other multivariate statistical analyses. In this example, we have two more scale variables, positive self-image (PSI) and negative self-image (NSI). Due to space limitation, we do not present the alpha coefficient analyses of these two variables, but they both had acceptable alpha coefficients ranging from .70 to .76. It should be noted that variables that have poor alpha coefficients will reduce the probability to reject the null hypothesis.

Cultural Marker as an Independent Variable

As discussed previously, we should analyze cultural variables as independent variables or as moderator variables. In the following regression analyses, we will illustrate the analysis of the variable country of origin, which is considered as a cultural marker.

$$Depression = a + b1(Country\ of\ Origin)$$

Before we run the regression analysis, it is a good practice to look at the mean of the dependent variable (e.g., depression) across the comparative groups.

```
. mean depress,over(COO)

Mean estimation                    Number of obs   =       3,123

        Cuba: COO = Cuba
      Mexico: COO = Mexico
 Philippines: COO = Philippines
     Vietnam: COO = Vietnam
```

Over	Mean	Std. Err.	[95% Conf. Interval]	
depress				
Cuba	6.41598	.0702966	6.278148	6.553812
Mexico	6.731444	.0946614	6.545839	6.917049
Philippines	6.726485	.0892376	6.551515	6.901456
Vietnam	6.747222	.1354177	6.481705	7.012739

We begin with the model that examines whether respondents' country origin (cultural groups) has a significant association with depression. Here, we view cultural groups as an independent variable. We want to know whether levels of depression are similar across these four cultural groups. The mean table above shows some variation of the mean of depression across the selected cultural groups, but we do not know whether the differences are statistically significant.

Running Regression Analysis. The command syntax: "*regress depress i.COO*" is used to perform a regression analysis of depression (depress) with its respective independent variable COO (country of origin). The prefix "i" declares that the independent variable "COO" is a categorical variable. Country of origin is a categorical variable; therefore, it must be transformed into dummy variables in order to perform a regression analysis. The rule of transforming a categorical variable into dummy variables is "C-1." C refers to the number of categories. The variable country of origin has four categories, thus there are three dummy variables. A dummy variable has values of 0 and 1. The category coded as 1 is the reference group. In the results above, the Cuban group was assigned as the base or reference group. By default, Stata uses the group that was assigned with the lowest numerical value to be the base (reference) group. In our data we coded the country of origin variable as 1 = Cuba, 2 = Mexico, 3 = Philippines, and 4 = Vietnam. It is possible to select a different category to be our base category as long as the categories are labeled correctly.

. `regress depress i.COO`

Source	SS	df	MS			
				Number of obs	=	3,123
				F(3, 3119)	=	3.91
Model	74.369202	3	24.789734	Prob > F	=	0.0084
Residual	19753.0378	3,119	6.3331317	R-squared	=	0.0038
				Adj R-squared	=	0.0028
Total	19827.407	3,122	6.35086707	Root MSE	=	2.5166

depress	Coef.	Std. Err.	t	P>|t|	[95% Conf. Interval]	
COO						
Mexico	.3154638	.1173179	2.69	0.007	.0854357	.5454918
Philippines	.3105049	.1142575	2.72	0.007	.0864773	.5345325
Vietnam	.331242	.1510258	2.19	0.028	.035122	.627362
_cons	6.41598	.0722271	88.83	0.000	6.274363	6.557598

Reading the Regression Output

The results above have two parts. The first part shows the statistics of the ANOVA table providing the information of the goodness of fit of the regression equation (model). The second part shows the statistics for estimates of each independent variable included in the model.

Dissecting the ANOVA Table

Source. There are three types of variance in a regression analysis. The *Model Variance* refers to the variance that is explained by the independent variables used in the regression model. The *Residual Variance* refers to variance that is not explained by the independent variables used in the analysis. This is sometimes referred to as the error of the estimates. The *Total Variance* of the regression model is the sum of the Model and Residual variance (Regression Analysis-Stata Annotated Output, https://stats.idre.ucla.edu/stata/output/regression-analysis/).

> **SS**—There are three sums of squares and each has a degree of freedom (df):
>
> **SSModel:** The squared differences between predicted value of y (dependent variable) and the mean of y.
>
> **SSResidual:** The sum of squared errors in prediction.
>
> **SSTotal:** The total variability around the mean.

Given the results above we can estimate the total sum of square as:

> 74.369202 (SSModel) + 19753.0378 (SSResidual) = 19827.407 (SSTotal)
>
> **df (SSModel)** = The degree of freedom of the SSModel equals the number of predictors (independent variables + constant −1). The results above show three regression estimates and a constant. Thus, the degree of freedom = 3 (estimates) + 1 (constant) −1 = 3 (df).
>
> **df (SSResidual)** = The degree of freedom of the sum of square residuals equal the degree of freedom of the total sum of square minus the degree of freedom of the sum of sum of square of the model (3,122 − 3 = 3,119).
>
> **df (SSTotal)** = The sample size minus 1 (3,123 − 1 = 3,122).

There are three mean squares (MS) associated with three sum of squares. The MS equals the sum of squares divided by their respective degree of freedom. For example, the mean square of the model equals 74.369202/3 = 24.789734.

Evaluating the Regression Equation

The F test value is the quotient of the Mean Square Model (24.789734) divided by the Mean Square Residual (6.3331317). The results above show the F value of 3.91 (24.789734/6.3331317 = 3.91). The level of significance associated with the F value is very small (p value = 0.0084) or less than .05.

$$F = \frac{Mean\ Square\ Model\ (24.789734)}{Mean\ Square\ Residual\ (6.3331317)} = 3.91$$

The F value and its level of significance (p value) is used to answer the question of whether the independent variables in the regression model have statistically significant associations with the dependent variable? The answer is "yes," given the F value and its level of statistical significance.

The R-squared value is the proportion of variance in the dependent explained by the independent variable. The R-squared value can range from 0.0 to 1.0, or from 0.00% to 100.00%. The R-squared is the quotient of the Model SS of square divided by the Total SS (74.369202/19827.407 = 0.0038). The Adjusted R-Squared can be estimated by this formula 1 − (Residual MS/Total MS) or 1− (6.3331317/6.35086707) = 0.0028.

$$R^2 = \frac{Model\ SS\ (74.369202)}{Total\ SS\ (19827.407)} = 0.0038$$

Although the R-Squared and the Adjusted R-Squared are the most commonly used statistics to determine the goodness of fit for the regression model, it should be noted that on their own they may not be reliable and should be interpreted with care (see Ford, 2015) (https://data.library. virginia.edu/is-r-squared-useless/).

Root Mean Square

The root mean square (RMS) error is a measure of the variability (spread) of all observed y values around the predicted values of y. It is the standard deviation of the error term of the regression model. Thus, the RMS error is measured on the same measurement units of y.

$$Root\ Mean\ Square = \sqrt{1 - \boxed{R^2}}$$

If there is no error in the dependent variable, the RMS is zero. The closer is the RMS to zero, the better the fit of the regression model.

Evaluating the Independent Variable (s)

In the second part of the result outputs, we see a table with seven columns. The first column lists the variables used in the analysis beginning with the dependent variable (depress), the independent variable, and the constant (cons). As explained earlier, the variable "country of origin" has four categories (i.e., four countries); therefore we have three dummy variables in the regression analysis. Each dummy variable has two categories and is coded as 1 and 0. The base category or the reference category should be always coded as 0. In this analysis, we compare the average of depression between Mexico (1) and Cuba (0), Philippines (1) and Cuba (0), and Vietnam (1) and Cuba (0).

The second column lists the unstandardized regression coefficient (b) of each independent variable. The third column lists the standard errors (SE) of the regression coefficients. Smaller standard errors indicate a better chance of the regression coefficient being statistically significant. If the independent variable is a continuous variable, we interpret the coefficient as the change in one unit of the dependent variable (Y) associated with a unit change in the independent variable (X). For the categorical variable of "country of origin" we should interpret the regression coefficient as the difference in the average of the dependent variable. For example, the regression coefficient indicates the difference of the average depression between Mexico and Cuba (base/reference) and so on. Based on the data presented above, the regression coefficient of Mexico is .3154638, which indicates that respondents whose country of origin is Mexico have an average depression .3154638 greater than those whose country of origin is Cuba. The constant (cons) is the mean of depression of the respondents whose country of origin is Cuba (base or reference group). If we add the constant to .3154638, we will have the average of depression score for respondents from Mexico (.3154638 + 6.41598 = 6.731444).

The fourth column lists the t-test value and the fifth column the p value of the t-test. This is the test of significance for each independent variable. For example, we test the null hypothesis that there is no difference in the average depression score between Mexico and Cuba. The t-test and its associated p value tell us whether we can reject that null hypothesis. Given the t-test value of 2.69 and p value of .007, which is less than 0.05, we can conclude that there is a statistically significant difference in average depression scores between respondents whose country of origin is Mexico and those whose country of origin is Cuba. The t-test value is the ratio of the regression coefficient over its standard error (.3154638/.1173179 = 2.69).

$$t = \frac{Coef.}{Std.Err.}$$

The sixth and seventh columns of the table list the lower and upper levels of 95% confidence intervals of the regression estimates. For a regression coefficient to be statistically significant, there should be no zero values for the lower and upper levels of 95% confidence intervals, and they should both be in the same direction. We can interpret the 95% confidence intervals as a measure of precision of the regression coefficient. In other words, the narrower the interval, the more precise the estimate.

Estimating the 95% Confidence Intervals

$$95\%\% C.I. = b \pm 1.96(SE\ b)$$

b = unstandardized regression coefficient
1.96 = t distribution value at .05 level of significant, two-tailed test
SE b = standard error of the unstandardized regression coefficient

In order to generate the exact t distribution value, we can use the Stata syntax below

```
. display invttail(e(df_r),0.025)
1.9607236
```

Using the t value of 1.9607236 with the equation above will generate similar values of the 95% confidence intervals produced by the Stata regression outputs.

Changing the Base or Reference Group

In the results above, Stata by default uses the group coded at the lowest numerical value as the base reference group. If we want to use Vietnam or another group as our base group for comparison, we can rerun the regression by changing the base or reference group. By using the prefix "b" and selecting a different category (4 = Vietnam), we can assign a different reference group for the analysis.

```
. codebook COO
```

COO			RECODE of V21 (Respondent national origin)
type:	numeric (long)		
label:	COO		
range:	[1,4]	units:	1
unique values:	4	missing .:	2,092/5,262
tabulation:	Freq.	Numeric	Label
	1,226	1	Cuba
	755	2	Mexico
	819	3	Philippines
	370	4	Vietnam
	2,092	.	

```
. regress depress b4.COO,base
```

Source	SS	df	MS
Model	74.369202	3	24.789734
Residual	19753.0378	3,119	6.3331317
Total	19827.407	3,122	6.35086707

```
Number of obs =      3,123
F(3, 3119)    =       3.91
Prob > F      =     0.0084
R-squared     =     0.0038
Adj R-squared =     0.0028
Root MSE      =     2.5166
```

depress	Coef.	Std. Err.	t	P>|t|	[95% Conf. Interval]	
COO						
Cuba	-.331242	.1510258	-2.19	0.028	-.627362	-.035122
Mexico	-.0157782	.1616749	-0.10	0.922	-.3327782	.3012217
Philippines	-.0207371	.1594681	-0.13	0.897	-.3334101	.2919359
Vietnam	0	(base)				
_cons	6.747222	.132635	50.87	0.000	6.487162	7.007283

Note that in the regression syntax, we use "b4.COO" instead of "i.COO." The prefix "b4" refers to the selection of group coded as "4" in the variable as the base group. We can change the base group using this prefix.

Group Comparisons

The results showed a statistically significant difference between respondents from Cuba and Vietnam (b = −.331242, p = 0 .028), though there was no statistically significant difference between respondents from Mexico and Vietnam (b = −.0157782, p = 0.922) and Philippines and Vietnam (b = −.0207371, p = 0.897). Are differences between Mexico and Cuba, Philippines and Cuba, and Philippines and Mexico statistically significant? We can use the *test* command to conduct further comparisons. The *test* command performs a Wald test of significance to test a null hypothesis. For example, to test the null hypothesis of no difference in the average depression score between respondents from Mexico (coded as 2) and Cuba (coded as 1), we can perform the following:

```
. test 1.COO=2.COO

 ( 1)   1.COO - 2.COO = 0

       F(  1,  3119) =     7.23
            Prob > F =   0.0072
```

The F value and its p value, which is less than 0.05, indicates that the difference in the average depression score is statistically significant between respondents from Mexico and Cuba as their countries of origin.

To compare Cuba and Philippines we run:

```
. test 1.COO=3.COO

 ( 1)   1.COO - 3.COO = 0

      F(   1,   3119) =      7.39
              Prob > F =    0.0066
```

The results show a statistically significant difference.

To compare Mexico and Philippines we run:

```
. test 2.COO=3.COO

 ( 1)   2.COO - 3.COO = 0

      F(   1,   3119) =      0.00
              Prob > F =    0.9691
```

The results show the difference was not statistically significant.

Additional Analysis

Following the regression command, we can perform a few more postestimations to generate additional information regarding the relationship between the independent variable(s) and dependent variable. Below the *margins* command generates the predicted values of the dependent variable across different categories of a categorical variable.

```
. margins COO
```

```
Adjusted predictions                        Number of obs    =    3,123
Model VCE   : OLS

Expression  : Linear prediction, predict()
```

	Margin	Delta–method Std. Err.	t	P>|t|	[95% Conf. Interval]	
COO						
Cuba	6.41598	.0722271	88.83	0.000	6.274363	6.557598
Mexico	6.731444	.0924486	72.81	0.000	6.550178	6.91271
Philippines	6.726485	.0885327	75.98	0.000	6.552897	6.900073
Vietnam	6.747222	.132635	50.87	0.000	6.487162	7.007283

These predicted averages of depression are the same as the mean of depression generated by the *mean* command.

```
. mean depress,over(COO)
```

After the *margins* command, we can generate a graph for the predicted means of depression across four cultural groups.

```
. marginsplot
```

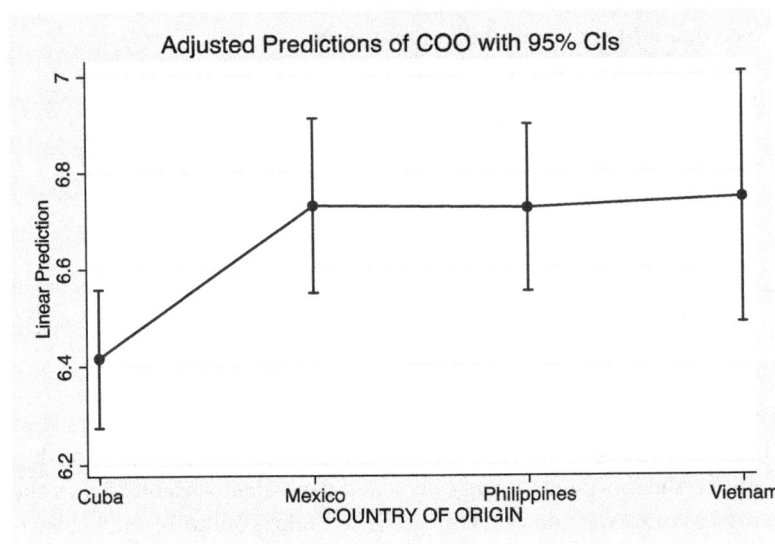

We can plot this as a bar chart instead of the line graph shown above.

```
. regress depress i.COO,base
. margins COO
. marginsplot, recast(bar) plotopts(barwidth(.5)) noci
```

The plot option (*plotopts*) allows us to set the size for the bars. We can adjust how the bars appear in the graph from .1 to 1, thereby adjusting the width of the bars. The option *noci* refers to no confidence intervals if we do not want the bars to include the 95% confidence intervals. We also can select this option for line graphs.

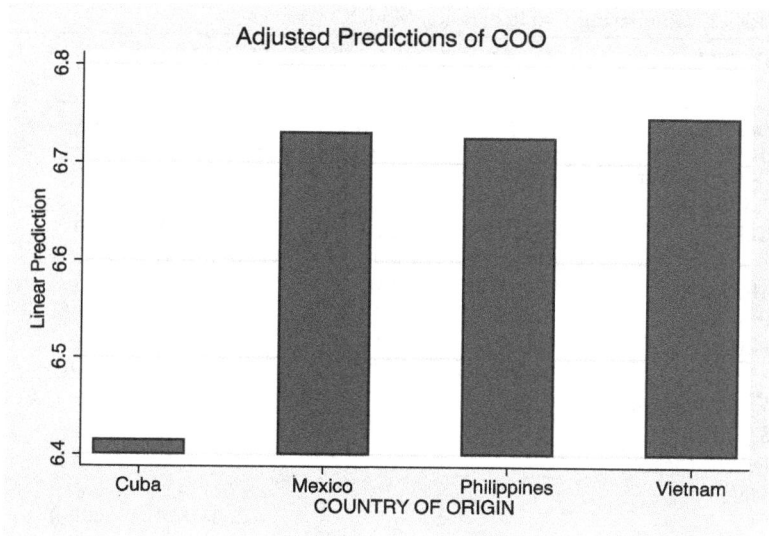

Adjusted Predictions of COO

Determining Cultural Differences and Similarities

The regression analysis of depression and cultural groups measured by countries of origin revealed differences and similarities among these groups. We need to perform further analyses to control for possible influences of other variables to identify cultural differences and similarities in the dependent variables among selected cultural groups. Let us theorize that cultural difference in depression scores might be influenced by sex. We add the sex variable to our regression analysis.

COMPARING THE MODELS

The summarized results presented in Table 4.2 show changes in the estimate values between the two models. The value of the F statistics changed from 3.91 to 37.95. The regression coefficients of the variable COO (country of origin) changed between Model 1 and Model 2. We also see changes in the goodness of fit measures between the two models. The R-squared value improved in Model 2 due to the addition of the sex variable into Model 2. The R-squared value will improve when

Table 4.2. Comparing Two Regression Models

Variables	Model 1 (N =3123)		Model 2 (N = 3223)	
Depression	b (SE)	t (p value)	B (SE)	t (p value)
COO (Country of Origin)				
Cuba	−.331242 (.1510258)	−2.19 (0.028)	−.3237203 (.1477811)	−2.19 (0.029)
Mexico	−.0157782 (.1616749)	−0.10 (0.922)	−.0197844 (.1582003)	−0.13 (0.900)
Philippines	−.0207371 (.1594681)	−0.13 (0.897)	−.039386 (.1560486)	−0.25 (0.801)
Vietnam (base)				
Sex				
Female (base)				
Male			−1.041592 (.0881804)	−11.81 (0.000)
Constant	6.747222 (.132635_	50.87 (0.000)	7.285378 (.1375487)	52.97 (0.000)

F(3, 3119) = 3.91
Prob > F = 0.0084
R-squared = 0.0038
Adj R-squared = 0.0028
Root MSE = 2.5166

F(4, 3118) = 37.95
Prob > F = 0.0000
R-squared = 0.0464
Adj R-squared = 0.0452
Root MSE = 2.4625

more variables are added to the regression equation even if the added variables are not statistically significant. The Root Mean Square Error (RMSE) was slightly smaller in Model 2 suggesting a better fit. Overall, by adding the sex variable into the analysis, we see some minor changes. We cannot definitively state, however, that our culture variable has an independent association with depression. Further analyses must be undertaken to arrive at this determination.

COMPARING TWO NESTED REGRESSION MODELS IN CROSS-CULTURAL ANALYSIS

We found minor differences and similarities in the association between depression scores among cultural groups and the association was somewhat influenced when the sex variable was introduced into the analysis. We can use the following command to compare the regression analysis model without the sex variable (m1) and the regression model with the sex variable (m2).

Step 1. Run the regression of depression and country of origin.

```
. regress depress b4.C00,base
```

Step 2. Save the regression results in m1 (m1 is an arbitrary label; you can use M1 or MA and so on to name the file that stores the results for further comparison).

```
. estimate store m1
```

Step 3. Run the same regression analysis in Step 1, adding sex as a control variable.

```
. regress depress b4.C00 i.sex,base
```

Step 4. Save the results of model 2.

```
. estimate store m2
```

Due to space limitations, we do not present the results here.
Step 5. Test the hypothesis m1 = m2.

```
. lrtest m1 m2

Likelihood-ratio test                          LR chi2(1)  =    136.71
(Assumption: m1 nested in m2)                  Prob > chi2 =    0.0000
```

The results of the Likelihood-ratio test show that the two regression models are statistically and significantly different, suggesting that adding the sex variable favorably changed the predictability of the overall model. We might want to find out whether sex moderates the association of cultural groups and depression. In other words, we can conduct moderation analysis to determine whether the association between countries of origin and average depression scores varies between females and males.

TESTING FOR POSSIBLE INTERACTION EFFECT BETWEEN CULTURAL GROUPS AND A MODERATING VARIABLE: STATISTICAL-MULTIPLICATIVE INTERACTION

Cultural differences could vary by known or unknown factors. Previous research and clinical observations could provide valuable insight for determining possible variables that can moderate the association between the cultural variable and the dependent variable. In the example above, we found that by adding the sex variable into the regression analysis, the association between country of origin and depression changed significantly. This is further supported by the results of the likelihood test comparing the model without the sex variable and the model with the sex variable. We want to know whether the association between country of origin and average depression varies between females and males across the four selected countries of origin, which is shown in the following analysis.

```
. regress depress i.COO##i.sex,base
```

Source	SS	df	MS		
				Number of obs	=	3,123
				F(7, 3115)	=	22.90
Model	970.400998	7	138.628714	Prob > F	=	0.0000
Residual	18857.006	3,115	6.05361348	R-squared	=	0.0489
				Adj R-squared	=	0.0468
Total	19827.407	3,122	6.35086707	Root MSE	=	2.4604

depress	Coef.	Std. Err.	t	P>|t|	[95% Conf. Interval]	
COO						
Cuba	0	(base)				
Mexico	.1669335	.1650527	1.01	0.312	-.1566896	.4905565
Philippines	.2493315	.1594383	1.56	0.118	-.0632834	.5619463
Vietnam	-.0978801	.212754	-0.46	0.646	-.5150324	.3192721
sex						
female	0	(base)				
male	-1.213853	.1413918	-8.59	0.000	-1.491083	-.9366223
COO#sex						
Mexico#male	.2634373	.2295457	1.15	0.251	-.1866388	.7135134
Philippines#male	.0615016	.2235178	0.28	0.783	-.3767555	.4997587
Vietnam#male	.8135933	.2955145	2.75	0.006	.2341703	1.393016
_cons	7.051903	.1023395	68.91	0.000	6.851243	7.252563

The regression command specifies that we only want to look at the interaction effect, not the main effects of the two independent variables. The results above only show the interaction effects between country of origin (COO) and sex. Cuba#female, or females from Cuba, is the base group for comparisons. These results are difficult to interpret, therefore, we should look at the predictive margins as discussed below.

MARGIN PREDICTIONS

The *margins* command produces the predicted probabilities for the interaction effect of country of origin and sex. The adjusted predictions of the means of depression below are presented in the following table with seven columns. The first column listed the interaction terms. For example, "Cuba#female" refers to the interaction term of Cuba as a country of origin and female. The second and the third columns present the predicted means of the interactions and their respective standard errors. The fourth and fifth columns present the t tests and their respective levels of significance. These t tests are similar to those found in the regression results. The t-test value for each predicted mean is the quotient derived from the margin predicted mean divided by its standard error. If we divide the predicted mean of "Cuba#female" by its standard error we will have the t value as presented in the result outputs (7.051903/.1023395 = 68.91). The last two columns are the 95% confidence intervals. A confidence interval is the range of likely values of the parameter (estimate $\pm$ margin of error). When there is a zero value within the range of a 95% confidence interval, we can conclude that the estimate is not statistically meaningful or statistically significant. If the confidence interval does not include the null value, then we conclude that an estimate is statistically significant. The t value and its level of significance corresponds to the 95% confidence interval. If the t value of an estimate is not significant, there is a zero value within the range of the 95% confidence interval of that estimate (Sullivan, L., Confidence Intervals, retrieved 2019 from http://sphweb.bumc. bu.edu/otlt/MPH-Modules/BS/BS704_Confidence_Intervals/BS704_ Confidence_Intervals_print.html).

All interaction terms in our example were found to be statistically significant, but our goal is to find out whether the association between country of origin and depression varies, or whether it is dependent on sex. This tests whether the combination of having a certain country of origin and being a female or a male would have different levels of depression. We need to test the differences in the adjusted predictions of the means of depression after the *margins* command.

```
. margins COO#sex

Adjusted predictions                    Number of obs    =      3,123
Model VCE    : OLS

Expression   : Linear prediction, predict()
```

	Margin	Delta-method Std. Err.	t	P>|t|	[95% Conf. Interval]	
COO#sex						
Cuba#female	7.051903	.1023395	68.91	0.000	6.851243	7.252563
Cuba#male	5.83805	.0975616	59.84	0.000	5.646759	6.029342
Mexico#female	7.218837	.1294952	55.75	0.000	6.964932	7.472741
Mexico#male	6.268421	.1262163	49.66	0.000	6.020945	6.515897
Philippines#female	7.301235	.1222587	59.72	0.000	7.061519	7.54095
Philippines#male	6.148883	.1225617	50.17	0.000	5.908573	6.389193
Vietnam#female	6.954023	.1865231	37.28	0.000	6.588302	7.319744
Vietnam#male	6.553763	.180406	36.33	0.000	6.200037	6.90749

COMPARING THE PREDICTED MEANS

We can use the command "*margins* r.COO, over (sex)" to compare predicted means. This command specifies the comparisons of the predicted means for depression scores of respondents from different countries of origin between female and male. For example, the predicted mean of depression of respondents with Vietnam as country of origin who are male (Vietnam#male) is 6.553763, and the predicted mean of respondents with Cuba as country of origin who are male is 5.83805. The difference between these two predicted means is (6.553763 − 5.83805 = .715713). We should ask whether the difference of .715713 is statistically significant? The "*margin* r" command provides the F test of significance for the comparisons. Let us look at the comparison of depression between Vietnam country of origin and Cuba country of origin for males. Do males from these two countries of origin have different means of depression? The results below have two parts, the first part includes the F test of significance for the comparisons and the second part has the difference of the predicted means of each comparison. The F value for the Vietnam versus Cuba male comparison is 12.18 and its p value is 0.0005. This result shows that the difference in predicted means of depression between respondents with these two countries of origin who are male is statistically different in such a way that male respondents from Vietnam as country of origin had a significantly greater predicted mean of depression as compared to male respondents from Cuba as country of origin.

```
. margins r.COO,over(sex)

Contrasts of predictive margins
Model VCE    : OLS

Expression   : Linear prediction, predict()
over         : sex
```

	df	F	P>F
COO@sex			
(Mexico vs Cuba) female	1	1.02	0.3119
(Mexico vs Cuba) male	1	7.28	0.0070
(Philippines vs Cuba) female	1	2.45	0.1180
(Philippines vs Cuba) male	1	3.94	0.0473
(Vietnam vs Cuba) female	1	0.21	0.6455
(Vietnam vs Cuba) male	1	12.18	0.0005
Joint	6	3.22	0.0037
Denominator	3115		

	Contrast	Delta-method Std. Err.	[95% Conf. Interval]	
COO@sex				
(Mexico vs Cuba) female	.1669335	.1650527	-.1566896	.4905565
(Mexico vs Cuba) male	.4303707	.1595269	.1175823	.7431592
(Philippines vs Cuba) female	.2493315	.1594383	-.0632834	.5619463
(Philippines vs Cuba) male	.3108331	.1566513	.0036828	.6179833
(Vietnam vs Cuba) female	-.0978801	.212754	-.5150324	.3192721
(Vietnam vs Cuba) male	.7157131	.2050965	.3135751	1.117851

ADDITIONAL TESTS FOR INTERACTION EFFECT

After running the regression analysis with the interaction term, we can use the *testparm* command to further verify the presence of the interaction effect.

```
. testparm COO##sex

( 1)   2.COO = 0
( 2)   3.COO = 0
( 3)   4.COO = 0
( 4)   1.sex = 0
( 5)   2.COO#1.sex = 0
( 6)   3.COO#1.sex = 0
( 7)   4.COO#1.sex = 0

       F(  7,  3115) =    22.90
            Prob > F =    0.0000
```

The value of the F test and its level of significance confirm the inter-action effect reported in the regression analysis.

We can use the *contrast* command to illustrate the interaction effect.

```
. contrast sex@COO

Contrasts of marginal linear predictions

Margins        : asbalanced
```

	df	F	P>F
sex@COO			
Cuba	1	73.70	0.0000
Mexico	1	27.62	0.0000
Philippines	1	44.31	0.0000
Vietnam	1	2.38	0.1231
Joint	4	37.00	0.0000
Denominator	3115		

The results above show that sex difference in the predicted means of depression was significant among respondents reporting Cuba, Mexico, and Philippines as countries of origin, but not for those reporting Vietnam as country of origin. These results are similar to the results of the "*margin* r.COO, over(sex)" command reported earlier.

COMPARING DEPRESSION AMONG FEMALES AND MALES ACROSS COUNTRIES OF ORIGIN

The command "*contrast* COO@sex" produces the test of significance to compare depression score among females and males across different countries of origin. The results below show that there was no statistically significant difference in the predicted means of depression among females from the four countries of origin. The difference was significant, however, among males across four countries of origin. Similar to what was presented earlier, we can verify this in the results of the command "*margin* r.COO, over (sex)."

```
. contrast COO@sex

Contrasts of marginal linear predictions

Margins          : asbalanced
```

	d f	F	P>F
COO@sex			
female	3	1.28	0.2803
male	3	5.16	0.0015
Joint	6	3.22	0.0037
Denominator	3115		

FURTHER COMPARISONS

We can make further comparisons using the pairwise comparison procedure as shown below. Stata will compute all possible pairwise comparisons generated by the combination of the two variables. We can use all available post hoc tests of significance such as Bonferroni, Sidak, Scheffe, and Tukey similar to one-way ANOVA tests. For this example, we will use the Bonferroni test. We will briefly look at a few pairwise comparisons extracted from the full table below.

		Delta-method	Bonferroni		Bonferroni	
	Contrast	Std. Err.	t	P>|t|	[95% Conf. Interval]	
COO#sex						
(Cuba#male) vs (Cuba#female)	-1.213853	.1413918	-8.59	0.000	-1.655905	-.7718007
(Mexico#female) vs (Cuba#female)	.1669335	.1650527	1.01	1.000	-.3490929	.6829598
(Mexico#male) vs (Cuba#female)	-.7834821	.1624929	-4.82	0.000	-1.291505	-.2754588
(Philippines#female) vs (Cuba#female)	.2493315	.1594383	1.56	1.000	-.2491418	.7478048

The above extracted results show that males and females from Cuba differed in levels of depression such that males had a lower predicted mean in depression scores compared to females ($t = -8.59$, $p < .001$). If we now look at the comparison between females from Cuba and females from Mexico, the results show the difference was not statistically significant ($t = 1.01$, $p > 0.05$). The full list of comparisons is included in the table below.

```
. margins COO#sex,pwcompare(effect) mcompare(bon)

Pairwise comparisons of adjusted predictions
Model VCE    : OLS

Expression   : Linear prediction, predict()
```

	Number of Comparisons
COO#sex	28

		Delta-method	Bonferroni		Bonferroni	
	Contrast	Std. Err.	t	P>|t|	[95% Conf. Interval]	
COO#sex						
(Cuba#male) vs (Cuba#female)	-1.213853	.1413918	-8.59	0.000	-1.655905	-.7718007
(Mexico#female) vs (Cuba#female)	.1669335	.1650527	1.01	1.000	-.3490929	.6829598
(Mexico#male) vs (Cuba#female)	-.7834821	.1624929	-4.82	0.000	-1.291505	-.2754588
(Philippines#female) vs (Cuba#female)	.2493315	.1594383	1.56	1.000	-.2491418	.7478048
(Philippines#male) vs (Cuba#female)	-.9030197	.1596708	-5.66	0.000	-1.40222	-.4038197
(Vietnam#female) vs (Cuba#female)	-.0978801	.212754	-0.46	1.000	-.7630414	.5672811
(Vietnam#male) vs (Cuba#female)	-.4981397	.2074119	-2.40	0.459	-1.146599	.1503198
(Mexico#female) vs (Cuba#male)	1.380786	.1621335	8.52	0.000	.8738866	1.887686
(Mexico#male) vs (Cuba#male)	.4303707	.1595269	2.70	0.196	-.0683794	.9291209
(Philippines#female) vs (Cuba#male)	1.463184	.1564144	9.35	0.000	.9741651	1.952203
(Philippines#male) vs (Cuba#male)	.3108331	.1566513	1.98	1.000	-.1789269	.800593
(Vietnam#female) vs (Cuba#male)	1.115973	.2104974	5.30	0.000	.4578666	1.774079
(Vietnam#male) vs (Cuba#male)	.7157131	.2050965	3.49	0.014	.0744925	1.356934
(Mexico#male) vs (Mexico#female)	-.9504155	.1808302	-5.26	0.000	-1.515769	-.3850618
(Philippines#male) vs (Mexico#female)	.082398	.1780904	0.46	1.000	-.47439	.639186
(Philippines#female) vs (Mexico#male)	-1.069953	.1782986	-6.00	0.000	-1.627392	-.5125145
(Vietnam#female) vs (Mexico#female)	-.2648136	.227068	-1.17	1.000	-.9747268	.4450996
(Vietnam#male) vs (Mexico#female)	-.6650731	.2220705	-2.99	0.077	-1.359362	.0292157
(Philippines#female) vs (Mexico#male)	1.032814	.1757207	5.88	0.000	.4834345	1.582193
(Philippines#male) vs (Mexico#male)	-.1195377	.1759316	-0.68	1.000	-.6695762	.4305009
(Vietnam#female) vs (Mexico#male)	.6856019	.2252142	3.04	0.066	-.0185154	1.389719
(Vietnam#male) vs (Mexico#male)	.2853424	.2201746	1.30	1.000	-.403019	.9737038
(Philippines#male) vs (Philippines#female)	-1.152351	.1731143	-6.66	0.000	-1.693582	-.6111207
(Vietnam#female) vs (Philippines#female)	-.3472116	.2230203	-1.56	1.000	-1.04447	.3500468
(Vietnam#male) vs (Philippines#female)	-.7474711	.21793	-3.43	0.017	-1.428815	-.0661273
(Vietnam#female) vs (Philippines#male)	.8051396	.2231866	3.61	0.009	.1073615	1.502918
(Vietnam#male) vs (Philippines#male)	.4048801	.2181002	1.86	1.000	-.2769956	1.086756
(Vietnam#male) vs (Vietnam#female)	-.4002595	.2594941	-1.54	1.000	-1.211551	.4110316

The above pairwise comparisons allow us to test several hypotheses within and between cultural groups stratified by sex.

SUBGROUP ANALYSIS

This section illustrates the use of subgroup or stratified analysis in cross-cultural comparison. We will compare sex differences in the sense of positive self-assessment as measured by five positive items of the Rosenberg's Self-Esteem Scale.

```
. des v101r–v107r

                  storage   display   value
variable name     type      format    label     variable label

v101r             long      %18.0g    vlabel    RECODE of v101 (I am a person of worth)
v102r             long      %18.0g    vlabel    RECODE of v102 (I have a number of good qualities)
v104r             long      %18.0g    vlabel    RECODE of v104 (I do things as well as other people)
v106r             long      %18.0g    vlabel    RECODE of v106 (I take a positive attitude toward myself)
v107r             long      %18.0g    vlabel    RECODE of v107 (I am satisfied with myself)
```

It is important to check the internal consistency of these five positive items between males and females. This is because our dependent should be comparable between the comparative groups to avoid biases of measurement (please see Tran, Nguyen, & Chan, 2016).

```
. bysort sex:alpha v101r–v107r

-> sex = female

Test scale = mean(unstandardized items)

Average interitem covariance:      .1860267
Number of items in the scale:             5
Scale reliability coefficient:       0.7364

-> sex = male

Test scale = mean(unstandardized items)

Average interitem covariance:      .1886803
Number of items in the scale:             5
Scale reliability coefficient:       0.7486
```

The results of the *alpha* analysis show these five items had comparable internal consistency. We can begin our subgroup analysis with the following procedure. We begin by reviewing the variables that will be used in this example.

```
. sum positive CNTYORIG english sex
```

Variable	Obs	Mean	Std. Dev.	Min	Max
positive	5,096	17.54749	2.50207	5	20
CNTYORIG	2,654	1.791635	.8199764	1	3
english	5,240	14.83779	1.943373	4	16
sex	5,262	.4893577	.4999342	0	1

After reviewing the variables to be used, we will run two separate regression models: one for male and one for female.

```
. regres positive i.CNTYORIG english i.usborn    ///
>    if sex==1,base
```

Source	SS	df	MS		
Model	939.413348	4	234.853337		
Residual	7958.36409	1,307	6.08903144		
Total	8897.77744	1,311	6.78701559		

Number of obs	=	1,312
F(4, 1307)	=	38.57
Prob > F	=	0.0000
R-squared	=	0.1056
Adj R-squared	=	0.1028
Root MSE	=	2.4676

positive	Coef.	Std. Err.	t	P>|t|	[95% Conf. Interval]	
CNTYORIG						
Cuba	0	(base)				
Mexico	-.5512355	.1710439	-3.22	0.001	-.8867861	-.215685
Indochina	-.5404517	.2064219	-2.62	0.009	-.9454061	-.1354972
english	.338021	.0358707	9.42	0.000	.2676506	.4083914
usborn						
Foreign Born	0	(base)				
U.S. Born	-.2285933	.1652974	-1.38	0.167	-.5528705	.0956839
_cons	12.99983	.5445021	23.87	0.000	11.93164	14.06802

All variables had significant associations with positive self-assessment with the exception of the US-born variable. We need to save this analysis for later comparison using a name that is easy to remember and related to the focus of our analysis. We will save the whole regression equation as "male" because the analysis was performed for males only.

```
. estimate store male
```

After saving or storing the analysis for males in the file named "male," we repeat the analysis for females only and store the results in the file named "female."

```
. regres positive i.CNTYORIG english i.usborn      ///
>    if sex==0,base
```

Source	SS	df	MS
Model	665.510501	4	166.377625
Residual	7658.89254	1,243	6.1616191
Total	8324.40304	1,247	6.67554374

Number of obs = 1,248
F(4, 1243)   = 27.00
Prob > F   = 0.0000
R-squared   = 0.0799
Adj R-squared = 0.0770
Root MSE   = 2.4823

positive	Coef.	Std. Err.	t	P>|t|	[95% Conf. Interval]	
CNTYORIG						
Cuba	0	(base)				
Mexico	.0089802	.1767169	0.05	0.959	-.3377162	.3556766
Indochina	-.3797225	.2002501	-1.90	0.058	-.7725879	.013143
english	.3208138	.0359832	8.92	0.000	.2502193	.3914082
usborn						
Foreign Born	0	(base)				
U.S. Born	-.2060954	.166752	-1.24	0.217	-.5332418	.121051
_cons	12.75252	.5472267	23.30	0.000	11.67893	13.82611

```
. estimate store female
```

Among females, countries of origin and US-born had no significant associations with positive self-assessment. We will compare the regression coefficients between the two regression models for subsequent analyses. First, we will use the *seemingly unrelated estimation* (*suest*) postestimation command to combine the two regression models that will allow us to compare the regression coefficients between the two models.

```
. suest male female

Simultaneous results for male, female
```

| | | | | | Number of obs | = | 2,560 |

	Coef.	Robust Std. Err.	z	P>|z|	[95% Conf. Interval]	
male_mean						
CNTYORIG						
Mexico	-.5512355	.1764255	-3.12	0.002	-.8970232	-.2054478
Indochina	-.5404517	.1934718	-2.79	0.005	-.9196494	-.161254
english	.338021	.0398016	8.49	0.000	.2600114	.4160306
usborn						
U.S. Born	-.2285933	.1554255	-1.47	0.141	-.5332218	.0760351
_cons	12.99983	.608528	21.36	0.000	11.80714	14.19252
male_lnvar						
_cons	1.806489	.0534497	33.80	0.000	1.70173	1.911248
female_mean						
CNTYORIG						
Mexico	.0089802	.1777878	0.05	0.960	-.3394774	.3574378
Indochina	-.3797225	.1945966	-1.95	0.051	-.7611248	.0016798
english	.3208138	.036585	8.77	0.000	.2491084	.3925191
usborn						
U.S. Born	-.2060954	.1652853	-1.25	0.212	-.5300486	.1178578
_cons	12.75252	.5585439	22.83	0.000	11.65779	13.84724
female_lnvar						
_cons	1.81834	.0496586	36.62	0.000	1.72101	1.915669

We now can test the equality of each regression coefficient between the separate models of male-only and female-only in the analyses. Let us compare the coefficients of countries of origin between males and females.

Hypothesis: Differences in positive self-assessment between respondents reporting Mexico and Cuba as countries of origin should be the same between males and females.

We use the test command to statistically determine the validity of this hypothesis.

```
. test _b[male_mean:2.CNTYORIG]=_b[female_mean:2.CNTYORIG]

( 1)   [male_mean]2.CNTYORIG - [female_mean]2.CNTYORIG = 0

           chi2(  1) =    5.00
         Prob > chi2 =    0.0253
```

_b *refers to the coefficient to be compared.*

male_mean *refers to the analysis stored in the file named male that contains the average score of the dependent variable (positive).*

2.CNTYORIG *refers to the category coded as 2 in the countries of origin variable that is Mexico. We must use the correct coding for each category of the variable under consideration.*

chi2(1) *refers to the χ^2 test of significance with 1 degree of freedom.*

Prob > chi2 *refers to the level of significance or the P value of the χ^2 test.*

Given the level of significance of .025, which is less than .05, we can conclude that among male respondents, those with Mexico as country of origin had lower average positive self-assessment than those from Cuba. Among female respondents, however, there was no statistically significant difference between Mexico and Cuba as countries of origin.

We can perform the same procedure to compare Indochina and Cuba as countries of origin:

```
. test _b[male_mean:3.CNTYORIG]=_b[female_mean:3.CNTYORIG]

( 1)   [male_mean]3.CNTYORIG - [female_mean]3.CNTYORIG = 0

           chi2(  1) =    0.34
         Prob > chi2 =    0.5581
```

The results of the comparison between Indochina and Cuba show no difference given the P value of the χ^2 test is greater than 0.05.

When we compare the coefficient of continuous variables such as English competency, we do not specify the exact numerical values for the range of the value.

```
. test _b[male_mean:english]=_b[female_mean:english]

( 1)  [male_mean]english - [female_mean]english = 0

          chi2(  1) =      0.10
         Prob > chi2 =      0.7503
```

Using subgroup or stratified analysis allows us to compare the influences of multiple independent and covariates across-groups. The "seemingly unrelated estimation (suest)" illustrated here is one useful tool for cross-cultural comparisons to compare different independent variables on the same outcome.

Applied Regression for Mediation Analysis in Cross-Cultural Comparisons

In this section, we will illustrate the use of mediation analysis for cross-cultural comparisons. Mediation analysis aims to identify the causal (longitudinal data) or noncausal (cross-sectional data) pathways between an independent variable and a dependent variable (Pearl, 2014). As discussed earlier, when cultural variables are operationalized as independent variables, we need to control or account for possible variables that might influence the direct association between a cultural variable and its respective dependent variable. In the interaction analysis, we examine whether the association between a cultural independent variable and its respective dependent variable depends on another variable. In mediation analysis, we aim to identify the pathways of the association between a cultural independent variable and its respective dependent variable by examining its direct effect, indirect effect, and total effect. Traditional path analysis via regression analysis can be used to test the mediation hypothesis. The Path Model present in Figure 4.1 illustrates a simple mediation hypothesis.

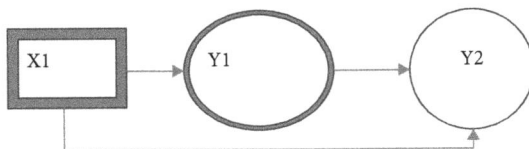

Figure 4.1. Mediation analysis path model.

The information presented in Figure 4.1 illustrates the pathways of X1 to Y2. We use the two waves of data.

X1 = Exogenous variable (Independent variable)
Y1 = Endogenous variable (Mediation variable)
Y2 =Endogenous variable (Dependent variable)

The analysis of the variables in Figure 4.1 involves two structural equations:

$$Y1 = a + b1\ X1$$

$$Y2 = a + b1Y1 + b2X1$$

Steps in Mediation Analysis Using Simple SEM with Stata

In this example, we will illustrate the use of simple path analysis with no latent variables to test the mediation effect of English ability. We hypothesize that the association between country of origin (cultural variable) and depression is mediated by English ability.

Variable Specification

Exogenous variables:

Country of origin (Independent variable)
Sex (Covariate)
Endogenous variables:
English ability (Mediation variable)
Depression (Dependent variable)

1. Model Specification

```
sem (english <- corigin2 corigin3 corigin4 sex) ///
   (depressw1 <- english corigin2 corigin3 corigin4 sex)
   estat teffects
```

The model specification can be written in two regression equations:

$$english = a + corigin2 + corigin3 + corigin4 + sex$$

$$depressw1 = a + english + corigin2 + corigin3 + corigin4 + sex$$

Endogenous Variables: dependent and mediation variables. These variables must be continuous variables.

Dependent variable:

depressw1 = depression measured at wave 1 (continuous)

Mediation variable:

english = English ability (continuous)

Exogenous Variables: Independent and Covariates or Control Variables. These variables can be dummy or continuous variables.

Independent variable (s):

corrigin2 = Mexico (dummy, reference = Cuba)
corigin3 = Philippines (dummy, reference = Cuba)
corigin4 = Vietnam (dummy, reference = Cuba)

The Country of origin variable was coded as:

1. Cuba
2. Mexico
3. Philippines
4. Vietnam

Covariate–Control variable:

sex = Respondents' sex (dummy, reference = Female)

Understanding The Stata Syntax:

```
. sem (english <- corigin2 corigin3 corigin4 sex) ///
>      (depressw1 <- english corigin2 corigin3 corigin4 sex)
(2150 observations with missing values excluded)

Endogenous variables

Observed:   english depressw1

Exogenous variables

Observed:   corigin2 corigin3 corigin4 sex
```

We used SEM commands to perform mediation analysis. All variables are treated as observed variables. We have to use lower case variable labels for observed variables and upper case variable labels for latent variables. The "*sem*" command specifies two structural equations.

In the first equation, English ability is the dependent variable and three dummy variables representing three countries of origin are the independent variables. The variable *country of origin* has four countries, therefore, only three dummy variables are allowed. One of the categories has to be the reference or the base for the three dummy variables. In this example, Cuba as country of origin is the base. Sex is the control variable and coded 1 for male and 0 for female. This equation examines the direct association (effect) of the cultural variable (country of origin) and English ability.

In the second equation, depression is the dependent variable; English, country of origin, and sex are the independent variables. Note that the mediation variable is both dependent and independent in the analysis.

Model Definitions (Hubert, 2014)

The **Saturated Model:** This model assumes that all variables in the model are to be correlated.

The **Baseline Model:** This model assumes no correlation among endogenous variables. Correlation among the exogenous variables, however, is assumed.

The **Specified Model:** Relationships among the variables are determined by the investigator.

```
Fitting target model:

Iteration 0:    log likelihood = -19227.21
Iteration 1:    log likelihood = -19227.21

Structural equation model                    Number of obs    =    3,112
Estimation method  = ml
Log likelihood     = -19227.21
```

	Coef.	OIM Std. Err.	z	P>|z|	[95% Conf. Interval]	
Structural						
english						
corigin2	-1.561771	.0851799	-18.33	0.000	-1.728721	-1.394821
corigin3	-.0344512	.0829239	-0.42	0.678	-.1969791	.1280768
corigin4	-1.916755	.1094039	-17.52	0.000	-2.131183	-1.702328
sex	-.1732304	.0653798	-2.65	0.008	-.3013725	-.0450882
_cons	15.50578	.0625644	247.84	0.000	15.38315	15.6284
depressw1						
english	-.0766306	.0199194	-3.85	0.000	-.1156718	-.0375893
corigin2	.0896403	.099634	0.90	0.368	-.1056387	.2849194
corigin3	.3520429	.0921484	3.82	0.000	.1714354	.5326503
corigin4	.2035774	.1274251	1.60	0.110	-.0461712	.453326
sex	-.8003782	.0727325	-11.00	0.000	-.9429314	-.657825
_cons	6.464463	.3165931	20.42	0.000	5.843952	7.084974
var(e.english)	3.322022	.0842166			3.160994	3.491253
var(e.depressw1)	4.101982	.1039894			3.903147	4.310946

```
LR test of model vs. saturated: chi2(0)    =       0.00, Prob > chi2 =      .
```

The results above refer to two structural equations; the first equation specifies English as the dependent variable and the second specifies depression as the dependent variable. These two structural equations were examined simultaneously by Stata. We can interpret the coefficients as the unstandardized regression coefficients. If we want to look at the standardized coefficients, we can use the standardized option in the SEM command syntax.

```
. sem (english <- corigin2 corigin3 corigin4 sex) ///
>     (depressw1 <- english corigin2 corigin3 corigin4 sex), standardized
```

READING THE RESULTS OF THE STRUCTURAL EQUATIONS

English as Dependent Variable

Let us look at the association between country of origin and English. Compared to respondents whose country of origin is Cuba (corigin1), respondents of Mexico as country of origin (corigin2) had a statistically significantly lower English ability (Coef. = −1.561771, p = .000). The z test of significance is similar to the t test in OLS regression analysis. The z test is estimated here:

$$z = \frac{Coef.}{stdandard\ roor} = \frac{-1.561771}{.0851779} = 18.33$$

When the coefficient is statistically significant, its 95% confidence intervals include no zero value. The narrower the range of intervals is, the more precise the prediction. The results show no statistically significant difference in English ability between Philippine country of origin (corigin3) and Cuban country of origin (coring1). Respondents with Vietnam as country of origin (corigin4) had lower English ability than those with Cuba as country of origin (corigin1). Finally, male respondents had a statistically significant lower English ability than females. The statistically significant association between the key independent variable (culture variable), country of origin, and English (mediation variable) satisfies the first requirement of the proposed mediation analysis.

Depression as the Dependent Variable

Let us look at the results of the second equation with depression (depressw1) as the dependent variable. In this model, English is the independent variable assuming the role of the mediation variable. For the mediation hypothesis to be supported, the association between English and depression must be statistically significant. The results show that the association between English ability and depression was statistically significant (Coef. = −.0766306, p = .000). The direction of the association indicates that respondents with greater English ability reported lower depression.

Decomposing the Associations: Direct, Indirect, and Total Associations (Effects)

The structural association of the exogenous and endogenous variables depicted in a path model includes three components: direct, indirect, and total effect. By convention, the term effect refers to both noncausal (cross-sectional data) and causal association (longitudinal data, experimental data).

$$Direct\ Effect + Indirect\ Effect = Total\ Effect$$

Direct Effect or Association

The direct effect or direct association between an independent variable on its respective dependent variable refers to the association that is not mediated by other variables in the model or after controlling for other variables in the model. The coefficients reported in the structural equations above are the same as those reported in the direct effect results below.

```
Direct effects
```

	Coef.	OIM Std. Err.	z	P>|z|	Std. Coef.
Structural					
english					
corigin2	−1.561771	.0851799	−18.33	0.000	−.3330187
corigin3	−.0344512	.0829239	−0.42	0.678	−.0075673
corigin4	−1.916755	.1094039	−17.52	0.000	−.3076319
sex	−.1732304	.0653798	−2.65	0.008	−.0434517
depressw1					
english	−.0766306	.0199194	−3.85	0.000	−.0736198
corigin2	.0896403	.099634	0.90	0.368	.0183632
corigin3	.3520429	.0921484	3.82	0.000	.0742888
corigin4	.2035774	.1274251	1.60	0.110	.0313897
sex	−.8003782	.0727325	−11.00	0.000	−.1928726

When English is the dependent variable, the culture variable (country of origin) has a statistically significant association with English proficiency in such a way that respondents whose country of origin (corigin3= Mexico) have a statistically significant lower English proficiency (Coefficient = −1.561, p = .00) than those whose country of origin is Cuba (corigin1). Respondents from Vietnam (corigin4) also had a statistically significant lower English proficiency that those whose country of origin is Cuba (Coefficient = −1.916, p = .00). There was no statically significant difference in English proficiency between Philippines as the country of origin (corigin2) and Cuba. Male respondents had a statistically significant lower English proficiency than female respondents (Coefficient = −.800, p = .00). To interpret the meaning of the association, we need to be clear about the coding of the variables used in the analysis. The more detailed the description of the measurement of the variables, the easier the interpretation of the statistical results will be.

Indirect Effect

Let us define the indirect effect of the independent variable X1 on Y2 in the model below:

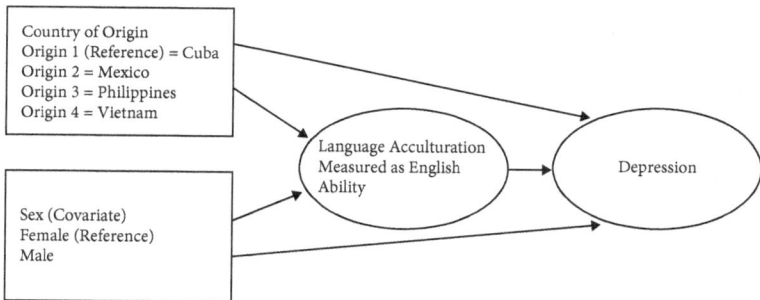

Figure 4.2. Mediation Model of English Ability Between Country of Origin and Depression.

a = direct effect of X (Sex) on Y1 (English)
b = direct effect of Y1 (English) on Y2 (Depression)
c = direct effect of X (Sex) on Y2 (Depression)
I.E. = Indirect effect of X (Sex) on Y2 (Depression)

$$I.E. = a * b$$

Indirect Effect of Sex on Depression = (−.1732304) * (−.0766306) = .0132747

Notes:
Direct effect of Sex on English = 0.1732304
Direct effect of English on Depression = −.0766306

Sex had a significant indirect effect on depression via its direct effect on English (the mediator variable). The z statistic (2.18) and its level of significance (P = .029) indicate the indirect effect is statistically significant. In addition, the corresponding 95% confidence intervals for sex include no zero value in-between, also thereby confirming that the indirect effect is statistically significant.

Indirect effects

	Coef.	OIM Std. Err.	z	P>|z|	[95% Conf. Interval]	
Structural						
english						
corigin2	0	(no path)				
corigin3	0	(no path)				
corigin4	0	(no path)				
sex	0	(no path)				
depressw1						
english	0	(no path)				
corigin2	.1196794	.0317869	3.77	0.000	.0573782	.1819806
corigin3	.00264	.0063915	0.41	0.680	−.009887	.015167
corigin4	.1468821	.0390902	3.76	0.000	.0702667	.2234974
sex	.0132747	.0060834	2.18	0.029	.0013515	.025198

Total Effect

The total effect of a variable on the dependent variable in a path model equals the sum of its direct effect and indirect effect.

$$TE = Direct\ Effect + Indirect\ Effect$$

The total effect of sex on depression equals the sum of its direct effect and its indirect effect via the mediator variable (English), that is:

$$Total\ Effect = (-.8003782) + (.0132747) = -.7871035$$

Total effects

		OIM				
	Coef.	Std. Err.	z	P>|z|		Std. Coef.
Structural						
english						
corigin2	-1.561771	.0851799	-18.33	0.000		-.3330187
corigin3	-.0344512	.0829239	-0.42	0.678		-.0075673
corigin4	-1.916755	.1094039	-17.52	0.000		-.3076319
sex	-.1732304	.0653798	-2.65	0.008		-.0434517
depressw1						
english	-.0766306	.0199194	-3.85	0.000		-.0736198
corigin2	.2093197	.0948775	2.21	0.027		.0428799
corigin3	.3546829	.0923647	3.84	0.000		.0748459
corigin4	.3504595	.1218593	2.88	0.004		.0540375
sex	-.7871035	.0728232	-10.81	0.000		-.1896737

Evaluation the Model: Goodness of Fit

In the chapter on structural equation modeling, we will further illustrate and explain the meanings of the goodness-of-fit measures. For the current path analysis model using the observed variables, we recommend the use of the significant path coefficients (direct, indirect, and total effects) and the coefficient of determination, (R squared) as the measures of the goodness of fit.

To estimate the coefficient of determination, we use the following command:

```
. estat gof, stats(residuals)
```

Fit statistic	Value	Description
Size of residuals		
SRMR	0.000	Standardized root mean squared residual
CD	0.199	Coefficient of determination

The option: stat (residuals) produces the standardized root mean squared residuals (SRMR) and the coefficient of determination (R^2). The SRMR compares the difference between the observed model tested by the sample data and the predicted model. The model fits well when

SRMR is close to 0.00. Hu and Bentler (1999) recommend this value should be close to .08 or below. The value of zero refers to a perfect fit, but there is no such thing as a perfect fit. The value of zero of our observed model only suggests that all hypothetical paths depicted in the model are statistically significant. We need to examine the relative magnitudes of the path coefficients to determine the strength of the model. The interpretation of the coefficient of determination is similar to the interpretation of the R squared in OLS regression analysis.

FURTHER INTERPRETATION OF THE MEDIATION ANALYSIS

To further explain how English ability may mediate the association between sex and depression, we calculate (1) the proportion of the total effect of sex on depression mediated by English ability, (2) the ratio of the indirect effect of sex on its direct effect, and (3) the ratio of total effect of sex to it direct effect. Note that although Stata outputs use the term "effect," it does not mean *causality* due to the use of cross-sectional data in our example.

We first compute the proportion of the total effect that is mediated by the mediation variable (English) as shown here.

Proportion of total Sex effect mediated
$$= .0132747 / -.7871035 = -.01686525$$

The result shows that better English ability reduced the negative effect of being a female on depression by −1.66%.

The ratio of the indirect effect to the direct effect is about −.165. Again, this ratio indicates the positive role of English ability in the association between sex and depression.

Ratio of Sex indirect to Sex to direct effect
$$= . 0132747 / -.8003782 = -.01658553$$

Finally, the total effect is about 98% the direct effect. That means the total effect is lessened by the mediation of English ability. We can reasonably interpret that better English ability helps female respondents to reduce their depression.

Ratio of total Sex to direct Sex effect = −.7871035/−.8003782 = .98341447

We illustrated a simple mediation analysis that can be useful for cross-cultural comparisons, especially when we want to identify and compare the pathways of independent variables to their respective dependent variables across cultural groups.

Seemingly Unrelated Regression

There are situations in which our variables of interest might be correlated with more than one dependent variable due to the fact that the dependent variables are correlated. For example, the concepts of self-esteem (positive self-image and negative self-image) and depression appear to be correlated because they both measure a person's psychological status or psychological well-being. Therefore, these concepts must be correlated. If we studied them separately, we would not be able to examine their correlated error terms. In this section, we will illustrate the application of Seemingly Unrelated Regression analysis in cross-cultural comparisons. As defined in the Stata's Manual, "seemingly unrelated regression models are so called because they appear to be joint estimates from several regression models, each with its own error term. The regressions are related because the (contemporaneous) errors associated with the dependent variables may be correlated (Cameron & Trivedi, 2010).

Analysis of Two Dependent Variables with the Same Independent Variables

Let us look at the variables that will be used in our *sureg* analysis.

```
. des  v101r-v107r rv103-rv110

              storage   display    value
variable name type      format     label     variable label
─────────────────────────────────────────────────────────────────────────────
v101r         long      %18.0g     vlabel    RECODE of v101 (I am a person of worth)
v102r         long      %18.0g     vlabel    RECODE of v102 (I have a number of good qualities)
v104r         long      %18.0g     vlabel    RECODE of v104 (I do things as well as other people)
v106r         long      %18.0g     vlabel    RECODE of v106 (I take a positive attitude toward myself)
v107r         long      %18.0g     vlabel    RECODE of v107 (I am satisfied with myself)
rv103         long      %9.0g                RECODE of v103 (I'm inclined to feel I'm a failure)
rv105         long      %9.0g                RECODE of v105 (I do not have much to be proud of)
rv108         long      %9.0g                RECODE of v108 (I wish I had more respect for myself)
rv109         long      %9.0g                RECODE of v109 (I certainly feel useless at times)
rv110         long      %9.0g                RECODE of v110 (At times I think I am no good at all)
```

We created two subscales from ten items of the Rosenberg Self-Esteem Scale: (1) positive self-assessment and (2) negative self-assessment.

Higher scores indicate higher positive assessment and higher negative assessment, on each respective subscale.

The table below summarizes the descriptive statistics for the variables used in the analysis.

```
. sum positive negative CNTYORIG english sex usborn
```

Variable	Obs	Mean	Std. Dev.	Min	Max
positive	5,096	17.54749	2.50207	5	20
negative	5,106	9.537015	3.488543	5	20
CNTYORIG	2,654	1.791635	.8199764	1	3
english	5,240	14.83779	1.943373	4	16
sex	5,262	.4893577	.4999342	0	1
usborn	5,262	.49981	.5000475	0	1

The syntax below shows two regression equations that were analyzed simultaneously and accounted for the correlation of the two dependent variables.

```
. sureg (positive i.CNTYORIG english i.sex i.usborn ) ///
>       (negative i.CNTYORIG english i.sex i.usborn),corr base
```

Note that positive and negative are our dependent variables and the remaining variables are our independent variables. The syntax *corr* refers to the correlation of the two dependent variables, and *base* tells Stata to list the reference groups for the categorical variables used in the model. The prefix "i." declares a categorical variable. We compare the coefficients between two different dependent variables, therefore, only unstandardized coefficients are reported. The summary statistics show the sample size or number of observations for each equation, the number of estimates including the number of independent variables and the intercept or the constant. The RMSE measures the accuracy of the model, wherein the smaller the value, the better the model. The R-square value is the amount of variance in the dependent variable explained by the independent variable. The χ^2 test indicates whether all or a few variables in the equation are statistically significant. The Breusch-Pagan test of independence determines the significance of the correlation of the errors (residuals) of the dependent variables used in the analysis. In this example, we have the same number of independent variables, but we can have a different number of independent variables.

```
. sureg (positive i.CNTYORIG english i.sex i.usborn ) ///
>        (negative i.CNTYORIG english i.sex i.usborn),corr base

Seemingly unrelated regression
```

Equation	Obs	Parms	RMSE	"R-sq"	chi2	P
positive	2,520	5	2.468164	0.0932	258.99	0.0000
negative	2,520	5	3.351965	0.1086	306.99	0.0000

	Coef.	Std. Err.	z	P>|z|	[95% Conf. Interval]	
positive						
CNTYORIG						
Cuba	0	(base)				
Mexico	-.2754579	.1234651	-2.23	0.026	-.5174451	-.0334707
Indochina	-.4254541	.1440952	-2.95	0.003	-.7078755	-.1430327
english	.3341269	.0257183	12.99	0.000	.28372	.3845338
sex						
female	0	(base)				
male	.3028703	.0986999	3.07	0.002	.109422	.4963186
usborn						
Foreign Born	0	(base)				
U.S. Born	-.2011649	.1177526	-1.71	0.088	-.4319557	.029626
_cons	12.64694	.3971933	31.84	0.000	11.86846	13.42543
negative						
CNTYORIG						
Cuba	0	(base)				
Mexico	.9042591	.1676755	5.39	0.000	.575621	1.232897
Indochina	1.347223	.1956928	6.88	0.000	.9636719	1.730774
english	-.3702371	.0349275	-10.60	0.000	-.4386937	-.3017805
sex						
female	0	(base)				
male	-.4644139	.1340424	-3.46	0.001	-.7271322	-.2016956
usborn						
Foreign Born	0	(base)				
U.S. Born	.0961986	.1599175	0.60	0.547	-.2172339	.409631
_cons	14.68987	.5394204	27.23	0.000	13.63263	15.74711

```
Correlation matrix of residuals:

          positive  negative
positive   1.0000
negative  -0.4492    1.0000

Breusch-Pagan test of independence: chi2(1) =   508.541, Pr = 0.0000
```

The results above show that the two regression models of positive and negative were statistically significant based on the results of the χ^2

tests reported in the summary. Both models explained a relatively small amount of variance (R square). The RSMEs are relatively small. Our interest is to show the association of the dependent variables with their respective independent variables between the two models. The z statistics and the 95% confidence intervals are more important to our goal than the R-square values or the RSME values. For both equations, only the US-born variable had no statistically significant association with either positive or negative dependent variables.

Our next step is to compare the coefficients between the two models. We use the *coeflegend* option to organize the results according to their respective dependent variables. Subsequently, we use the *test* procedure to test the equality of the coefficients between the regression models.

```
. sureg, coeflegend

Seemingly unrelated regression
```

Equation	Obs	Parms	RMSE	"R-sq"	chi2	P
positive	2,520	5	2.468164	0.0932	258.99	0.0000
negative	2,520	5	3.351965	0.1086	306.99	0.0000

	Coef.	Legend
positive		
CNTYORIG		
Mexico	-.2754579	_b[positive:2.CNTYORIG]
Indochina	-.4254541	_b[positive:3.CNTYORIG]
english	.3341269	_b[positive:english]
sex		
male	.3028703	_b[positive:1.sex]
usborn		
U.S. Born	-.2011649	_b[positive:1.usborn]
_cons	12.64694	_b[positive:_cons]
negative		
CNTYORIG		
Mexico	.9042591	_b[negative:2.CNTYORIG]
Indochina	1.347223	_b[negative:3.CNTYORIG]
english	-.3702371	_b[negative:english]
sex		
male	-.4644139	_b[negative:1.sex]
usborn		
U.S. Born	.0961986	_b[negative:1.usborn]
_cons	14.68987	_b[negative:_cons]

With the above results, we can use the *test* command to make comparisons for the coefficients between the two models.

Let us compare the association of the *country of origin* variable with positive and negative self-assessments. To make it easier to interpret the comparisons, we will review the coding of the variable *country of origin* as below.

```
. codebook CNTYORIG

CNTYORIG                                                          Country of origin

            type:  numeric (float)
           label:  ctry

           range:  [1,3]                        units:  1
   unique values:  3                        missing .:  2,608/5,262

      tabulation:  Freq.    Numeric  Label
                   1,226       1     Cuba
                     755       2     Mexico
                     673       3     Indochina
                   2,608       .
```

The first comparison is between Mexico and Cuba as Cuba is the reference (base) group in the regression equation.

```
. test  _b[positive:2.CNTYORIG]= _b[negative:2.CNTYORIG]

 ( 1)  [positive]2.CNTYORIG - [negative]2.CNTYORIG = 0

          chi2(  1) =    22.46
          Prob > chi2 =    0.0000
```

The coefficient of the difference between Mexico and Cuba with respect to positive assessment (coef = −.275) is much smaller than that with respect to negative assessment (.904). The χ^2 test has the p value < 0.001 indicating a statistically significant difference.

We repeat to compare Vietnam and Cuba as follows:

```
. test  _b[positive:3.CNTYORIG]= _b[negative:3.CNTYORIG]

 ( 1)   [positive]3.CNTYORIG - [negative]3.CNTYORIG = 0

           chi2(  1) =    37.23
           Prob > chi2 =    0.0000
```

The results above are statistically significant. We can further perform within-model comparisons. For example, we can compare Mexico and Vietnam for both positive and negative assessment as dependent variables. The results below show no statistically significant difference between Mexico and Vietnam with respect to positive assessment, but there was a statistically significant difference with respect to negative assessment.

```
.
. test  _b[positive:2.CNTYORIG]= _b[positive:3.CNTYORIG]

 ( 1)   [positive]2.CNTYORIG - [positive]3.CNTYORIG = 0

           chi2(  1) =     1.04
           Prob > chi2 =    0.3075


.
. test  _b[negative:2.CNTYORIG]= _b[negative:3.CNTYORIG]

 ( 1)   [negative]2.CNTYORIG - [negative]3.CNTYORIG = 0

           chi2(  1) =     4.92
           Prob > chi2 =    0.0265
```

We can apply the same comparison procedure to other independent variables in the models.

Two Dependent Variables with Different Independent Variables

In this example, we add the variable *discrimination* to the negative equation to show that the procedure *sureg* can be used when the independent variables in the two equations are not the same. Let us assume that we use two different measures of English ability, one is ability to speak (Speak) and the other is to understand English (Understand). We would expect that the *speak English* variable must have a positive association with the dependent variable *positive assessment* and the *understand English* variable must have a negative association with the dependent variable *negative assessment (higher scores refer to higher negative self-assessment)*. The results of the analysis below indicate that the associations of these two different independent variables are significant and in the expected directions. Looking at the two regression equations below, we see the independent variables are not the same. We can run two separate regression analyses, but such analyses cannot take into the account the correlated errors between the two dependent variables, especially that these two dependent variables represent two separate dimensions of self-esteem.

$$Positive = a + b1(CNTYORIG) + b2(Speak) + b3(U.S.Born)$$

$$Negative = a + b1(CNTYORIG) + b2(Understand) \\ + b3(U.S.Born) + b4(Discriminated)$$

The results of the analyses of the two different equations are reported below.

```
. sureg (positive i.CNTYORIG Speak i.sex i.usborn ) ///
>      (negative i.CNTYORIG Understand i.sex i.usborn i.Discriminated),corr base
```

Seemingly unrelated regression

Equation	Obs	Parms	RMSE	"R-sq"	chi2	P
positive	2,512	5	2.482046	0.0824	206.81	0.0000
negative	2,512	6	3.355875	0.1071	298.18	0.0000

	Coef.	Std. Err.	z	P>|z|	[95% Conf. Interval]	
positive						
CNTYORIG						
Cuba	0	(base)				
Mexico	-.3760722	.1236794	-3.04	0.002	-.6184793	-.1336651
Indochina	-.5391818	.1442376	-3.74	0.000	-.8218823	-.2564813
Speak	.9765322	.090089	10.84	0.000	.799961	1.153103
sex						
female	0	(base)				
male	.2581063	.0992072	2.60	0.009	.0636638	.4525487
usborn						
Foreign Born	0	(base)				
U.S. Born	-.1019389	.117766	-0.87	0.387	-.3327561	.1288783
_cons	13.93699	.3556952	39.18	0.000	13.23984	14.63414
negative						
CNTYORIG						
Cuba	0	(base)				
Mexico	.8696157	.1701378	5.11	0.000	.5361517	1.20308
Indochina	1.147357	.20222	5.67	0.000	.7510134	1.543701
Understand	-1.180436	.1331565	-8.87	0.000	-1.441418	-.9194545
sex						
female	0	(base)				
male	-.3836496	.13417	-2.86	0.004	-.6466181	-.1206811
usborn						
Foreign Born	0	(base)				
U.S. Born	-.0909201	.157898	-0.58	0.565	-.4003945	.2185542
Discriminated						
No	0	(base)				
Yes	.707484	.1246483	5.68	0.000	.4631779	.9517901
_cons	13.44735	.5302541	25.36	0.000	12.40807	14.48663

Correlation matrix of residuals:

```
          positive  negative
positive   1.0000
negative  -0.4534    1.0000
```

Breusch–Pagan test of independence: chi2(1) =   516.307, Pr = 0.0000

If we want to compare the equality of *speaking English* and *understanding English* on the two dimensions of self-esteem, we must indicate to Stata to report the regression coefficients according to their respective dependent variables then run the *test* procedure.

```
. sureg,coeflegend
```

Seemingly unrelated regression

Equation	Obs	Parms	RMSE	"R-sq"	chi2	P
positive	2,512	5	2.482046	0.0824	206.81	0.0000
negative	2,512	6	3.355875	0.1071	298.18	0.0000

	Coef.	Legend
positive		
CNTYORIG		
Mexico	-.3760722	_b[positive:2.CNTYORIG]
Indochina	-.5391818	_b[positive:3.CNTYORIG]
Speak	.9765322	_b[positive:Speak]
sex		
male	.2581063	_b[positive:1.sex]
usborn		
U.S. Born	-.1019389	_b[positive:1.usborn]
_cons	13.93699	_b[positive:_cons]
negative		
CNTYORIG		
Mexico	.8696157	_b[negative:2.CNTYORIG]
Indochina	1.147357	_b[negative:3.CNTYORIG]
Understand	-1.180436	_b[negative:Understand]
sex		
male	-.3836496	_b[negative:1.sex]
usborn		
U.S. Born	-.0909201	_b[negative:1.usborn]
Discriminated		
Yes	.707484	_b[negative:1.Discriminated]
_cons	13.44735	_b[negative:_cons]

TEST FOR THE EQUALITY OF SPEAKING ENGLISH
AND UNDERSTANDING ENGLISH

The equality comparison revealed that the association between *speaking English* and positive (b = .975, p < .001) is significantly smaller than the association between *understanding English* and negative (b = −1,18, p < .001).

```
. test _b[positive:Speak]=_b[negative:Understand]

( 1)   [positive]Speak - [negative]Understand = 0

         chi2(  1) =    134.54
       Prob > chi2 =     0.0000
```

THREE DEPENDENT VARIABLES

In this example, we illustrate the analysis of three dependent variables as described below.

```
. sum positive negative depress
```

Variable	Obs	Mean	Std. Dev.	Min	Max
positive	5,096	17.54749	2.50207	5	20
negative	5,106	9.537015	3.488543	5	20
depress	5,163	6.616889	2.540192	4	16

We use these three dependent variables because they appear to measure different but related dimensions of psychological well-being. Thus, there must be some degree of correlation among their errors. *Seemingly Unrelated Regression* allows us to take their correlated errors into consideration. The interpretations of the results below should be similar to the analysis with two dependent variables. Should we want to compare the regression coefficients across the three regression models, we can use the *test* procedure as we did in the previous examples.

```
. sureg (positive i.CNTYORIG english i.sex ) (negative i.CNTYORIG english i.sex) ///
>       (depress i.CNTYORIG english i.sex ),corr base

Seemingly unrelated regression
```

Equation	Obs	Parms	RMSE	"R-sq"	chi2	P
positive	2,492	4	2.468123	0.0908	249.00	0.0000
negative	2,492	4	3.354854	0.1062	296.05	0.0000
depress	2,492	4	2.43495	0.0459	119.77	0.0000

	Coef.	Std. Err.	z	P>|z|	[95% Conf. Interval]	
positive						
CNTYORIG						
Cuba	0	(base)				
Mexico	-.2692428	.1242332	-2.17	0.030	-.5127355	-.0257502
Indochina	-.3177978	.1325827	-2.40	0.017	-.5776551	-.0579404
english	.322291	.025081	12.85	0.000	.2731331	.371449
sex						
female	0	(base)				
male	.2844803	.0990997	2.87	0.004	.0902486	.4787121
_cons	12.69938	.3998278	31.76	0.000	11.91574	13.48303
negative						
CNTYORIG						
Cuba	0	(base)				
Mexico	.9248583	.1688669	5.48	0.000	.5938853	1.255831
Indochina	1.285252	.1802162	7.13	0.000	.9320344	1.638469
english	-.3597911	.034092	-10.55	0.000	-.4266102	-.292972
sex						
female	0	(base)				
male	-.4689322	.1347035	-3.48	0.000	-.7329462	-.2049182
_cons	14.58883	.5434752	26.84	0.000	13.52364	15.65402
depress						
CNTYORIG						
Cuba	0	(base)				
Mexico	.1203971	.1225634	0.98	0.326	-.1198228	.3606171
Indochina	-.043509	.1308007	-0.33	0.739	-.2998738	.2128557
english	-.1051333	.0247439	-4.25	0.000	-.1536305	-.0566361
sex						
female	0	(base)				
male	-.9731057	.0977677	-9.95	0.000	-1.164727	-.7814846
_cons	8.556937	.3944538	21.69	0.000	7.783822	9.330053

```
Correlation matrix of residuals:

          positive  negative   depress
positive   1.0000
negative  -0.4526    1.0000
depress   -0.2720    0.3377    1.0000

Breusch-Pagan test of independence: chi2(3) =   979.096, Pr = 0.0000
```

If we want to compare the regression coefficients across the three equations, we might wish to begin with overall comparisons for all three dependent variables, then perform pairwise comparisons.

```
. sureg, coeflegend

Seemingly unrelated regression
```

Equation	Obs	Parms	RMSE	"R-sq"	chi2	P
positive	2,492	4	2.468123	0.0908	249.00	0.0000
negative	2,492	4	3.354854	0.1062	296.05	0.0000
depress	2,492	4	2.43495	0.0459	119.77	0.0000

	Coef.	Legend
positive		
CNTYORIG		
Mexico	-.2692428	_b[positive:2.CNTYORIG]
Indochina	-.3177978	_b[positive:3.CNTYORIG]
english	.322291	_b[positive:english]
sex		
male	.2844803	_b[positive:1.sex]
_cons	12.69938	_b[positive:_cons]
negative		
CNTYORIG		
Mexico	.9248583	_b[negative:2.CNTYORIG]
Indochina	1.285252	_b[negative:3.CNTYORIG]
english	-.3597911	_b[negative:english]
sex		
male	-.4689322	_b[negative:1.sex]
_cons	14.58883	_b[negative:_cons]
depress		
CNTYORIG		
Mexico	.1203971	_b[depress:2.CNTYORIG]
Indochina	-.043509	_b[depress:3.CNTYORIG]
english	-.1051333	_b[depress:english]
sex		
male	-.9731057	_b[depress:1.sex]
_cons	8.556937	_b[depress:_cons]

```
.
end of do-file
```

Below are the tests for equality of the English variable across three equations. If the overall comparison is not statistically significant, we do not need to perform pair comparisons. In this example, the test of significance for the comparisons across three dependent variables is statistically significant as reported below, so we can continue our pairwise comparisons. The results show all equality comparisons are statistically significant.

```
. test _b[positive:english] = _b[negative:english]=_b[depress:english]

 ( 1)   [positive]english - [negative]english = 0
 ( 2)   [positive]english - [depress]english = 0

            chi2(  2) =   183.18
          Prob > chi2 =    0.0000


.
. test _b[positive:english] = _b[negative:english]

 ( 1)   [positive]english - [negative]english = 0

            chi2(  1) =   181.36
          Prob > chi2 =    0.0000


.
. test _b[positive:english] =_b[depress:english]

 ( 1)   [positive]english - [depress]english = 0

            chi2(  1) =   115.70
          Prob > chi2 =    0.0000


.
. test _b[negative:english]=_b[depress:english]

 ( 1)   [negative]english - [depress]english = 0

            chi2(  1) =    53.83
          Prob > chi2 =    0.0000
```

CHECK FOR VIOLATION OF OUTLIER, HOMOSCEDASTICITY, AND COLLINEARITY

We conclude this chapter with a brief discussion of the potential violations of assumptions in doing regression analysis and illustrate a few procedures to handle these violations (https://www.stata.com/manuals13/rregresspostestimation.pdf).

When one or more independent variables in our analysis have extreme values, it is possible that this will influence the estimates of the regression coefficients and the standard errors. The Stata command *rreg* or "robust regression" helps us to deal with this problem. We will demonstrate the use of robust regression below.

Check for Outliers

Outliers or extreme values in the variables cause biases in the estimates. We can use robust regression to handle this potential problem.

First, we can run a regression analysis without the robust procedure, then we run the same analysis with robust regression to illustrate the differences.

Ordinary Least Squares Regression (OLS)

We can check for the potential influence of outliers on the outcome of a regression model. We will present a regression analysis and then repeat the analysis using the procedure for robust regression *rreg*. Stata's *rreg* "first performs an initial screening based on Cook's distance being greater than 1 to eliminate gross outliers before calculating starting values, and subsequently performing Huber iterations followed by biweight iterations," as suggested by Li (1985) (https://www.stata.com/manuals/rrreg.pdf).

Analysis Without Robust Regression

`. reg positive Understand age i.sex`

Source	SS	df	MS			
				Number of obs	=	5,088
				F(3, 5084)	=	106.64
Model	1886.83654	3	628.945512	Prob > F	=	0.0000
Residual	29984.4935	5,084	5.89781539	R-squared	=	0.0592
				Adj R-squared	=	0.0586
Total	31871.33	5,087	6.26525064	Root MSE	=	2.4285

positive	Coef.	Std. Err.	t	P>|t|	[95% Conf. Interval]	
Understand	1.261857	.073023	17.28	0.000	1.118701	1.405014
age	-.0580562	.0400217	-1.45	0.147	-.1365159	.0204035
sex						
male	.218865	.0681871	3.21	0.001	.0851889	.3525411
_cons	13.48663	.6661218	20.25	0.000	12.18075	14.79252

Let us check for the possibility of outliers by generating studentized residuals. In regression analysis, the errors are assumed to be independent and have the same variance. Residuals, however, are estimates from the observed data that are not true errors. The residual estimates, therefore, are not independent. The distribution of the residuals can tell us whether there are outliers in our analysis. We will illustrate the procedures to generate residuals and their distribution below.

. predict r, rstudent
(174 missing values generated)

The *predict* command generates the residuals and saves them in a variable named "r." We can then generate a stem and leaf plot of the residuals as shown below. The results of the leaf plot show that there are a few extreme values, such as −53.7422 and 23.99. Given that there is the possibility of having outliers in multiple regression especially with survey data, we recommend the use of robust regression analysis when we are not sure that outliners can be ruled out in our analysis.

```
. stem r

Stem-and-leaf plot for r (Studentized residuals)

r rounded to nearest multiple of .01
plot in units of .01

  -53*  7442
  -52*  555
  -51*
  -50*
  -49*  1
  -48*  4
  -47*
  -46*
  -45*  4
  -44*  2000
  -43*
  -42*
  -41*  0
  -40*
  -39*
  -38*
  -37*  1
  -36*  9962000
  -35*  777
  -34*  96
  -33*  000
  -32*  7777555311
  -31*  888888877664
  -30*  841
  -29*  0
  -28*  86666444411
  -27*  99997777755553311
  -26*  966644222
  -25*
  -24*  7777777555555555222222000
  -23*  8888888888666666666666666444443333333333322221
  -22*  9995555531
  -21*  2
  -20*  6666444444444444444441111111111111111
  -19*  99977777777777777775555555555555555555555555555555553333333322222 ... (81)
  -18*  8888664444111111
  -17*  9
  -16*  75555555555555222222222222222222222222222222222220000000000000000 ... (72)
  -15*  8888888866666666666666444443333333333333333333333333333332 ... (88)
  -14*  999999999999999999755555333333333333333311000000000
  -13*  9888882
  -12*  99744444444444444444444444444441111111111111111111111111111111111 ... (96)
  -11*  99999999999999999999999999999999999999766666444444444444444 ... (213)
  -10*  888888888888888877777777766666644444444211111111111111111111
   -9*  99999999999999775111
   -8*  82222222222222222222222222000000000000000000000000000000000000 ... (88)
   -7*  888888888888888888888888888888888886655555553333333333333333 ... (182)
   -6*  99999999999999999999999999999999999999999999999999999999999999 ... (143)
   -5*  88888888888886654
   -4*  9753111111111111111111111111111111111111111
   -3*  99999999999999999999999999999999999999999999999999999999999999 ... (337)
   -2*  888888888888888888888877777777777777777777777777777777777777 ... (135)
   -1*  999999999999999999977777777777777777777777777554444442
   -0*  88888866322
    0*  00000000000000000000000000000000000000000000000002222222222 ... (344)
    1*  11111111111111111111111111111111111111111111111111111111111111 ... (320)
    2*  00000000022222222222222222224444555555555555555555555677777
    3*  13355999
    4*  01111111111111111111111111111111111111111111111111111111111111 ... (360)
    5*  00000000000000000000000000000000000000000000000000000000000000 ... (394)
    6*  01111111111133333333333333333333355666666666666666666688888888888
    7*  00479
    8*  00122222222222222222222222222222222222222222222222222222222222 ... (660)
    9*  00000000000000000000000000000000000000000001111111111111111111 ... (746)
   10*  00022234555555555555555555555555577777777777777777777777799999999
   11*  6668
   12*  009
   13*  44444444777777777777777777777777777777777799999999999999999999999
   14*  2222222444444666666666666666666688888888888888888888888
   15*  111113999
   16*  1
   17*
   18*
   19*  111468
   20*  33
   21*  2
   22*
   23*  99
```

Analysis Using Robust Regression

```
. rreg positive Understand age i.sex

    Huber iteration 1:  maximum difference in weights = .73487414
    Huber iteration 2:  maximum difference in weights = .07143296
    Huber iteration 3:  maximum difference in weights = .00947734
 Biweight iteration 4:  maximum difference in weights = .29325835
 Biweight iteration 5:  maximum difference in weights = .02860602
 Biweight iteration 6:  maximum difference in weights = .0074733
```

```
Robust regression                      Number of obs    =      5,088
                                       F(  3,    5084) =     136.52
                                       Prob > F         =     0.0000
```

positive	Coef.	Std. Err.	t	P>|t|	[95% Conf. Interval]	
Understand	1.360752	.0691012	19.69	0.000	1.225284	1.49622
age	-.038702	.0378722	-1.02	0.307	-.1129479	.0355439
sex						
male	.2253081	.064525	3.49	0.000	.0988113	.3518049
_cons	13.06844	.6303465	20.73	0.000	11.83269	14.30419

Let us compare the results from the OLS regression analysis and from the robust regression. Results from the robust regression are slightly improved compared to the OLS regression coefficients. Therefore, if having outliers is a problem in the data, we should use the robust regression procedure. We can check for outliers by running frequencies for all variables before carrying out our analysis. In our example, the problem of outliers is not serious because the two outcomes are somewhat similar. In our example, the results of the robust regression give us more accurate estimates of the regression coefficients and their standard errors. For example, the regression coefficient of the variable *understand* (English) improves from 1.261 with a standard error of .073 (rounded up) in the analysis without robust estimates, and is changed to 1.360 with a standard deviation of .069 with robust estimates. Consequently, the t value in the robust regression was greater than the t value in the nonrobust regression analysis. We recommend that it is preferable to use robust regression (*rreg*) procedure when the sample size is relatively small or when we suspect the possibility of outliers in our analysis.

Check for Heteroscedasticity: Unequal Variance

Homogeneity of variance of the residuals is one of the assumptions for the ordinary least squares (OLS) regression. When the variance of the residuals is similar, we can say that the residual variance is "heteroscedastic." If this problem occurs in our data, the results could be biased. Stata allows us to use the robust variance procedure to account for unequal variance. A few different tests can be used to check for this assumption, but we will illustrate the use of the *hettest* to check whether this problem exists in our data.

Analysis Without Robust Variance

```
. reg negative i.CNTYORIG psupport i.sex age,base
```

Source	SS	df	MS		
Model	4912.59959	5	982.519919		
Residual	27641.6442	2,566	10.7722698		
Total	32554.2438	2,571	12.662094		

Number of obs	=	2,572
F(5, 2566)	=	91.21
Prob > F	=	0.0000
R-squared	=	0.1509
Adj R-squared	=	0.1493
Root MSE	=	3.2821

negative	Coef.	Std. Err.	t	P>|t|	[95% Conf. Interval]	
CNTYORIG						
Cuba	0	(base)				
Mexico	1.251749	.1551732	8.07	0.000	.9474711	1.556026
Indochina	1.574973	.1639631	9.61	0.000	1.25346	1.896487
psupport	.7361493	.0467101	15.76	0.000	.6445559	.8277427
sex						
female	0	(base)				
male	-.4140903	.1296381	-3.19	0.001	-.6682962	-.1598844
age	.0611286	.0741215	0.82	0.410	-.0842154	.2064726
_cons	6.057094	1.055726	5.74	0.000	3.986933	8.127255

We can check for the equal variance assumption for the above analysis using the procedure *estat hettest*. The procedure gives us the results of Breusch-Pagan / Cook-Weisberg test for heteroscedasticity. The null hypothesis is that there is no heteroscedasticity (which is preferable) in the regression model above, meaning there is no violation of the equal variance assumption in the model.

The results below show that the null hypothesis was rejected due to the significance value or the p value of the χ^2 test being less than .05. Thus, the model violates the homoscedasticity assumption.

```
. estat hettest

Breusch-Pagan / Cook-Weisberg test for heteroskedasticity
        Ho: Constant variance
        Variables: fitted values of negative

        chi2(1)      =      5.79
        Prob > chi2  =     0.0161
```

We can take care of the problem by redoing the analysis to produce correct variance estimates for the model as below.

Analysis Using Robust Variance

Let us compare the results of the OLS regression analysis without robust variance above with the analysis with robust variance below. The two analyses have the same regression coefficients but different standard errors. The robust standard errors are more accurate that the nonrobust standard errors, thus giving us more accurate tests of significance for the estimates. Although we do not find vast differences between the two models, we should be concerned with this problem when we attempt to draw comparisons of the results across cultural groups.

```
. regress negative i.CNTYORIG   Speak i.sex age, robust
```

```
Linear regression                          Number of obs   =      2,584
                                           F(5, 2578)      =      63.01
                                           Prob > F        =     0.0000
                                           R-squared       =     0.1021
                                           Root MSE        =     3.3703
```

negative	Coef.	Robust Std. Err.	t	P>|t|	[95% Conf. Interval]	
CNTYORIG						
Mexico	.9931347	.1692097	5.87	0.000	.6613341	1.324935
Indochina	1.43916	.176208	8.17	0.000	1.093637	1.784684
Speak	−1.191264	.1222104	−9.75	0.000	−1.430904	−.9516232
sex						
male	−.419416	.1331703	−3.15	0.002	−.6805475	−.1582844
age	.0122229	.0770503	0.16	0.874	−.1388639	.1633097
_cons	13.51245	1.251176	10.80	0.000	11.05903	15.96586

TAKING CARE OF COLLINEARITY: EXTREME CORRELATION BETWEEN INDEPENDENT VARIABLES

In a multiple regression model, the independent variables should not be highly correlated. When two or more independent variables are highly correlated or their correlations are close to 1.00, most statistical software would remove the variables from the analysis by default. When the variables are highly correlated but not close to 1.00, however, the results could potentially be severely biased. We will demonstrate a situation with the correlation of two independent variables in the 0.80 range and illustrate different ways to check for this violation and how to handle it. Let us look at the analysis below.

. reg positive i.CNTYORIG Speak Understand i.sex,base

Source	SS	df	MS			
				Number of obs	=	2,562
				F(5, 2556)	=	46.04
Model	1426.00332	5	285.200663	Prob > F	=	0.0000
Residual	15832.7902	2,556	6.19436236	R-squared	=	0.0826
				Adj R-squared	=	0.0808
Total	17258.7935	2,561	6.73908376	Root MSE	=	2.4888

positive	Coef.	Std. Err.	t	P>|t|	[95% Conf. Interval]	
CNTYORIG						
Cuba	0	(base)				
Mexico	-.3220232	.1233497	-2.61	0.009	-.5638987	-.0801477
Indochina	-.4431261	.1338268	-3.31	0.001	-.705546	-.1807062
Speak	1.014141	.1548459	6.55	0.000	.7105052	1.317777
Understand	.0632108	.1709848	0.37	0.712	-.2720721	.3984936
sex						
female	0	(base)				
male	.2398198	.0984438	2.44	0.015	.0467821	.4328575
_cons	13.4791	.4055024	33.24	0.000	12.68395	14.27425

It is logical to accept that the two variables measuring English speaking ability (*speak*) and understand English (*understand*) have similarities in their associations with the dependent variable. As shown in the table above, the variable *speak* has a statistically significant association with the dependent variable while the variable *understand* has no significant association. Let us review the correlation among the variables used in the analysis.

The correlation matrix below shows that the two variables *speak* and *understand* have a correlation at .8441, which is considered very high, suggesting that the regression analysis has a multicollinearity problem.

. cor positive CNTYORIG Speak Understand sex
(obs=2,562)

	positive	CNTYORIG	Speak	Unders~d	sex
positive	1.0000				
CNTYORIG	-0.1700	1.0000			
Speak	0.2745	-0.3864	1.0000		
Understand	0.2418	-0.4248	0.8441	1.0000	
sex	0.0458	-0.0260	-0.0093	-0.0129	1.0000

We also can use the variance inflation factor (VIF) as an indicator to detect multicollinearity in a regression analysis. Although there are no clear directions on how to interpret the value of VIF, we recommend that the average of VIF in a model should not be greater than 1. Below are the results of the VIF estimates. The procedure *estat vif* produces the results below.

```
. estat vif
```

Variable	VIF	1/VIF
CNTYORIG		
2	1.27	0.787128
3	1.39	0.718875
Speak	3.55	0.282019
Understand	3.64	0.274673
1.sex	1.00	0.998594
Mean VIF	2.17	

.

Both the correlation matrix among the variables used in the analysis and the average of the VIF value at 2.12 (greater than 1) confirm that our analysis suffers from the problem of multicollinearity. We recommend two approaches to handle this situation. First, if there is a good reason to combine the variables that have high intercorrelations, we can create a composite index or scale to represent a single construct. Let us say that the variables *speak* and *understand* (English) represent a construct of English Ability. We combine these two variables into one and rerun the analysis.

```
. gen English=Speak+Understand
```

```
. sum English
```

Variable	Obs	Mean	Std. Dev.	Min	Max
English	5,244	7.51106	.9701199	2	8

Our newly created variable English has scores that range from 2 to 8. Note that the sample size is for the entire survey. In our analysis we only use respondents from four countries of origin and not the whole sample.

Now we can see that in the results below, the variable *English* has a statistical significance with the dependent variable in the expected direction, meaning respondents with stronger English ability have greater sense of positive self-image.

```
. reg positive i.CNTYORIG English i.sex,base
```

Source	SS	df	MS			
				Number of obs	=	2,562
				F(4, 2557)	=	55.03
Model	1367.86608	4	341.966519	Prob > F	=	0.0000
Residual	15890.9274	2,557	6.21467636	R-squared	=	0.0793
				Adj R-squared	=	0.0778
Total	17258.7935	2,561	6.73908376	Root MSE	=	2.4929

positive	Coef.	Std. Err.	t	P>|t|	[95% Conf. Interval]	
CNTYORIG						
Cuba	0	(base)				
Mexico	-.3378966	.1234427	-2.74	0.006	-.5799545	-.0958387
Indochina	-.4049455	.1334635	-3.03	0.002	-.6666531	-.1432379
English	.5646265	.0495577	11.39	0.000	.4674492	.6618039
sex						
female	0	(base)				
male	.2424454	.0986014	2.46	0.014	.0490988	.435792
_cons	13.26155	.3998904	33.16	0.000	12.47741	14.04569

If we wish to compare whether ability to understand English has the same association with positive self-image as ability to speak English, we can perform two separate regression models and subsequently compare the regression coefficients of these two variables as illustrated below.

```
. reg positive i.CNTYORIG Speak i.sex
. estimates store speak
. reg positive i.CNTYORIG Understand i.sex
. estimates store understand
. suest speak understand
```

The above command syntax was used to estimate the results below. As illustrated, we ran the regression model with the variable *speak*, saved the results in the file named *speak* then ran another model with the variable *understand*, and saved the results in the file named *understand*. The procedure *suest* (Seemingly Unrelated Estimation) was used to compare the two models for further analysis.

```
. suest speak understand

Simultaneous results for speak, understand

                                              Number of obs   =     2,565
```

	Coef.	Robust Std. Err.	z	P>|z|	[95% Conf. Interval]	
speak_mean						
CNTYORIG						
Mexico	−.3258958	.1262809	−2.58	0.010	−.5734019	−.0783897
Indochina	−.4557879	.1302257	−3.50	0.000	−.7110255	−.2005503
Speak	1.061241	.0947042	11.21	0.000	.8756239	1.246858
sex						
male	.2370411	.0984585	2.41	0.016	.044066	.4300162
_cons	13.54704	.3859068	35.10	0.000	12.79068	14.3034
speak_lnvar						
_cons	1.822845	.0363828	50.10	0.000	1.751536	1.894154
understand_mean						
CNTYORIG						
Mexico	−.4303794	.1246941	−3.45	0.001	−.6747755	−.1859834
Indochina	−.4762134	.1335401	−3.57	0.000	−.7379471	−.2144796
Understand	.9780863	.1064484	9.19	0.000	.7694513	1.186721
sex						
male	.2414654	.099259	2.43	0.015	.0469213	.4360094
_cons	13.84027	.4287909	32.28	0.000	12.99985	14.68068
understand_lnvar						
_cons	1.839696	.0365658	50.31	0.000	1.768028	1.911364

Given the results above, we can now use the *test* procedure to compare the regression coefficients of the variables *speak* and *understand*.

```
. test _b[speak_mean:Speak]=_b[understand_mean:Understand]

 ( 1)   [speak_mean]Speak - [understand_mean]Understand = 0

         chi2(  1) =    1.35
         Prob > chi2 =    0.2460
```

The results above show that there is no statistically significant difference between the association of *speak* and *understand*. We demonstrated two approaches to handle the problem of multicollinearity in multiple regression analysis. The decision to use either approach depends on theory, informed experience with the variables that are used, and practicality in applying the analysis.

In this chapter, we explain the basic concepts of multiple linear regression analysis or ordinary least squares regression analysis (OLS). We illustrate the use of Stata commands to perform regression analysis for cross-cultural research. We then illustrate and demonstrate the applications of multiple regression in cross-cultural data analysis and comparisons. We expanded the application of multiplicative interaction and subgroup analyses. Special types of analyses, such as mediation analysis, and seemingly unrelated regression are explained and demonstrated with concrete examples.

REFERENCES

Daniel, W. (2005). *Biostatistics: A foundation for analysis in the health sciences* (8th ed.). Hoboken, NJ: Wiley.

Cameron, A. C., & Trivedi, P. K. (2010). *Micrometrics Using Stata*, Revised edition. College Station: Stata Press.

Ford, C. (2015). Is R-square Useless? University of Virginia Library, Research Data Services + Sciences. Retrieved from https://data.library.virginia.edu/is-r-squared-useless/.

Hu, L., & Bentler, P. M. (1999). Cutoff criteria for fit indexes in covariance structure analysis: Conventional criteria versus new alternatives. *Structural Equation Modeling, 6,* 1–55.

Huber, C. (2014). Introduction to structural equation modeling using Stata. Retrieved from: http://www.cair.org/wp-content/uploads/sites/474/2015/07/HuberC-SEMWorkshop.pdf.

Li, G. (1985). Robust regression. In D. C. Hoaglin, C. F. Mosteller, & J. W. Tukey (Eds.). *Exploring data tables, trends, and shapes* (pp. 281–340). New York: Wiley.

Pearl, J. (2014). Interpretation and identification of causal mediation. *Psychological Methods, 19*(4), 459–481. https://doi.org/10.1037/a0036434

Portes, A., Rumbaut, R. G. (2007). *Children of Immigrants Longitudinal Study (CILS), 1991–2006*. Irvine, CA: University of California-Irvine & Inter-University Consortium for Political Social Research.

Rosenberg, M. (1965). *Society and the adolescent self-image*. Princeton, NJ: Princeton University Press.

Skriner, L., Chu, B., & Reynolds, C. R. (2014). Cross-ethnic measurement invariance of the SCARED and CES–D in a youth sample. *Psychological Assessment, 26*(1), 332–337.

Tran, T. V., Nguyen, T. H., & Chan, K. T. (2016). *Developing Cross-Cultural Measurement in Social Work Research and Evaluation* (2nd ed.). New York, NY: Oxford University Press.

5

Comparing a Binary Dependent Variable Across Cultural Groups Using Applied Logistic Regression

In this chapter, we will review the basic ideas of logistic regression involving a binary dependent regressed on independent variables, along with assumptions for analysis and interpretations of results. We will provide strategies and practical guides for data analysis using Stata (StataCorp, 2017). We used Stata 15 in this book, but readers can easily replicate our examples with the newest version of Stata 16. As mentioned earlier, our position of making cross-cultural comparisons requires the application of testing nested models, assessing and evaluating the possibility of interaction effects between cultural marker variables and their moderators, or between an independent variable and the cultural marker variable. Thus, cultural marker variables such as race, religion, sex, and linguistic identification can be operationalized

Applied Cross-Cultural Data Analysis for Social Work. Thanh V. Tran and Keith T. Chan,
Oxford University Press. © Oxford University Press 2021. DOI: 10.1093/oso/9780190888510.003.0005

as either independent variables or as moderator variables. We will introduce the concept of biological interaction or additive interaction at the end of this chapter.

INTRODUCTION TO LOGISTIC REGRESSION FOR CROSS-CULTURAL RESEARCH

Unlike Ordinary Least Square regression (OLS), which requires a continuous dependent variable or variables that are measured on a range of scores from low to high (e.g., earned annual income "$0.00 to $100,000," or a composite score of constructs such as self-esteem, life satisfaction, and depression), logistic regression requires the dependent variable to be binary with the values of 0 and 1 (i.e., whether a patient diagnosed with a mental health condition after receiving a treatment was able to recover from an illness, as in yes "1" or not yet "0").

Y = Binary dependent variable (0 = (Not recovered)
    (1 = (Recovered))
Yi = 1 if the patient was recovered
Yi = 0 if the patient was not recovered
X = (X_1, X_2, X_3, ... X_k) represents a set of the independent and
    control (covariate) variables.

The independent and control variables can be measured as categorical (e.g., race, sex) or continuous (e.g., chronological age, annual earned income).

$$Outcome\ (Dependent\ Variable) = \Pr(Yi = 1|Xi = x1) = \frac{\exp(Bo + B1xi)}{1 + \exp(Bo + B1xi)}$$

$$logit\,(Oi) = \log\left(\frac{Oi}{1 - Oi}\right)$$

= B_0 + B_1 X_i (Simple Logistic Model)
= B_0 + B_1 X_1 + ... B_k X_k (Multiple Logistic Model)
Or we can write the multiple logistic regression equation with four independent variables, as follows:

$$Logit(E(Yi)) = Log\left(\frac{Pi}{1-Pi}\right) = Intercept + B1X_1 + B2X_2 + B3X_3 + B4X_4$$

BASIC ASSUMPTIONS

Researchers should be aware of some basic assumptions when applying logistic regression in their analysis.

> **Assumption #1:** As mentioned, the dependent **variable** or the outcome variable must consist of **two independent (unrelated) values** such as recovered "1" versus not recovered "0." For example, the dependent variable is originally measured on a continuous scale, that is, the Center for Epidemiologic Studies–Depression (CES-D) scale consisting of twenty items with scores ranging from 0 to 60. We can transform this continuous scale into a binary or dichotomous variable so a score of 16 or greater is coded as "1," which can be classified as at risk for clinical depression, while a score of 16 or lower is coded as "0" or not at risk for clinical depression. We need to have a sound reason to transform a continuous variable into a categorical or dichotomous variable. In the case of the CES-D scale, a substantive body of previous research has confirmed the utility of using a cutoff score of 16 or greater (Lewinsohn, Seeley, Roberts, & Allen, 1997).
>
> **Assumption #2:** We can use two or more independent and control variables, which are measured as continuous (age, income, etc.) or categorical (race, foreign-born status, etc.) variables. The number of independent variables and control variables included in the analysis should be guided by the researchers' hypothesis and the availability of the data. Although we can have numerous independent and control variables in an analysis, the more variables we include in the model, the more difficult it is to interpret the results and draw meaningful conclusions. There are a few matters we should consider in selecting the independent and control variables for cross-cultural analysis. First, all variables used in an analysis should be well-defined

and bear similar meaning among the comparative groups. The variables should have a reasonable degree of reliability across the comparative groups (i.e., similar Cronbach's alpha coefficient) if they were created by the summation of multiple items, indicators or questions. Among variables, there should be enough observations for each comparative group. Long and Freese (2014) suggest that each variable in the model should have at least ten observations. We recommend at least twenty observations for each variable in cross-cultural analysis. Thus, if the analysis involves a comparison of a dependent variable across three cultural groups using three independent variables, we should have sixty observations for each group and the total sample size should be at least 180 observations. It is important to note that this is a rule of thumb, and results from too few observations should be treated with caution. It is also noteworthy to consider the number of independent variables and the number of observations based on the statistical power of a model (VanVoorhis & Morgans, 2007). For cross-cultural program evaluation, The Abdul Latif Jameel Poverty Action Lab (J-PAL) offers six rules of thumb that are practical and useful for researchers (J-PAL, 2020).

Assumption #3: The data we use in an analysis must be drawn from independent observations. More specifically, there must be no relationship among the observations.

Assumption #4: The selected independent and control variables should not be highly correlated. If two of our independent or control variables are highly correlated, we can have a statistical problem called **multicollinearity**. Most statistical packages would give a warning when multicollinearity occurs in an analysis. Conceptually, when two independent variables are highly correlated, it's difficult to distinguish the contribution of each variable on the dependent variable. If the two variables appear to represent a single concept, we should combine them into one variable. If two variables have a high inverse correlation, check their coding and examine their correlation again. If the problem persists, we may consider dropping one of the two variables from the analysis with consideration to their respective conceptual importance.

Assumption #5: There should be a linear relationship between the logit transformation of the binary dependent variable and the continuous independent variables.

Assumption #6: There should be no outliers (i.e., extreme values) among the variables used in the analysis. If there are outliers, we can use the robust option to obtain robust variance estimates. (Tabatabai, Eby, Kengwoung-Kueymom Manne, Bae, Fouad, & Singh, 2014).

APPLIED LOGISTIC REGRESSION TO EXAMINE THE ASSOCIATION OF SEX, RACE, AND DEPRESSION

We demonstrate the strategies to perform cross-cultural analysis via logistic regression in the following examples using the Behavioral Risk Factor Surveillance System 2017 data set (https://www.cdc.gov/brfss/annual_data/2017/pdf/overview-2017-508.pdf). Below is a brief description of this data set from the Centers for Disease Control and Prevention website.

> The Behavioral Risk Factor Surveillance System (BRFSS) is a collaborative project between all of the states in the United States (US) and participating US territories and the Centers for Disease Control and Prevention (CDC). The BRFSS is administered and supported by CDC's Population Health Surveillance Branch, under the Division of Population Health at the National Center for Chronic Disease Prevention and Health Promotion. The BRFSS is a system of ongoing health-related telephone surveys designed to collect data on health-related risk behaviors, chronic health conditions, and use of preventive services from the noninstitutionalized adult population (≥ 18 years) residing in the United States.

In order to demonstrate cross-cultural analysis using logistic regression, gender and race are used to illustrate their roles as both biological and cultural variables for interpretation. Gender and race are variables that imply a set of shared inherited values, lifestyles, and common social influences that resulted from the socialization process in a particular socioeconomic environment. In the BRFSS, gender was coded as male and female. Based on this categorization, we hypothesize that females have a greater prevalence or probability of being diagnosed as depressed than males. We further hypothesize, however, that the prevalence or probability of depression varies among racial groups. More specifically, women and men from different racial groups would experience a different prevalence of depression compared to non-Hispanic Whites and each other.

EXAMINING THE CODEBOOK

Almost all well-established secondary data sets should have a detailed codebook that contains relevant information on variables that researchers plan to use for a project. In this example, we used three variables and provided basic descriptive information and variable layouts, which are described below in the BRFSS data codebook. We imported the BRFSS data set that was prepared for users of SAS-Statistical Analysis Software (https://www.sas.com/en_us/home.html). Therefore the variable values are not included in our Stata data. We used the BRFSS 2027 codebook as a guide to assign the variable values to all the selected variables used in this chapter.

For the respondent's sex variable, the results from Stata are displayed below:

```
. tab sex
```

RESPONDENTS SEX	Freq.	Percent	Cum.
1	198,725	44.16	44.16
2	251,007	55.78	99.94
9	284	0.06	100.00
Total	450,016	100.00	

Label: Respondents Sex
Section Name: Demographics
Core Section Number: 8
Question Number: 1
Column: 125
Type of Variable: Num
SAS Variable Name: SEX
Question Prologue:
Question: Indicate sex of respondent.

Value	Value Label	Frequency	Percentage	Weighted Percentage
1	Male	198,725	44.16	48.64
2	Female	251,007	55.78	51.31
9	Refused	284	0.06	0.06

Using the information provided in the codebook above, we recoded the sex variable as below.

```
. recode sex (1=0 "male") (2=1 "female") (9=.),gen (Sex_F)
(450016 differences between sex and Sex_F)

. tab Sex_F
```

RECODE of sex (RESPONDENTS SEX)	Freq.	Percent	Cum.
male	198,725	44.19	44.19
female	251,007	55.81	100.00
Total	449,732	100.00	

Notes: (9 =.) refers to missing data. Those who refused to answer regarding their sex are treated as missing data. In the future, large-scale data sets can benefit from including nonbinary categories as responses in order to capture gender minority populations.

Here is the coding information of the variable Sex_F after recoding:

```
. codebook Sex_F
```

Sex_F	RECODE of sex (RESPONDENTS SEX)

```
                 type:  numeric (double)
                label:  Sex_F

                range:  [0,1]                    units:  1
        unique values:  2                      missing .:  284/450,016

          tabulation:  Freq.   Numeric  Label
                       198,725       0  male
                       251,007       1  female
                       284          .
```

Label: Imputed race/ethnicity value
Section Name: Weighting Variables
Module Section Number: 1
Question Number: 12
Column: 1519-1520
Type of Variable: Num
SAS Variable Name: _IMPRACE
Question Prologue:
Question: Imputed race/ethnicity value   (This value is the reported race/ethnicity or an imputed race/ethnicity, if the respondent refused to give a race/ethnicity. The value of the imputed race/ethnicity will be the most common race/ethnicity response for that region of the state)

Value	Value Label	Frequency	Percentage	Weighted Percentage
1	White, Non-Hispanic	344,800	76.62	63.06
2	Black, Non-Hispanic	36,199	8.04	11.66
3	Asian, Non-Hispanic	9,963	2.21	5.37
4	American Indian/Alaskan Native, Non-Hispanic	8,497	1.89	1.01
5	Hispanic	37,233	8.27	16.81
6	Other race, Non-Hispanic	13,324	2.96	2.08

Label: Ever told you had a depressive disorder
Section Name: Chronic Health Conditions
Core Section Number: 6
Question Number: 10
Column: 115
Type of Variable: Num
SAS Variable Name: ADDEPEV2
Question Prologue:
Question: (Ever told) you have a depressive disorder (including depression, major depression, dysthymia, or minor depression)?

Value	Value Label	Frequency	Percentage	Weighted Percentage
1	Yes	89,209	19.82	19.03
2	No	358,683	79.71	80.50
7	Don't know/Not sure	1,661	0.37	0.39
9	Refused	460	0.10	0.08
BLANK	Not asked or Missing	3	.	.

The description of the three selected variables from the 2017 BRFSS presented above has five important pieces of information needed to use the data for this study appropriately.

A. Value: This refers to how observations of the variable were coded.
B. Value Label: Once the data are entered into a computer database as 1, 2, 7, or 9, we need to know what these numbers represent. The value labels inform the data analyst that participants who reported they had a depressive disorder through their healthcare professionals were assigned a value of 1, a value of 2 was assigned for those reporting no depressive disorder, 7 for those who reported "don't know/not sure," and 9 for those who refused to report. Some secondary data sets might not have the complete value labels. For example, the variable _imprace has no value labels when we import the data form SAS format to Stata.
C. Frequency: This reports the number of responses to each category or value of the variable.
D. Percentage: This refers to the valid percentage for each response category. Stata excludes missing data when computing the valid percentage, unless their inclusion is requested by the user.
E. Weighted Percentage: This statistic is estimated using weighted population data. We will illustrate the procedure that Stata uses to compute the weighted percentage in the following examples.

```
. tab _imprace
```

IMPUTED RACE/ETHNIC ITY VALUE	Freq.	Percent	Cum.
1	344,800	76.62	76.62
2	36,199	8.04	84.66
3	9,963	2.21	86.88
4	8,497	1.89	88.77
5	37,233	8.27	97.04
6	13,324	2.96	100.00
Total	450,016	100.00	

The frequency table above only has the unweighted frequencies and percentages. The unweighted results assume that the data were collected using a simple random sampling design, which cannot be accurately applied for the BRSFF data set. To generate the weighted frequencies, we have to declare in Stata that the analysis will apply weights from complex survey designs. Before we demonstrate how to declare complex survey designs using Stata, we should give the numerical values of the *race* variable their respective labels as described in the codebook. As a matter of practicality, we will combine those numerical values coded as "Don't Know/Not Sure," "Refused," and "Blank" as missing data. Stata use the "." to refer to missing data. The Frequency column reports the number of observations for each category of the variable.

```
. recode _imprace (1=1 "White") (2=2 "Black") (3=3 "Asian") ///
>        (4=4 "American Indian") (5=5 "Hispanic") (6=6 "Others"), gen (Race_6)
(0 differences between _imprace and Race_6)
```

We now have a new variable named Race_6. As noted above: "("0" differences between _imprace and Race_6). This means that the data in the original variable _imprace remains the same in the newly created variable from the "recode" procedure.

```
. tab Race_6
```

RECODE of _imprace (IMPUTED RACE/ETHNICITY VALUE)	Freq.	Percent	Cum.
White	344,800	76.62	76.62
Black	36,199	8.04	84.66
Asian	9,963	2.21	86.88
American Indian	8,497	1.89	88.77
Hispanic	37,233	8.27	97.04
Others	13,324	2.96	100.00
Total	450,016	100.00	

Let's declare weights for the BRSFF data using complex survey design and rerun the frequency for the variable *Race_6*. We used the *svyset* command to declare survey design for the data as below:

```
. svyset [pweight= _llcpwt], strata(_ststr) psu(_psu)

      pweight: _llcpwt
          VCE: linearized
  Single unit: missing
     Strata 1: _ststr
        SU 1: _psu
       FPC 1: <zero>
```

The above *svyset* command syntax works for population weight only because the "single unit" is missing. We must use the following *svyset* command syntax to declare the survey design before using the data set. If we do not declare "single unit certainty" in the *svyset* command syntax, Stata will not estimate the standard error for the logit estimates, and there will be no test of significance for the logit estimate. We will illustrate this in the next section of logistic regression.

```
. svy: tab Race_6
(running tabulate on estimation sample)

Number of strata   =     1,659        Number of obs    =      450,016
Number of PSUs     =   450,016        Population size  =  255,653,205
                                      Design df        =      448,357


RECODE of  |
_imprace   |
(IMPUTED   |
RACE/ETHN  |
ICITY      |
VALUE)     |  proportion
-----------+------------
   White   |      .6306
   Black   |      .1166
   Asian   |      .0537
American   |      .0101
Hispanic   |      .1681
  Others   |      .0208
-----------+------------
   Total   |          1

Key:  proportion  =  cell proportion
```

We should always refer to the codebook to verify our analysis to be sure that our process of data manipulation and transformation does not corrupt the original data. The weighted proportions in the above results can be converted to the weighted percentage to reflect the information provided in the 2017 BRFSS data codebook.

```
. display    .6306*100
63.06
```

```
Label: Imputed race/ethnicity value
Section Name: Weighting Variables
Module Section Number: 1
Question Number: 12
Column: 1519-1520
Type of Variable: Num
SAS Variable Name: _IMPRACE
Question Prologue:
Question:   Imputed race/ethnicity value   (This value is the reported race/ethnicity or an imputed race/ethnicity, if the
respondent refused to give a race/ethnicity. The value of the imputed race/ethnicity will be the most common
race/ethnicity response for that region of the state)
```

Value	Value Label	Frequency	Percentage	Weighted Percentage
1	White, Non-Hispanic	344,800	76.62	63.06
2	Black, Non-Hispanic	36,199	8.04	11.66
3	Asian, Non-Hispanic	9,963	2.21	5.37
4	American Indian/Alaskan Native, Non-Hispanic	8,497	1.89	1.01
5	Hispanic	37,233	8.27	16.81
6	Other race, Non-Hispanic	13,324	2.96	2.08

We see that the results from the weighted percentage using the "svy: tab Race_6" command are the same. The codebook provides the percentage in raw frequencies, and Stata provides the weighted proportion. Using the "display" command, we can simply convert the proportion of White (.6306) to percentage by multiplying the proportion by 100 to arrive to 63.06%.

CHECKING THE CODING OF THE VARIABLES

In addition to the checking of the distribution of the variables, we also can use the "summarize" command, or "sum" for short (Stata allows for abbreviated commands whenever possible), to look at the full range of values for each variable before performing logistic regression.

```
. summarize Sex_F Race_6 depression
```

Variable	Obs	Mean	Std. Dev.	Min	Max
Sex_F	449,732	.5581257	.4966105	0	1
Race_6	450,016	1.66035	1.402448	1	6
depression	447,892	.1991752	.3993806	0	1

The above table shows that all three variables have the correct values as coded, especially the dependent variable *depression*, which was coded properly as a dummy variable.

SIMPLE LOGISTIC REGRESSION

We can use either Logit or Logistic commands to arrive at the same information.

```
. logit depression i.Sex_F

Iteration 0:    log likelihood = -223459.77
Iteration 1:    log likelihood = -220408.53
Iteration 2:    log likelihood = -220381.91
Iteration 3:    log likelihood = -220381.91
```

```
Logistic regression                           Number of obs   =   447,621
                                              LR chi2(1)      =   6155.73
                                              Prob > chi2     =    0.0000
Log likelihood = -220381.91                   Pseudo R2       =    0.0138
```

depression	Coef.	Std. Err.	z	P>|z|	[95% Conf. Interval]	
Sex_F						
Female	.6070236	.007889	76.95	0.000	.5915615	.6224856
_cons	-1.75778	.0063497	-276.83	0.000	-1.770225	-1.745334

To shorten the outputs, we can use the option "nolog." The number of iterations and log likelihood for each iteration is not reported in the outputs when "nolog" is used, as shown below.

```
. logit depression i.Sex_F,nolog
```

```
Logistic regression                           Number of obs   =   447,621
                                              LR chi2(1)      =   6155.73
                                              Prob > chi2     =    0.0000
Log likelihood = -220381.91                   Pseudo R2       =    0.0138
```

depression	Coef.	Std. Err.	z	P>|z|	[95% Conf. Interval]	
Sex_F						
Female	.6070236	.007889	76.95	0.000	.5915615	.6224856
_cons	-1.75778	.0063497	-276.83	0.000	-1.770225	-1.745334

Let's study the Stata output of a simple logistic regression using unweighted data.

SUMMARY STATISTICS OF THE LOGISTIC REGRESSION MODEL

1. Log likelihood = −220381.91
2. Number of obs = 447,621
3. LR chi2(1) = 6155.73
4. Prob > chi2 = 0.0000
5. Pseudo R2 = 0.0138

1. Log likelihood refers to the last iteration when the logistic regression model converged. Logistic regression uses a maximum likelihood approach to estimate the association between the dependent variable and its respective independent variable. We note that there is a list of the log likelihoods from 0 to 3. The analysis starts with the null or empty model identified as iteration 0. This null model has no predictor or independent variable. The iterative process in maximum likelihood estimations continues until the differences between the null model and each subsequent model become very small. This is referred to as *tolerance*, and by default the tolerance in Stata is set at a difference of less than 0.0000001 for the model to achieve *convergence* (Long & Freese, 2014). If the model does not converge, do not interpret the results because they may be unreliable. It is possible in Stata or other statistical packages to ensure that the model will converge by using specific procedures to designate a set number of iterations for convergence or increase the acceptable tolerance. We do not recommend this approach, however, due to nonlinearity inherent in maximum likelihood estimations, which can lead to misleading results unless an acceptable tolerance is achieved.

2. Number of obs refers to the sample size used in the analysis excluding the missing data.

3. LR ch2(1) is the likelihood ratio (LR) chi-square test. The likelihood chi-square test statistic can be calculated by hand or by using the "display" command as $2*((−223459.77)−(−220381.91)) = −6155.72$. The LR chi-square equals two times the difference between the first iteration (−223459) and the last iteration (220381.91). The number in the parenthesis (1) indicates the number of degrees of freedom or the number of the independent variable(s) included in the model. In the above model, there is only one independent variable. This LR

chi-square test tells us whether the regression model is significantly statistically different compared to a value of 0.

```
. display 2*((-223459.77)-(-220381.91))
-6155.72
```

4. If the Prob > chi square or the p value of the test equals or is smaller than 0.05, we can say that the model is supported or our research hypothesis is supported by the data. In a simple logistic regression model, this test tells us whether the independent variable has a statistically significant association with the dependent variable. In a multiple regression model that has more than one independent variable, this test will tell us whether one or all independent variables have a significant association with the dependent variable.

5. The Pseudo R^2 reported by Stata is the McFadden's R^2. It could be viewed as the goodness-of-fit measure for the model. This test, however, does not give us the same information as the R square of the ordinary least square regression, which is a measure of linearity. The utility of this test in logistic regression is limited because of the inherent nonlinearity of estimations in the use of the maximum likelihood approach.

$$McFadden's\ Pseudo\ R^2 = 1 - \frac{LLm}{LL0} = 1 - \frac{-220381.91}{-223459.77} = 0.0138$$

LLm is Iteration 3: log likelihood = –220381.91 or the last iteration.

LL0 is Iteration 0: log likelihood = –223459.77 or the first iteration.

We also can calculate the Pseudo R^2 using the "display" command as below.

```
. display 1-( -220381.91/-223459.77)
.01377366
```

INTERPRETATION OF THE ESTIMATES

Coefficients. On its own, the logit command provides us with the logit coefficient or the log odds of the association between depressive disorder and sex, which is not very informative. Given the results, all we can say is that females tend to report that they were told by their healthcare professionals that they had a depressive disorder more often than males.

Standard Error. The standard error of the logit coefficient is an estimate of its *standard deviation* indicating the amount it varies across cases used in the analysis. This can be viewed as a measure of the precision of the logit coefficient, wherein the smaller the standard error, the greater the probability that the coefficient is statistically significant.

Test of Significance Z. If we look at the results of the "logit" analysis, we can see that the log odds coefficient is .6070236 with the correspondent z statistics of 76.95 and its P value or significance value of 0.000. The z value equals to the log odds coefficient divided by its standard error (z = .6070235/.007889 = 76.94557). We can use the "display" command to compute the z test of significance for the log odds coefficient. The log odds coefficient of the variable *Sex_F* is also within the lower and upper 95% confidence intervals.

$$Z = \frac{Coef.}{Std.Err.} = \frac{.6070235}{.007889} = 76.94557$$

```
. display   .6070236/.007889
76.94557
```

95% C.I. The *95% confidence interval* indicates that we can be 95% confident that the logit coefficient falls within the specified 95% confidence interval. If the interval does not contain 0, the p value of the logit coefficient will be 0.05 or less. The p value and the 95% C.I. are related because they are determined by the standard error. The 95% C.I. is useful to interpret because it gives us a sense of the predictability of a coefficient when comparing other coefficients in a multiple logistic regression model. A narrower range between the lower and the upper C.I. intervals indicates more precision in the estimates and better predictability and reliability.

We can manually compute the 95% C.I. using the Stata Codes as below

For the lower interval (see the results above):

```
. display 0.6070236-invnormal(0.975)*0.007889
.59156144
```

For the upper interval (see the results above):

```
. display 0.6070236+invnormal(0.975)*0.007889
.62248576                                          I
```

Notes:
.6070236 is the logit coefficient (see table above)
Invnormal(p) is the inverse cumulative standard normal distribution: if normal(z) = p, then invnormal(p) = z (Stata [2017] *STATA Functions Reference Manual Release 15*, p. 88).
-normal()- is the cumulative standard normal distribution. (It is also a function in Stata.) Assume z is an arbitrary number, then p is the corresponding cumulative standard normal distribution. The command invnormal() in Stata produces the inverse function of normal(). So invnormal (0.975) produces a value wherein the cumulative standard normal distribution is set at 0.975, or 97.5% (communication with Stata Technical Consultant, 4/2020).

It's more informative to report the odds ratio than the log odds coefficients. There are two options for generating the odds ratios. First, we can add the option "or" to the logit command to estimate the odds ratio of sex on depression or we can use the "logistic" command. Both give us the same outcomes.

```
. logit depression i.Sex_F,nolog
```

Logistic regression				Number of obs	=	447,621
				LR chi2(1)	=	6155.73
				Prob > chi2	=	0.0000
Log likelihood = -220381.91				Pseudo R2	=	0.0138

depression	Coef.	Std. Err.	z	P>|z|	[95% Conf. Interval]	
Sex_F						
female	.6070236	.007889	76.95	0.000	.5915615	.6224856
_cons	-1.75778	.0063497	-276.83	0.000	-1.770225	-1.745334

```
. logit depression i.Sex_F,or nolog
```

```
Logistic regression                        Number of obs   =   447,621
                                           LR chi2(1)      =   6155.73
                                           Prob > chi2     =    0.0000
Log likelihood = -220381.91                Pseudo R2       =    0.0138
```

depression	Odds Ratio	Std. Err.	z	P>|z|	[95% Conf. Interval]	
Sex_F						
Female	1.834962	.0144759	76.95	0.000	1.806808	1.863554
_cons	.1724273	.0010949	-276.83	0.000	.1702947	.1745866

Note: **_cons** estimates baseline odds.

ODDS RATIOS

Now we can use the odds ratio (OR) to explain these findings. For females, the odds of having a depressive disorder (vs. not having a depressive disorder) are 1.834962 times or 83% higher compared to males. To put it simply, the results indicate that females were more likely to have a depressive disorder than males. Note that z test of 76.95 is based on the ratio of the regression coefficient divided by its standard error (.6070236/.007889 = 76.95). The 95% C.I. should not have a 0 included in the range. If the 95% C.I. includes a zero value, the p value is not statistically significant. We can calculate the 95% C.I. for the odds ratio as follows.

$$OR * e^{-1.96(S.E.\ of\ OR)}$$

$$OR * e^{+1.96(S.E.\ of\ OR)}$$

```
. display    1.834962 -invnormal(0.975)*.0144759
1.8065898
```

```
. display    1.834962+invnormal(0.975)*.0144759
1.8633342
```

Due to the computing process, the values generated by the "display "commands above differ slightly from those in the results of the logistic regression. They are, however, approximately the same.

UNDERSTANDING THE ODDS AND THE ODDS RATIO

To further understand how Stata computes the odds and odds ratio, we examine the association between depressive disorder and sex via the crosstab analysis of these two variables.

```
. tab depression Sex_F,col
```

```
┌─────────────────────────┐
│ Key                     │
├─────────────────────────┤
│      frequency          │
│  column percentage      │
└─────────────────────────┘
```

RECODE of addepev2 (EVER TOLD YOU HAD A DEPRESSIVE DISORDER)	RECODE of Sex (RECODE of sex (RESPONDENTS SEX))		Total
	Male	Female	
No	168,645	189,834	358,479
	85.29	75.96	80.09
Yes	29,079	60,063	89,142
	14.71	24.04	19.91
Total	197,724	249,897	447,621
	100.00	100.00	100.00

Notes:

Tab is the abbreviation of **tabulate.** This command executes the cross-tabulation analysis for the dependent and the independent variables.

It is useful to list the dependent variable (*depression*) before the independent variable (*Sex_F*).

Col is the abbreviation of **column.** This option gives us the column percentage.

Using the data in the 2X2 Table above we calculate:

The odds of having a depressive disorder for male is:

$$Odds = \frac{29070 \,(yes)}{168645 \,(no)} = .17242729$$

The odds of having a depressive disorder for female is:

$$Odds = \frac{60063}{189834} = .31639748$$

The odds ratio of depressive disorder between the female group and the male group is:

$$Odds\,Ratio\,Female\,over\,Male = \frac{.31639748}{.17242729} = 1.8349617$$

```
. display (.31639748/.17242729)
1.8349617
```

Or

$$Odds\,Ratio\,Female\,over\,Male = \frac{\left(\dfrac{60063}{189834}\right)}{\left(\dfrac{29079}{168645}\right)} = 1.8349618$$

```
. display (60063/189834)/(29079/168645)
1.8349618
```

```
. logit depression i.Sex_F,nolog
```

```
Logistic regression                    Number of obs    =      447,621
                                       LR chi2(1)       =      6155.73
                                       Prob > chi2      =       0.0000
Log likelihood = -220381.91            Pseudo R2        =       0.0138
```

depression	Coef.	Std. Err.	z	P>|z|	[95% Conf. Interval]	
Sex_F						
Female	.6070236	.007889	76.95	0.000	.5915615	.6224856
_cons	-1.75778	.0063497	-276.83	0.000	-1.770225	-1.745334

The constant (_cons) or the intercept of –1.75778 in the table above is the log of the odds of male (.17242729). We know this because male is coded as the reference group (Sex_F = 0).

Let's rerun the logit analysis and add the "base" option to see the reference group listed in the outputs. By specifying the "base" option, Stata will list the group that is considered as the reference group for a factor variable or a categorical variable. As discussed in the previous chapters, we do not have to create dummy variables for a multiple categorical or multiple factor variable such as ethnicity, race, sex, religion, and other similar variables.

```
. logit depression i.Sex_F,base nolog
```

Logistic regression

Number of obs   =   447,621
LR chi2(1)   =   6155.73
Prob > chi2   =   0.0000
Log likelihood = -220381.91

Pseudo R2   =   0.0138

depression	Coef.	Std. Err.	z	P>|z|	[95% Conf. Interval]
Sex_F						
Male	0	(base)				
Female	.6070236	.007889	76.95	0.000	.5915615	.6224856
_cons	-1.75778	.0063497	-276.83	0.000	-1.770225	-1.745334

We can use the "display" command or a hand calculator to calculate logit coefficient using the odds ratio of the constant at .17243729, as reported in the constant as follows:

```
. display log(.17242729)
-1.7577796
```

```
. logistic depression i.Sex_F,or nolog
```

Logistic regression

Number of obs   =   447,621
LR chi2(1)   =   6155.73
Prob > chi2   =   0.0000
Log likelihood = -220381.91

Pseudo R2   =   0.0138

depression	Odds Ratio	Std. Err.	z	P>|z|	[95% Conf. Interval]
Sex_F						
female	1.834962	.0144759	76.95	0.000	1.806808	1.863554
_cons	.1724273	.0010949	-276.83	0.000	.1702947	.1745866

Note: _cons estimates baseline odds.

SURVEY DATA

The above simple logistic regression analysis did not take complex survey design into account. In general, statistical packages assume that all data used in the analysis were collected by simple random sampling. However, most large-scale survey data, such as the 2017 BRFSS data set, used complex survey design. Therefore, the standard errors are likely to be biased (https://stats.idre.ucla.edu/stata/seminars/survey-data-analysis-with-stata-15/) if we do not account for the weights that are used by declaring that the data in the analysis were collected using complex survey designs. Without designating the use of these weights, Stata and other statistical packages including SAS and SPSS will treat the data as collected by simple random sampling design.

As noted earlier the following command syntax is appropriate for frequency analysis but not for analyses that require the estimates for the tests of significance (https://www.cdc.gov/copd/pdfs/brfss_copd_syntax.pdf).

```
. svyset [pweight=_llcpwt], strata(_ststr) psu(_psu)

       pweight: _llcpwt
           VCE: linearized
   Single unit: missing
     Strata 1: _ststr
        SU 1: _psu
       FPC 1: <zero>

. svy:logistic depression i.Sex_F,or nolog
(running logistic on estimation sample)

Survey: Logistic regression

Number of strata   =       1,659        Number of obs    =        447,621
Number of PSUs     =     447,621        Population size  =    254,297,821
                                        Design df        =        445,962
                                        F(   0, 445962)  =              .
                                        Prob > F         =              .
```

depression	Odds Ratio	Linearized Std. Err.	t	P>|t|	[95% Conf. Interval]	
Sex_F						
female	1.914259	.	.	.	.	.
_cons	.1638758	.	.	.	.	.

```
Note: _cons estimates baseline odds.
Note: Missing standard errors because of stratum with single sampling unit.
```

Note that the above results are not complete due to the lack of the estimates for the standard errors, test of significance, and 95% confidence intervals. The problem was caused by missing single unit weights. To correct this problem we add "singleunit(certainty)" to the command "svyset" as below.

```
. svyset [pweight=_llcpwt], singleunit(certainty) strata(_ststr) vce(linearized)

       pweight: _llcpwt
           VCE: linearized
   Single unit: certainty
     Strata 1: _ststr
         SU 1: <observations>
        FPC 1: <zero>

. svy:logistic depression i.Sex_F,or nolog
(running logistic on estimation sample)

Survey: Logistic regression

Number of strata   =       1,659        Number of obs       =        447,621
Number of PSUs     =     447,621        Population size     =    254,297,821
                                        Design df           =        445,962
                                        F(   1, 445962)     =        1509.54
                                        Prob > F            =         0.0000
```

depression	Odds Ratio	Linearized Std. Err.	t	P>|t|	[95% Conf. Interval]	
Sex_F						
female	1.914259	.0319922	38.85	0.000	1.852571	1.978001
_cons	.1638758	.0021246	−139.50	0.000	.1597641	.1680934

```
Note: _cons estimates baseline odds.
Note: Strata with single sampling unit treated as certainty units.

.
```

COMPARING THE RESULTS OF THE COMPLEX SURVEY AND SIMPLE SAMPLING SURVEY

Simple Random Sampling Survey

```
. logit depression  i.Sex_F, nolog
```

Logistic regression

Number of obs	=	447,621
LR chi2(1)	=	6155.73
Prob > chi2	=	0.0000
Pseudo R2	=	0.0138

Log likelihood = -220381.91

depression	Coef.	Std. Err.	z	P>|z|	[95% Conf. Interval]	
Sex_F						
female	.6070236	.007889	76.95	0.000	.5915615	.6224856
_cons	-1.75778	.0063497	-276.83	0.000	-1.770225	-1.745334

```
. logistic depression i.Sex_F,or nolog
```

Logistic regression

Number of obs	=	447,621
LR chi2(1)	=	6155.73
Prob > chi2	=	0.0000
Pseudo R2	=	0.0138

Log likelihood = -220381.91

depression	Odds Ratio	Std. Err.	z	P>|z|	[95% Conf. Interval]	
Sex_F						
female	1.834962	.0144759	76.95	0.000	1.806808	1.863554
_cons	.1724273	.0010949	-276.83	0.000	.1702947	.1745866

Note: _cons estimates baseline odds.

Complex Survey Results

```
. svy:logit depression i.Sex_F,nolog
(running logit on estimation sample)
```

Survey: Logistic regression

```
Number of strata   =      1,659          Number of obs      =       447,621
Number of PSUs     =    447,621          Population size     =   254,297,821
                                         Design df          =       445,962
                                         F(   1, 445962)    =       1509.54
                                         Prob > F           =        0.0000
```

depression	Coef.	Linearized Std. Err.	t	P>|t|	[95% Conf. Interval]	
Sex_F						
female	.6493305	.0167126	38.85	0.000	.6165744	.6820867
_cons	−1.808646	.0129649	−139.50	0.000	−1.834057	−1.783235

Note: Strata with single sampling unit treated as certainty units.

Survey: Logistic regression

```
Number of strata   =      1,659          Number of obs      =       447,621
Number of PSUs     =    447,621          Population size     =   254,297,821
                                         Design df          =       445,962
                                         F(   1, 445962)    =       1509.54
                                         Prob > F           =        0.0000
```

depression	Odds Ratio	Linearized Std. Err.	t	P>|t|	[95% Conf. Interval]	
Sex_F						
female	1.914259	.0319922	38.85	0.000	1.852571	1.978001
_cons	.1638758	.0021246	−139.50	0.000	.1597641	.1680934

Note: _cons estimates baseline odds.
Note: Strata with single sampling unit treated as certainty units.

Let's compare the analysis from results that did not consider complex survey design with results where complex survey design weights were declared as presented in the tables above. We see that the changes in the regression coefficients and the odds ratios are relatively small, but the changes in the standard errors are considerably larger. This indicates that the analysis without taking complex survey design into consideration can underestimate the standard errors of the estimates, which can impact the tests of significance of the estimates. In short, this can result in estimates that are inaccurately reported as significant (Type 1 error), or confidence intervals that appear more precise than when they are appropriately examined with survey weights.

Applied Multiple Logistic Regression for Cross-Cultural Comparisons

In the previous example, we illustrated and discussed the application of a simple regression for cross-cultural comparison. In this section, we will illustrate the application of multiple logistic regression to compare the association of race with depression. The first research question is to determine whether people who identified as Asians, Blacks, Hispanics, or Whites have the same probability of reporting a depressive disorder. Subsequently, if the association between race and depression was not independent, we will examine whether the association of race and depression is moderated by sex. This second question refers to the possibility of a statistical interaction effect between race and sex on depression. To simplify our presentation and discussion, we will include only one control variable in the analysis. We will repeat the basic steps of the analytical process and illustrate the use of both descriptive statistics and multiple logistic regression for cross-cultural comparison. Some of the following data transformation procedures are redundant, but we think it is important to demonstrate these procedures in the following example.

Dependent Variable. The dependent or outcome variable of a simple or multiple logistic regression analysis must be a binary variable. We use the variable depression in our example. Let's look at the data of this variable in the 2017 BRFSS data codebook again.

Label: Ever told you had a depressive disorder
Section Name: Chronic Health Conditions
Core Section Number: 6
Question Number: 10
Column: 115
Type of Variable: Num
SAS Variable Name: ADDEPEV2
Question Prologue:
Question: (Ever told) you have a depressive disorder (including depression, major depression, dysthymia, or minor depression)?

Value	Value Label	Frequency	Percentage	Weighted Percentage
1	Yes	89,209	19.82	19.03
2	No	358,683	79.71	80.50
7	Don't know/Not sure	1,661	0.37	0.39
9	Refused	460	0.10	0.08
BLANK	Not asked or Missing	3	.	.

If we just run a multiple regression of this variable without doing data transformation, we will get the results below.

```
. logistic addepev2 i.Race i.Sex_F
outcome does not vary; remember:
                              0 = negative outcome,
          all other nonmissing values = positive outcome
r(2000);
```

The result above indicates that we must transform the variable "addepev2" into a binary or dummy variable with 0 and 1 values.

```
. recode addepev2 (1=1 "Yes") (2=0 "No") (7 9=.),gen (depression)
(360804 differences between addepev2 and depression)

. tab depression
```

RECODE of addepev2 (EVER TOLD YOU HAD A DEPRESSIVE DISORDER)	Freq.	Percent	Cum.
No	358,683	80.08	80.08
Yes	89,209	19.92	100.00
Total	447,892	100.00	

To verify that the value of No is coded as "0" and Yes is coded as "1," we can use the *codebook* command.

```
. codebook depression
```

depression	RECODE of addepev2 (EVER TOLD YOU HAD A DEPRESSIVE DISORDER)

```
              type:  numeric (double)
             label:  depression

             range:  [0,1]                    units:  1
     unique values:  2               missing .:  2,124/450,016

        tabulation:  Freq.   Numeric  Label
                     358,683       0  No
                      89,209       1  Yes
                       2,124       .
```

The coding of our newly recoded variable (depression) has correct values of 0 and 1 that are appropriate for it to be the dependent variable of our forthcoming logistic regression analyses. We present the original coding of income level, age, and education which was extracted from the BRFSS codebook to illustrate the procedure needed to handle these variables in such a way that we can use them appropriately in our logistic regression analyses.

Label: Income Level
Section Name: Demographics Core
Section Number: 8
Question Number: 17
Column: 180–181

Type of Variable: Num

SAS Variable Name: INCOME2

Question Prologue:

Question: Is your annual household income from all sources: (If respondent refuses at any income level, code "Refused.")

Value	Value Label	Frequency	Percentage	Weighted Percentage
1	Less than $10,000 Notes: If "no," code 02	18,346	4.11	5.02
2	Less than $15,000 ($10,000 to less than $15,000) Notes: If "no," code 03; if "yes," ask 01	19,334	4.33	4.34
3	Less than $20,000 ($15,000 to less than $20,000) Notes: If "no," code 04; if "yes," ask 02	27,735	6.21	6.45
4	Less than $25,000 ($20,000 to less than $25,000) Notes: If "no," ask 05; if "yes," ask 03	34,222	7.66	7.78
5	Less than $35,000 ($25,000 to less than $35,000) Notes: If "no," ask 06	39,751	8.90	8.71
6	Less than $50,000 ($35,000 to less than $50,000) Notes: If "no," ask 07	53,148	11.90	11.07
7	Less than $75,000 ($50,000 to less than $75,000) Notes: If "no," code 08	59,632	13.35	12.26
8	$75,000 or more	122,763	27.48	28.50
77	Don't know/Not sure	33,328	7.46	8.40
99	Refused	38,426	8.60	7.48
BLANK	Not asked or Missing	3,331	.	.

Label: *Imputed Age value collapsed above*
80 Section Name: Calculated Variables
Module Section Number: 8
Question Number: 13
Column: 2031-2032

Type of Variable:

Num

SAS Variable Name: _AGE80_

Question Prologue:

Question: Imputed Age value collapsed above 80

Value	Value Label	Frequency	Percentage	Weighted Percentage
18-24	Imputed Age 18 to 24	26,236	5.83	12.53
25-29	Imputed Age 25 to 29	22,397	4.98	8.03
30-34	Imputed Age 30 to 34	24,835	5.52	9.32
35-39	Imputed Age 35 to 39	26,451	5.88	8.17
40-44	Imputed Age 40 to 44	25,649	5.70	8.13
45-49	Imputed Age 45 to 49	31,263	6.95	7.69
50-54	Imputed Age 50 to 54	38,639	8.59	8.95
55-59	Imputed Age 55 to 59	45,412	10.09	8.28
60-64	Imputed Age 60 to 64	51,165	11.37	8.40
65-69	Imputed Age 65 to 69	51,403	11.42	6.77
7074	Imputed Age 70 to 74	41,456	9.21	5.34
75-79	Imputed Age 75 to 79	29,279	6.51	3.94
80-99	Imputed Age 80 or older	35,831	7.96	4.45

Label: Education Level
Section Name: Demographics Core
Section Number: 8
Question Number: 7
Column: 163
Type of Variable: Num
SAS Variable Name: EDUCA
Question Prologue:
Question: What is the highest grade or year of school you completed?

Value	Value Label	Frequency	Percentage	Weighted Percentage
1	Never attended school or only kindergarten	629	0.14	0.31
2	Grades 1 through 8 (Elementary)	10,434	2.32	4.61
3	Grades 9 through 11 (Some high school)	21,624	4.81	8.63
4	Grade 12 or GED (High school graduate)	122,577	27.24	27.90
5	College 1 year to 3 years (Some college or technical school)	124,655	27.70	30.92
6	College 4 years or more (College graduate)	168,390	37.42	27.24
9	Refused	1,701	0.38	0.40
BLANK	Not asked or Missing	6	.	.

The description of the age variable in the codebook as presented on page 159 can be confusing because the age variable was reported in brackets, but the actual coding presented below shows that the age of participants ranged from 18 to 80 with 63 unique values.

```
_age80                                              IMPUTED AGE VALUE COLLAPSED ABOVE 80


                type:  numeric (double)

               range:  [18,80]                   units:  1
       unique values:  63                    missing .:  0/450,016

                mean:  55.0702
           std. dev:  17.3237

         percentiles:        10%      25%      50%      75%      90%
                             29       42       58       69       78
```

Because this is an imputed variable, the codebook that is included in the data download will oftentimes be more informative regarding how the various categories are captured in the variable. As indicated in the BRFSS codebook, the _age80 variable includes age from 18 to 80.

We will treat both income and education as continuous variables in our analysis. It is important to note that as we review the codebook information of these two variables, we should declare the categories "Refused" or "Don't Know" as missing data. We also need to create two new variables because it is important to not corrupt the original data.

```
. recode educa (9=.),gen(edu)

. recode income2 (77 99=.),gen(income)
```

Let's look at the coding of the variables that will be used in the analyses.

```
. codebook depression Race Sex_F age edu income
```

---

depression   RECODE of addepev2 (EVER TOLD YOU HAD A DEPRESSIVE DISORDER)

```
              type:  numeric (double)
             label:  depression

             range:  [0,1]                          units:  1
     unique values:  2                            missing .:  2,124/450,016

       tabulation:  Freq.   Numeric  Label
                    358,683       0  No
                     89,209       1  Yes
                      2,124       .
```

Race   RECODE of _race (COMPUTED RACE-ETHNICITY GROUPING)

```
              type:  numeric (double)
             label:  race4

             range:  [1,4]                          units:  1
     unique values:  4                            missing .:  30,152/450,016

       tabulation:  Freq.   Numeric  Label
                    337,166       1  White
                     35,765       2  Black
                      9,855       3  Asian
                     37,078       4  Hispanic
                     30,152       .
```

Sex_F   RECODE of sex (RESPONDENTS SEX)

```
              type:  numeric (double)
             label:  Sex_F

             range:  [0,1]                          units:  1
     unique values:  2                            missing .:  284/450,016

       tabulation:  Freq.   Numeric  Label
                    198,725       0  male
                    251,007       1  female
                        284       .
```

```
age                                    RECODE of _age80 (IMPUTED AGE VALUE COLLAPSED ABOVE 80)


               type:  numeric (double)

              range:  [18,80]                    units:  1
      unique values:  63                       missing .:  0/450,016

               mean:  55.0702
           std. dev:  17.3237

        percentiles:          10%      25%     50%     75%     90%
                               29       42      58      69      78
```

```
edu                                                    RECODE of educa (EDUCATION LEVEL)


               type:  numeric (double)

              range:  [1,6]                      units:  1
      unique values:  6                        missing .:  1,707/450,016

         tabulation:  Freq.  Value
                        629  1
                     10,434  2
                     21,624  3
                    122,577  4
                    124,655  5
                    168,390  6
                      1,707  .
```

```
income                                                RECODE of income2 (INCOME LEVEL)


               type:  numeric (double)

              range:  [1,8]                      units:  1
      unique values:  8                        missing .:  75,085/450,016

         tabulation:  Freq.  Value
                     18,346  1
                     19,334  2
                     27,735  3
                     34,222  4
                     39,751  5
                     53,148  6
                     59,632  7
                    122,763  8
                     75,085  .

.
```

How should we read the information provided by the codebook command? First, we should look at the range to verify whether the lowest value and the highest value are consistent with what the variable should be. For example, the range of the variable *Sex_F* is [0,1] and 0 refers to male and 1 refers to female. The information is exactly what the variable supposes to be. We should also look at the summary description of the variables that will be included on the analysis.

```
. sum depression Race Sex_F age edu income
```

Variable	Obs	Mean	Std. Dev.	Min	Max
depression	447,892	.1991752	.3993806	0	1
Race	419,864	1.397055	.9034408	1	4
Sex_F	449,732	.5581052	.4966105	0	1
age	450,016	55.0702	17.32375	18	80
edu	448,309	4.930287	1.033939	1	6
income	374,931	5.852485	2.152269	1	8

The command "sum" stands for "summarize." The results give us descriptive information for each variable. In the case of a dummy variable coded as 0 and 1, the mean refers to the percentage of the category coded as 1. For example, 19.91752% of respondents reported that they were told by their healthcare professionals that they had a depressive disorder. However, the standard error of depression is not meaningful. The "Min" and "Max" provide information that can be used to verify the data is coded as expected based on the codebook and whether the values reflect the true coding of each variable.

Logistic Regression with Two Independent Variables. We begin this section with an example of a logistic regression analysis of depression with two independent variables: (1) race and (2) sex.

```
. logit depression i.Race i.Sex_F,  base nolog
```

Logistic regression				Number of obs	=	417,867
				LR chi2(4)	=	7558.15
				Prob > chi2	=	0.0000
Log likelihood = -204113.07				Pseudo R2	=	0.0182

depression	Coef.	Std. Err.	z	P>|z|	[95% Conf. Interval]	
Race						
White	0	(base)				
Black	-.3352435	.0150744	-22.24	0.000	-.3647889	-.3056981
Asian	-1.007918	.0368086	-27.38	0.000	-1.080062	-.9357746
Hispanic	-.2011456	.0144092	-13.96	0.000	-.2293871	-.1729042
Sex_F						
male	0	(base)				
female	.6247325	.0082322	75.89	0.000	.6085977	.6408673
_cons	-1.717794	.0068437	-251.00	0.000	-1.731207	-1.70438

```
. logistic depression i.Race i.Sex_F,  base nolog

Logistic regression                            Number of obs   =   417,867
                                               LR chi2(4)      =   7558.15
                                               Prob > chi2     =    0.0000
Log likelihood = -204113.07                    Pseudo R2       =    0.0182
```

depression	Odds Ratio	Std. Err.	z	P>|z|	[95% Conf. Interval]	
Race						
White	1	(base)				
Black	.7151639	.0107807	-22.24	0.000	.6943432	.736609
Asian	.364978	.0134343	-27.38	0.000	.3395746	.3922819
Hispanic	.8177933	.0117837	-13.96	0.000	.7950207	.8412182
Sex_F						
male	1	(base)				
female	1.867746	.0153757	75.89	0.000	1.837852	1.898126
_cons	.1794617	.0012282	-251.00	0.000	.1770705	.1818851

Note: **_cons** estimates baseline odds.

The negative regression coefficients using the *logit* command correspond to the same model using the *logistic* command where the odds ratios are less than 1. For example, the regression coefficient of Black is −0.3352435 and its odds ratio is 0.7151639 (*e* -.3352435).

```
. display exp(-.3352435 )
.71516392
```

depression	Coef.	Std. Err.	z	P>|z|	[95% Conf. Interval]	
Race						
White	0	(base)				
Black	-.3352435	.0150744	-22.24	0.000	-.3647889	-.3056981
Asian	-1.007918	.0368086	-27.38	0.000	-1.080062	-.9357746
Hispanic	-.2011456	.0144092	-13.96	0.000	-.2293871	-.1729042

depression	Odds Ratio	Std. Err.	z	P>|z|	[95% Conf. Interval]	
Race						
White	1	(base)				
Black	.7151639	.0107807	-22.24	0.000	.6943432	.736609
Asian	.364978	.0134343	-27.38	0.000	.3395746	.3922819
Hispanic	.8177933	.0117837	-13.96	0.000	.7950207	.8412182

The "Number of obs" indicates that the analysis was performed with a sample of 417,867 respondents. The LR chi2(4) has the value of 7558.15 with four degrees of freedom because the model has four estimates. The likelihood ratio (LR) chi-square test determines whether the overall model is statistically significant. The results show that the logistic regression model with two independent variables is statistically significant with a p-value that is less than 0.001. The pseudo R-squared is provided here, but should not be interpreted as the same R-squared that is found in OLS regression. As previously discussed, we do not recommend the use of the pseudo R-squared as a measure of fit for the logistic regression model. We can interpret the regression coefficients and the odds ratios of the Race variables in relation to White as the reference group. Compared with Whites, the Black, Asian, and Hispanic respondents were less likely to report that they were told by their healthcare providers that they had a depressive disorder. We can change the base reference group in the analysis and choose any other racial group as our reference group. Let's select Hispanic as our reference group and run another logit and logistic regression.

```
. logit depression b4.Race i.Sex_F, base nolog
```

```
Logistic regression                          Number of obs    =     417,867
                                             LR chi2(4)       =     7558.15
                                             Prob > chi2      =      0.0000
Log likelihood = -204113.07                  Pseudo R2        =      0.0182
```

depression	Coef.	Std. Err.	z	P>|z|	[95% Conf. Interval]	
Race						
White	.2011456	.0144092	13.96	0.000	.1729042	.2293871
Black	-.1340979	.0199504	-6.72	0.000	-.1731999	-.0949958
Asian	-.8067725	.0390606	-20.65	0.000	-.8833299	-.7302151
Hispanic	0	(base)				
Sex_F						
male	0	(base)				
female	.6247325	.0082322	75.89	0.000	.6085977	.6408673
_cons	-1.918939	.0147697	-129.92	0.000	-1.947887	-1.889991

Note that the Race variable was coded as:

```
. codebook Race
```

Race	RECODE of _race (COMPUTED RACE-ETHNICITY GROUPING)

```
              type:  numeric (double)
              label:  race4

              range:  [1,4]                    units:  1
      unique values:  4                      missing .:  30,152/450,016

        tabulation:  Freq.    Numeric  Label
                    337,166         1  White
                     35,765         2  Black
                      9,855         3  Asian
                     37,078         4  Hispanic
                     30,152         .
```

In the logit or logistic command, we select the category 4 if we want Hispanic to be our reference group.

```
. logit depression b4.Race i.Sex_F, base nolog
```

The syntax *b4.Race* informs Stata that we wish to designate the group that was coded with a value of "4" as the reference group. If we wish to use Black as our reference group, we can declare *b2.Race* in the command. When using a categorical variable such as Race as the independent variable, we can only compare the results of each group with the reference group. It is possible to examine all possible combinations for comparison, such as Black compared with White, Asian with White, and Hispanic with White. In addition, we can compare the regression coefficient or the odds ratio between Black and Asian, Black and Hispanic, and Asian and Hispanic. In the following analyses, we will use the *lincom* command to compare the regression coefficient between Black and Asian, and the odds ratio of the difference between Black and Asian.

```
. logit depression i.Race i.Sex_F,base nolog
```

```
Logistic regression                      Number of obs   =     417,867
                                         LR chi2(4)      =     7558.15
                                         Prob > chi2     =      0.0000
Log likelihood = -204113.07              Pseudo R2       =      0.0182
```

depression	Coef.	Std. Err.	z	P>|z|	[95% Conf. Interval]	
Race						
White	0	(base)				
Black	-.3352435	.0150744	-22.24	0.000	-.3647889	-.3056981
Asian	-1.007918	.0368086	-27.38	0.000	-1.080062	-.9357746
Hispanic	-.2011456	.0144092	-13.96	0.000	-.2293871	-.1729042
Sex_F						
male	0	(base)				
female	.6247325	.0082322	75.89	0.000	.6085977	.6408673
_cons	-1.717794	.0068437	-251.00	0.000	-1.731207	-1.70438

```
. lincom 2.Race-3.Race
```

```
( 1)  [depression]2.Race - [depression]3.Race = 0
```

depression	Coef.	Std. Err.	z	P>|z|	[95% Conf. Interval]	
(1)	.6726746	.0393155	17.11	0.000	.5956176	.7497316

The regression coefficient of 0.6726746 indicates that Black respondents were more likely to have a depressive disorder compared to Asian respondents and the difference is statistically significant given the p value of the z test is less than 0.001 and there is no zero value in the 95% confidence interval.

```
. display ((-.3352435)-(-1.007918 ))
.6726745
```

We also can look at the odds ratio of the difference between Black and Asian as illustrated in the analysis below.

```
. logistic depression i.Race i.Sex_F,base nolog
```

```
Logistic regression                          Number of obs    =    417,867
                                             LR chi2(4)       =    7558.15
                                             Prob > chi2      =     0.0000
Log likelihood = -204113.07                  Pseudo R2        =     0.0182
```

depression	Odds Ratio	Std. Err.	z	P>|z|	[95% Conf. Interval]	
Race						
White	1	(base)				
Black	.7151639	.0107807	-22.24	0.000	.6943432	.736609
Asian	.364978	.0134343	-27.38	0.000	.3395746	.3922819
Hispanic	.8177933	.0117837	-13.96	0.000	.7950207	.8412182
Sex_F						
male	1	(base)				
female	1.867746	.0153757	75.89	0.000	1.837852	1.898126
_cons	.1794617	.0012282	-251.00	0.000	.1770705	.1818851

```
Note: _cons estimates baseline odds.
```

```
. lincom 2.Race-3.Race
```

```
( 1)  [depression]2.Race - [depression]3.Race = 0
```

depression	Odds Ratio	Std. Err.	z	P>|z|	[95% Conf. Interval]	
(1)	1.959471	.0770376	17.11	0.000	1.814151	2.116432

```
. display  (.7151639/.364978 )
1.9594713
```

The results of the logistic regression above show racial differences in depression using White as the reference group. In order to compare the odds for depression between Black and Asian, we use the "lincom" command which uses the Wald test to estimate whether the odd ratios of depression of Black respondents is statistically similar to the odds ratio of Asian respondents. We use the "display" command as shown above to provide this result. The odds ratio for Black compared to Asian is 1.959471. We can interpret this to mean that compared to Asians, Black respondents were 96% more likely to report they have been told by a health professional that they have a depressive disorder. This odds ratio is statistically significant given the p value of the z test is at less than 0.001 and there is no zero value in the 95% confidence interval.

Check for Appropriateness of Logistic Regression Model Specification

Stata has the command *linktest*, which allows us to verify that the logistic regression model we specified is appropriate. More specifically, "The link test is based on the idea that if a regression or regression-like equation is properly specified, you should be able to find no additional independent variables that are significant except by chance" (https://www.stata.com/manuals13/rlinktest.pdf).

Let's rerun the logistic regression model:

$$logit(p\ depression) = bo + b1Race + b2Sex\_F$$

The null hypothesis is that this logistic regression model (equation) is not mis-specified, and that this is a correct model.

The results below show that the LR chi2(4) is statistically significant suggesting that both independent variables or one of them is statistically significant. In addition, all odds ratios of the independent variables are statistically significant. We can conclude that both Race and Sex are significant predictors of depression. We should not be complacent with the results yet. It is important to determine whether the regression model (equation) includes all appropriate independent variables. To answer this question, we can perform the *linktest* procedure.

```
. logistic depression i.Race i.Sex_F,base nolog
```

```
Logistic regression                          Number of obs    =    417,867
                                             LR chi2(4)       =    7558.15
                                             Prob > chi2      =     0.0000
Log likelihood = -204113.07                  Pseudo R2        =     0.0182
```

depression	Odds Ratio	Std. Err.	z	P>|z|	[95% Conf. Interval]	
Race						
White	1	(base)				
Black	.7151639	.0107807	-22.24	0.000	.6943432	.736609
Asian	.364978	.0134343	-27.38	0.000	.3395746	.3922819
Hispanic	.8177933	.0117837	-13.96	0.000	.7950207	.8412182
Sex_F						
male	1	(base)				
female	1.867746	.0153757	75.89	0.000	1.837852	1.898126
_cons	.1794617	.0012282	-251.00	0.000	.1770705	.1818851

```
Note: _cons estimates baseline odds.
```

```
. linktest,nolog
```

```
Logistic regression                          Number of obs    =    417,867
                                             LR chi2(2)       =    7575.10
                                             Prob > chi2      =     0.0000
Log likelihood = -204104.6                   Pseudo R2        =     0.0182
```

depression	Coef.	Std. Err.	z	P>|z|	[95% Conf. Interval]	
_hat	1.401175	.0967533	14.48	0.000	1.211543	1.590808
_hatsq	.1337918	.0319445	4.19	0.000	.0711818	.1964019
_cons	.2837205	.0700429	4.05	0.000	.146439	.4210021

In order for us to accept that the current logistic regression model has no specification problem, the _hatsq coefficient must have a p value that is greater than 0.05. In this example, the p value of the z test for the _hatsq coefficient is less than .001 (0.000). Given the result, we should reconsider our model. Previous literature and research related to the topic of our interest can be a good source and serve as a guide for revising our current model. Our aim is to use logistic regression for cross-cultural comparison; therefore, we should ask whether the association of depression and race is moderated by sex. More specifically, we seek to determine if the association between race and depression differs between females and males. This question assumes that race is not an independent predictor of depression, but its association with depression depends on sex. We may assume that the probability of having a depressive disorder among different racial groups varies between female and male respondents. We are now examining the multiplicative interaction or the statistical interaction effect of race and sex on depression.

Let's run a logistic regression with an interaction of race and sex. We will present two different ways to run a logistic regression with interaction terms. Stata uses the hashtag (#) for interaction. We use one hashtag (#) in the first analysis and two hashtags (##) in the second analysis. Both analyses arrive at the same outcomes.

Interaction Model with One Hashtag (#)

```
. logistic depression i.Race i.Sex_F i.Race#i.Sex_F, base nolog

Logistic regression                          Number of obs   =    417,867
                                             LR chi2(7)      =    7607.95
                                             Prob > chi2     =     0.0000
Log likelihood = -204088.17                  Pseudo R2       =     0.0183
```

depression	Odds Ratio	Std. Err.	z	P>|z|	[95% Conf. Interval]	
Race						
White	1	(base)				
Black	.8288307	.0221233	-7.03	0.000	.7865844	.8733459
Asian	.3967598	.0225432	-16.27	0.000	.3549473	.4434977
Hispanic	.8626548	.0208321	-6.12	0.000	.8227758	.9044667
Sex_F						
male	1	(base)				
female	1.911103	.0172075	71.93	0.000	1.877673	1.945129
Race#Sex_F						
Black#female	.8086438	.0261193	-6.58	0.000	.7590378	.8614918
Asian#female	.8703827	.0648672	-1.86	0.063	.7520949	1.007275
Hispanic#female	.9209909	.0277003	-2.74	0.006	.8682685	.9769147
_cons	.1768069	.0012845	-238.49	0.000	.1743071	.1793426

Note: **_cons** estimates baseline odds.

Interaction Model With Two Hashtags (##)

```
. logistic depression i.Race##i.Sex_F, base nolog
```

Logistic regression

Log likelihood = -204088.17

Number of obs	=	417,867
LR chi2(7)	=	7607.95
Prob > chi2	=	0.0000
Pseudo R2	=	0.0183

depression	Odds Ratio	Std. Err.	z	P>|z|	[95% Conf. Interval]	
Race						
White	1	(base)				
Black	.8288307	.0221233	-7.03	0.000	.7865844	.8733459
Asian	.3967598	.0225432	-16.27	0.000	.3549473	.4434977
Hispanic	.8626548	.0208321	-6.12	0.000	.8227758	.9044667
Sex_F						
male	1	(base)				
female	1.911103	.0172075	71.93	0.000	1.877673	1.945129
Race#Sex_F						
Black#female	.8086438	.0261193	-6.58	0.000	.7590378	.8614918
Asian#female	.8703827	.0648672	-1.86	0.063	.7520949	1.007275
Hispanic#female	.9209909	.0277003	-2.74	0.006	.8682685	.9769147
_cons	.1768069	.0012845	-238.49	0.000	.1743071	.1793426

Note: _cons estimates baseline odds.

The results of the model using one hashtag (#) and the model using two hashtags (##) are identical. We recommend using two hashtags for interaction specification. The results show two interaction terms are statistically significant suggesting that the association of race and depression is not the same for females and males. It's difficult to interpret the interaction terms as reported in the results above. We will address this issue later. Before we decide whether to accept this interaction model, we should use the *linktest* command to verify the model specification.

```
. linktest,nolog
```

```
Logistic regression                         Number of obs    =    417,867
                                            LR chi2(2)       =    7607.95
                                            Prob > chi2      =     0.0000
Log likelihood = -204088.17                 Pseudo R2        =     0.0183
```

depression	Coef.	Std. Err.	z	P>|z|	[95% Conf. Interval]	
_hat	1	.1089321	9.18	0.000	.7864972	1.213503
_hatsq	6.02e-08	.0366724	0.00	1.000	-.0718764	.0718766
_cons	1.42e-07	.0772445	0.00	1.000	-.1513963	.1513966

The results of the *linktest* show that the interaction model of race and sex is acceptable given the significance of the z test. We also can use the *testparm* command to test the interaction effect.

. testparm Race##Sex_F

```
( 1)   [depression]2.Race = 0
( 2)   [depression]3.Race = 0
( 3)   [depression]4.Race = 0
( 4)   [depression]1.Sex_F = 0
( 5)   [depression]2.Race#1.Sex_F = 0
( 6)   [depression]3.Race#1.Sex_F = 0
( 7)   [depression]4.Race#1.Sex_F = 0
```

$$chi2(\ 7) = 7149.82$$
$$Prob > chi2 =\ \ \ 0.0000$$

The results produced by the *testparm* command also confirm that the interaction model is statistically significant.

We can compare the model without the interaction term and the model with the interaction term to determine whether they are statistically the same. If they are statistically the same, there is no justification for estimating the interaction effect. Here are the steps we should follow:

1. Run the model without the interaction effect.

. `logit depression i.Race i.Sex_F,base nolog`

2. Use the *estimate store* command to save the results of this model in the file named M1. You can use any name you wish.

. `estimate store M1`

3. Run the model with the interaction effect. Note that when you add more variables in the equation, the sample size could be changed. To keep the sample sizes of the two models the same, we use the option "if e(sample)" in the command syntax.

. `logit depression i.Race##i.Sex_F if e(sample),base nolog`

4. Save the results of model as M2.

. `estimate store M2`

5. Use the likelihood-ratio test to compare the two models.

. `lrtest M1 M2`

Here are the results:

```
. logit depression i.Race i.Sex_F,base nolog
```

```
Logistic regression                          Number of obs   =    417,867
                                             LR chi2(4)      =    7558.15
                                             Prob > chi2     =     0.0000
Log likelihood = -204113.07                  Pseudo R2       =     0.0182
```

depression	Coef.	Std. Err.	z	P>|z|	[95% Conf. Interval]	
Race						
White	0	(base)				
Black	-.3352435	.0150744	-22.24	0.000	-.3647889	-.3056981
Asian	-1.007918	.0368086	-27.38	0.000	-1.080062	-.9357746
Hispanic	-.2011456	.0144092	-13.96	0.000	-.2293871	-.1729042
Sex_F						
male	0	(base)				
female	.6247325	.0082322	75.89	0.000	.6085977	.6408673
_cons	-1.717794	.0068437	-251.00	0.000	-1.731207	-1.70438

```
. estimate store M1
```

```
. logit depression i.Race##i.Sex_F if e(sample),base nolog
```

```
Logistic regression                          Number of obs   =    417,867
                                             LR chi2(7)      =    7607.95
                                             Prob > chi2     =     0.0000
Log likelihood = -204088.17                  Pseudo R2       =     0.0183
```

depression	Coef.	Std. Err.	z	P>|z|	[95% Conf. Interval]	
Race						
White	0	(base)				
Black	-.1877394	.0266922	-7.03	0.000	-.2400552	-.1354236
Asian	-.9244243	.0568182	-16.27	0.000	-1.035786	-.8130628
Hispanic	-.1477407	.0241488	-6.12	0.000	-.1950716	-.1004098
Sex_F						
male	0	(base)				
female	.6476806	.009004	71.93	0.000	.6300331	.665328
Race#Sex_F						
Black#female	-.2123967	.0323001	-6.58	0.000	-.2757037	-.1490897
Asian#female	-.1388223	.0745272	-1.86	0.063	-.2848928	.0072483
Hispanic#female	-.0823051	.0300766	-2.74	0.006	-.1412542	-.023356
_cons	-1.732697	.0072652	-238.49	0.000	-1.746937	-1.718457

```
. estimate store M2
```

```
. lrtest M1 M2
```

```
Likelihood-ratio test                        LR chi2(3)  =      49.80
(Assumption: M1 nested in M2)                 Prob > chi2 =     0.0000
```

The likelihood-ratio (LR) test indicates that the model without the interaction and the model with the interaction differ significantly, given the probability of the LR test is smaller than 0.05. In conclusion, both the *linktest* procedure for model specification and the LR test provide evidence to support examining the interaction effect between race and sex on depression.

As we mentioned earlier, the results of the logistic regression of the interaction model indicate that the association of depression and race depends on sex or varies by sex. We use the *margins* command to further illustrate these interaction effects. Stata states that "margins are statistics calculated from predictions of a previously fit model at fixed values of some covariates and averaging or otherwise integrating over the remaining covariates" (https://www.stata-press.com/manuals/users-guide/). There are different options when using the command *margins*. In this example, we will focus on the predictive probabilities of the interaction.

Let's estimate the predictive probabilities of depression across four racial groups.

```
. margins Race Sex_F

Predictive margins                          Number of obs    =     417,867
Model VCE    : OIM

Expression   : Pr(depression), predict()
```

	Margin	Delta–method Std. Err.	z	P>|z|	[95% Conf. Interval]	
Race						
White	.2076151	.000695	298.74	0.000	.206253	.2089772
Black	.159684	.0019334	82.59	0.000	.1558946	.1634734
Asian	.0873879	.0029368	29.76	0.000	.0816318	.093144
Hispanic	.1768067	.0019787	89.35	0.000	.1729285	.1806849
Sex_F						
male	.1447704	.0008219	176.15	0.000	.1431596	.1463812
female	.2397008	.0008801	272.35	0.000	.2379758	.2414258

The predictive probabilities of depression among the racial groups and between sex are similar to the results from the crosstabulation of depression and race and depression and sex as below.

```
. tab depression Race,col
```

```
┌─────────────────┐
│ Key             │
├─────────────────┤
│     frequency   │
│ column percentage│
└─────────────────┘
```

RECODE of addepev2 (EVER TOLD YOU HAD A DEPRESSIVE DISORDER)	RECODE of _race (COMPUTED RACE-ETHNICITY GROUPING)				Total
	White	Black	Asian	Hispanic	
No	266,163	29,773	8,975	30,379	335,290
	79.26	83.70	91.60	82.36	80.20
Yes	69,633	5,798	823	6,506	82,760
	20.74	16.30	8.40	17.64	19.80
Total	335,796	35,571	9,798	36,885	418,050
	100.00	100.00	100.00	100.00	100.00

```
. tab depression Sex_F,col
```

```
┌─────────────────┐
│ Key             │
├─────────────────┤
│     frequency   │
│ column percentage│
└─────────────────┘
```

RECODE of addepev2 (EVER TOLD YOU HAD A DEPRESSIVE DISORDER)	RECODE of sex (RESPONDENTS SEX)		Total
	male	female	
No	168,645	189,834	358,479
	85.29	75.96	80.09
Yes	29,079	60,063	89,142
	14.71	24.04	19.91
Total	197,724	249,897	447,621
	100.00	100.00	100.00

Predictive Probabilities of Interaction Effect between Race and Sex

. margins Race#Sex_F

```
Adjusted predictions                      Number of obs    =    417,867
Model VCE   : OIM

Expression  : Pr(depression), predict()
```

	Margin	Delta-method Std. Err.	z	P>|z|	[95% Conf. Interval]	
Race#Sex_F						
White#male	.1502429	.0009276	161.98	0.000	.148425	.1520609
White#female	.2525579	.001004	251.55	0.000	.25059	.2545257
Black#male	.1278129	.0028632	44.64	0.000	.1222011	.1334247
Black#female	.1846504	.0026187	70.51	0.000	.1795179	.1897829
Asian#male	.0655515	.0034518	18.99	0.000	.0587861	.0723168
Asian#female	.1044937	.0044855	23.30	0.000	.0957023	.113285
Hispanic#male	.1323386	.0026444	50.04	0.000	.1271556	.1375216
Hispanic#female	.211641	.0028567	74.09	0.000	.2060419	.2172401

The adjusted predicted probability of having a depressive disorder among White male respondents is 0.1502429, or approximately 15%. The adjusted predictive probability of having a depressive disorder among Hispanic female respondents was 0.211642, or approximately 21.12%. These predictive probabilities are the interaction effect between race and sex on having a depressive disorder. We can see that they are more informative than interaction coefficients reported in the earlier results of logistic regression.

Graphing the Interaction Effect

We can present the predictive probabilities of the interaction effect in a graph by using the command "marginsplot" after the command "margins."

. marginsplot

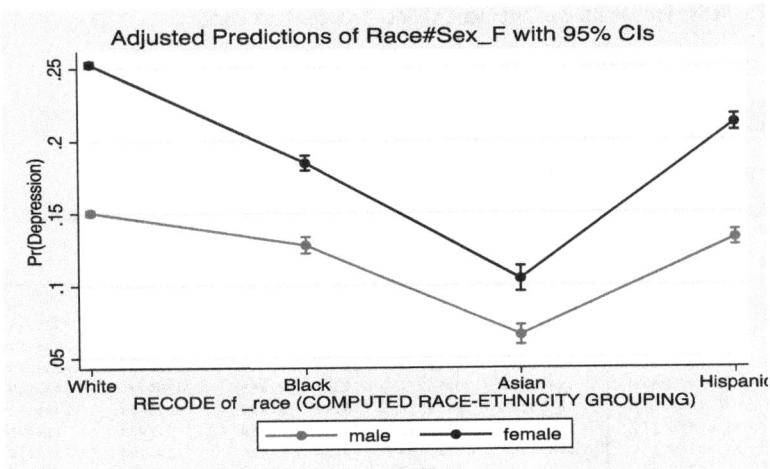

Adjusted Predictions of Race#Sex_F with 95% CIs

If the lines on the graph are parallel, there is no interaction effect. The two lines (female–male) in the graph above are not parallel as reported in the predicted margins above. Although females had the highest predicted probability of having a depressive disorder (.2525579), Asian males had the lowest predicted probability of having a depressive disorder in this analysis (.0655515).

Comparing the Predicted Probabilities

We can compare the predicted probabilities of having a depressive disorder for each racial group between females and males by using the *margins.rRace@Sex_F* command.

```
. margins r.Race@Sex_F
```

Contrasts of adjusted predictions
Model VCE   : OIM

Expression : Pr(depression), predict()

	df	chi2	P>chi2
Race@Sex_F			
(Black vs White) male	1	55.54	0.0000
(Black vs White) female	1	586.29	0.0000
(Asian vs White) male	1	561.45	0.0000
(Asian vs White) female	1	1037.66	0.0000
(Hispanic vs White) male	1	40.82	0.0000
(Hispanic vs White) female	1	182.59	0.0000
Joint	6	2195.89	0.0000

	Contrast	Delta-method Std. Err.	[95% Conf. Interval]	
Race@Sex_F				
(Black vs White) male	-.02243	.0030097	-.028329	-.0165311
(Black vs White) female	-.0679075	.0028045	-.0734043	-.0624107
(Asian vs White) male	-.0846915	.0035742	-.0916969	-.0776861
(Asian vs White) female	-.1480642	.0045964	-.1570731	-.1390554
(Hispanic vs White) male	-.0179043	.0028024	-.0233969	-.0124118
(Hispanic vs White) female	-.0409169	.003028	-.0468517	-.0349821

The above results show the comparison of Black, Asian, and Hispanic to White. This is because in our logistic regression model we assigned White as our reference group. In this example, the difference in the predicted probability of having a depressive disorder between Black males and White males was statistically significant given that the χ^2 test with one degree of freedom returned a value of 55.54 with a significance that is less than .001. If we examine the results in the *Delta-method*, we find that Black males had .02243 or −2.243% lower predicted probability of having a depressive disorder compared to White males (.1278129 (Black male) − .1502429 (White male) = −0.02243. See the Adjusted Predictions above). These comparisons are limited, however, to each racial group as compared with Whites. It may be useful to expand our comparisons across all groups simultaneously.

The following comparisons provide us with extensive comparisons, which are more informative compared to the previous comparisons.

The results show that twenty-eight pairwise comparisons are generated by the interaction effect between race and sex. There are twenty-eight pairwise comparisons because the Race variable has four categories and the Sex_F variable has two categories. We can use the formula n!/(2!*(n-2)!) to determine the number of categories where the symbol! is the factorial notation. We can calculate the number of comparisons with the command *display* 8!/(2!*6!), which is equal to 4*7, to produce a value of 28. (Communication with Stata consultant, May 2020).

```
. margins Race#Sex_F,pwcompare(effect) mcompare(bon)

Pairwise comparisons of adjusted predictions
Model VCE    : OIM

Expression   : Pr(depression), predict()
```

	Number of Comparisons
Race#Sex_F	28

	Contrast	Delta-method Std. Err.	Bonferroni z	P>|z|	Bonferroni [95% Conf. Interval]	
Race#Sex_F						
(White#female) vs (White#male)	.102315	.0013669	74.85	0.000	.0980451	.1065848
(Black#male) vs (White#male)	-.02243	.0030097	-7.45	0.000	-.0318316	-.0130285
(Black#female) vs (White#male)	.0344075	.0027781	12.39	0.000	.0257295	.0430855
(Asian#male) vs (White#male)	-.0846915	.0035742	-23.69	0.000	-.0958565	-.0735265
(Asian#female) vs (White#male)	-.0457493	.0045804	-9.99	0.000	-.0600571	-.0314415
(Hispanic#male) vs (White#male)	-.0179043	.0028024	-6.39	0.000	-.0266582	-.0091504
(Hispanic#female) vs (White#male)	.0613981	.0030035	20.44	0.000	.0520158	.0707803
(Black#male) vs (White#female)	-.124745	.0030342	-41.11	0.000	-.1342229	-.1152671
(Black#female) vs (White#female)	-.0679075	.0028045	-24.21	0.000	-.0766681	-.0591468
(Asian#male) vs (White#female)	-.1870064	.0035948	-52.02	0.000	-.1982358	-.1757771
(Asian#female) vs (White#female)	-.1480642	.0045964	-32.21	0.000	-.1624223	-.1337061
(Hispanic#male) vs (White#female)	-.1202193	.0028286	-42.50	0.000	-.1290551	-.1113834
(Hispanic#female) vs (White#female)	-.0409169	.003028	-13.51	0.000	-.0503756	-.0314582
(Black#female) vs (Black#male)	.0568375	.0038801	14.65	0.000	.044717	.068958
(Asian#male) vs (Black#male)	-.0622615	.0044847	-13.88	0.000	-.0762706	-.0482523
(Asian#female) vs (Black#male)	-.0233193	.0053214	-4.38	0.000	-.0399419	-.0066966
(Hispanic#male) vs (Black#male)	.0045257	.0038976	1.16	1.000	-.0076493	.0167007
(Hispanic#female) vs (Black#male)	.0838281	.0040446	20.73	0.000	.0711938	.0964624
(Asian#male) vs (Black#female)	-.119099	.0043327	-27.49	0.000	-.1326332	-.1055648
(Asian#female) vs (Black#female)	-.0801568	.0051939	-15.43	0.000	-.0963812	-.0639324
(Hispanic#male) vs (Black#female)	-.0523118	.0037216	-14.06	0.000	-.0639371	-.0406865
(Hispanic#female) vs (Black#female)	.0269906	.0038753	6.96	0.000	.014885	.0390961
(Asian#female) vs (Asian#male)	.0389422	.0056599	6.88	0.000	.0212623	.0566221
(Hispanic#male) vs (Asian#male)	.0667872	.0043483	15.36	0.000	.0532042	.0803702
(Hispanic#female) vs (Asian#male)	.1460895	.0044806	32.60	0.000	.1320933	.1600857
(Hispanic#male) vs (Asian#female)	.027845	.0052069	5.35	0.000	.0115798	.0441101
(Hispanic#female) vs (Asian#female)	.1071473	.0053179	20.15	0.000	.0905356	.1237591
(Hispanic#male) vs (Hispanic#female)	.0793024	.0038928	20.37	0.000	.0671423	.0914624

The above comparisons offer both within and between racial group comparisons of the probability of having a depressive disorder with respect to sex. We are more interested in cross-group comparisons than within-group comparisons, but this information is useful to us in understanding the interactions between race and sex on depression. In the current analysis, we used the Bonferroni's adjustment test for pairwise comparisons, but we also can use other tests, such as Sidak's adjustment test and the Scheffe's adjustment test. Note that only the first three letters of the test name are needed in the command syntax. We want to remind readers that the dot (.) shown at the beginning of the command line with the results must be omitted before any command syntax.

Let's look at a few cross-racial comparisons between females and males. Black males had a statistically and significantly lower (–.02246) probability of having a depressive disorder than White males. On the other hand, Black females had a statistically and significantly greater (.0344075) probability of having a depressive disorder than White males. With respect to Asians and Whites, Asian females had a statistically and significantly lower (–.1480645) probability of having a depressive disorder than White Females. The post logistic regression multigroup comparisons illustrated here are useful for examining cross-cultural differences. Although the analysis presented here is purely heuristic, we can conclude that the association of depression and race varies between the sex groups. The following "margins" commands are provided as examples to generate post hoc pairwise comparisons across selected cultural, racial or gender groups using three multiple comparison statistics procedures, which include Bonferroni, Sidak, and Sheffe tests.

```
. margins Race#Sex_F,pwcompare(effect) mcompare(bon)
. margins Race#Sex_F,pwcompare(effect) mcompare(sid)
. margins Race#Sex_F,pwcompare(effect) mcompare(sche)
```

Selection of Control Variables

Although the previous logistic regression analysis shows that race and sex have a statistically significant association with depression, we might want to ask whether this association is constant or remains the same across other variables such as age, education, and income. If these variables do influence the association of the independent variable with the dependent variable, we want to control for their possible effects by bring them into our analysis. The control variables or covariates should be selected for good reason. We can decide which variables should be included as control variables based on previous research literature or our own clinical observations. This information can provide us with some guidance in selecting the correct control variable. We also can use the *linktest* to test the specification of a logistic regression model with and without the control variables. In this example, we plan to use age, education, and income as our three possible control variables. We will run the logistic regression analyses below.

. logit depression i.Race##i.Sex_F c.age, base nolog

```
. linktest,nolog

Logistic regression                    Number of obs   =   417,867
                                       LR chi2(2)      =  10209.48
                                       Prob > chi2     =    0.0000
Log likelihood = -202787.4             Pseudo R2       =    0.0246
```

depression	Coef.	Std. Err.	z	P>|z|	[95% Conf. Interval]	
_hat	1.461585	.0600234	24.35	0.000	1.343941	1.579228
_hatsq	.1609757	.0205746	7.82	0.000	.1206503	.2013011
_cons	.3057647	.0417731	7.32	0.000	.2238909	.3876385

The results of the *linktest* show that age is not a good control variable to be included in the analysis. The *_hatsq* coefficient in the results above is statistically significant due to the p value smaller than 0.05, indicating that when age is included in the analysis the model become mis-specified.

The next step is to replace age with education and repeat the above steps.

1. Run a logistic regression with *education* as a control variable. (Results are not reported.)

. logit depression i.Race##i.Sex_F c.edu, base nolog

2. Run the *linktest*.

```
. linktest,nolog
```

Logistic regression

				Number of obs	=	416,760
				LR chi2(2)	=	8805.80
				Prob > chi2	=	0.0000
Log likelihood = -203015.58 | | | | Pseudo R2 | = | 0.0212 |

depression	Coef.	Std. Err.	z	P>|z|	[95% Conf. Interval]
_hat	.9752055	.0800697	12.18	0.000	.8182718 1.132139
_hatsq	-.0085295	.0272873	-0.31	0.755	-.0620116 .0449526
_cons	-.0168495	.0560554	-0.30	0.764	-.1267161 .0930171

The *linktest* results above show that the model with education as a control variable was correctly specified as the p value of the *_hatsq* coefficient is greater than .05. We continue and run the next model with *income* as an additional control variable.

```
. logit depression i.Race##i.Sex_F c.income, base nolog
```

```
. linktest,nolog
```

Logistic regression

				Number of obs	=	350,381
				LR chi2(2)	=	16537.41
				Prob > chi2	=	0.0000
Log likelihood = -168444.04 | | | | Pseudo R2 | = | 0.0468 |

depression	Coef.	Std. Err.	z	P>|z|	[95% Conf. Interval]
_hat	.9897351	.0311797	31.74	0.000	.928624 1.050846
_hatsq	-.0040217	.0118079	-0.34	0.733	-.0271647 .0191213
_cons	-.0053847	.0193569	-0.28	0.781	-.0433234 .0325541

The results of the *linktest* above indicate that the logistic regression model with *income* as an additional control variable was correctly specified due to the p value of the *_hatsq* coefficient is greater than .05. Finally, we include both education and income in the regression coefficient.

```
. logit depression i.Race##i.Sex_F c.edu c.income , base nolog
```

```
Logistic regression                        Number of obs    =    349,924
                                           LR chi2(9)       =   16637.54
                                           Prob > chi2      =     0.0000
Log likelihood = -168179.51                Pseudo R2        =     0.0471
```

depression	Coef.	Std. Err.	z	P>|z|	[95% Conf. Interval]
Race					
White	0	(base)			
Black	-.4442059	.0297364	-14.94	0.000	-.5024882 -.3859237
Asian	-.9778515	.0618398	-15.81	0.000	-1.099055 -.8566476
Hispanic	-.4007031	.0266197	-15.05	0.000	-.4528767 -.3485295
Sex_F					
male	0	(base)			
female	.6235261	.0098335	63.41	0.000	.6042529 .6427994
Race#Sex_F					
Black#female	-.2327491	.0358469	-6.49	0.000	-.3030077 -.1624905
Asian#female	-.1369372	.0818159	-1.67	0.094	-.2972935 .023419
Hispanic#female	-.1410543	.0331246	-4.26	0.000	-.2059772 -.0761314
edu	.0494642	.0047878	10.33	0.000	.0400802 .0588482
income	-.2008136	.0022041	-91.11	0.000	-.2051335 -.1964937
_cons	-.7422178	.0231131	-32.11	0.000	-.7875185 -.696917

```
. linktest,nolog
```

```
Logistic regression                        Number of obs    =    349,924
                                           LR chi2(2)       =   16637.71
                                           Prob > chi2      =     0.0000
Log likelihood = -168179.42                Pseudo R2        =     0.0471
```

depression	Coef.	Std. Err.	z	P>|z|	[95% Conf. Interval]
_hat	.9875342	.0307318	32.13	0.000	.927301 1.047767
_hatsq	-.0049007	.011669	-0.42	0.675	-.0277714 .0179701
_cons	-.0064956	.0190589	-0.34	0.733	-.0438503 .0308591

Note that when we use the logistic command we will have the odds ratios of the regression coefficients, and that other information, such as the tests of significance, remain the same as those reported in the logit command.

Final Analysis

Based on the series of our incremental analyses to find the control variables that can be included in the final analysis, we now can proceed with our postregression analysis to further our cross-cultural (racial) comparisons of race and sex on depression.

```
. logistic depression i.Race##i.Sex_F c.edu c.income, base nolog
```

```
Logistic regression                          Number of obs   =     349,924
                                             LR chi2(9)      =    16637.54
                                             Prob > chi2     =      0.0000
Log likelihood = -168179.51                  Pseudo R2       =      0.0471
```

depression	Odds Ratio	Std. Err.	z	P>|z|	[95% Conf. Interval]	
Race						
White	1	(base)				
Black	.6413333	.019071	-14.94	0.000	.6050233	.6798224
Asian	.3761183	.0232591	-15.81	0.000	.3331857	.4245831
Hispanic	.6698489	.0178312	-15.05	0.000	.6357966	.7057251
Sex_F						
male	1	(base)				
female	1.865494	.0183443	63.41	0.000	1.829885	1.901797
Race#Sex_F						
Black#female	.7923523	.0284034	-6.49	0.000	.7385934	.8500242
Asian#female	.8720249	.0713455	-1.67	0.094	.742826	1.023695
Hispanic#female	.8684422	.0287668	-4.26	0.000	.8138516	.9266945
edu	1.050708	.0050306	10.33	0.000	1.040894	1.060614
income	.8180649	.0018031	-91.11	0.000	.8145386	.8216065
_cons	.476057	.0110031	-32.11	0.000	.4549724	.4981186

Note: _cons estimates baseline odds.

```
. linktest,nolog
```

```
Logistic regression                          Number of obs   =     349,924
                                             LR chi2(2)      =    16637.71
                                             Prob > chi2     =      0.0000
Log likelihood = -168179.42                  Pseudo R2       =      0.0471
```

depression	Coef.	Std. Err.	z	P>|z|	[95% Conf. Interval]	
_hat	.9875342	.0307318	32.13	0.000	.927301	1.047767
_hatsq	-.0049007	.011669	-0.42	0.675	-.0277714	.0179701
_cons	-.0064956	.0190589	-0.34	0.733	-.0438503	.0308591

Marginal Predicted Probabilities of the Interaction

```
. margins Race#Sex_F

Predictive margins                          Number of obs   =    349,924
Model VCE   : OIM

Expression  : Pr(depression), predict()
```

	Margin	Delta-method Std. Err.	z	P>|z|	[95% Conf. Interval]	
Race#Sex_F						
White#male	.1644869	.0010581	155.45	0.000	.1624131	.1665608
White#female	.2647998	.0011107	238.42	0.000	.262623	.2669767
Black#male	.1131524	.0028099	40.27	0.000	.1076452	.1186597
Black#female	.1574626	.0025176	62.54	0.000	.1525281	.162397
Asian#male	.0702059	.003949	17.78	0.000	.0624661	.0779458
Asian#female	.1086072	.0050594	21.47	0.000	.0986908	.1185235
Hispanic#male	.1174984	.0025702	45.72	0.000	.1124609	.1225359
Hispanic#female	.1757096	.0027473	63.96	0.000	.1703251	.1810941

If we compare these predicted margins and those from the logistic regression without the control variables, we can see the changes in the current coefficients because they were adjusted for the influences of education and income (See pp. 180–181). The changes also are reflected in the graph below (See pp. 179–180).

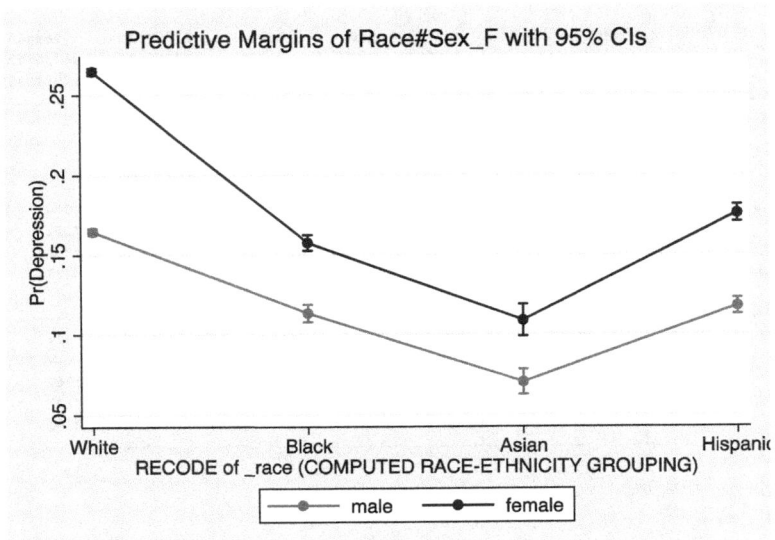

Predictive Margins of Race#Sex_F with 95% CIs

Comparing the Racial Groups with Whites

The *margins r.* command below provides us with the comparison of Whites with the remaining racial groups with respect to sex. The results show that the χ^2 tests for all comparisons are statistically significant. The magnitude of the differences are reported in the column "Contrast." For example, the difference of the predicted probability of depressive disorder between Black males and White males was −.0513345, indicating that the probability of having a depressive disorder was about 5% lower among Black men compared to White men.

```
. margins r.Race@Sex_F

Contrasts of predictive margins
Model VCE   : OIM

Expression  : Pr(depression), predict()
```

	df	chi2	P>chi2
Race@Sex_F			
(Black vs White) male	1	290.91	0.0000
(Black vs White) female	1	1520.37	0.0000
(Asian vs White) male	1	532.27	0.0000
(Asian vs White) female	1	910.17	0.0000
(Hispanic vs White) male	1	283.91	0.0000
(Hispanic vs White) female	1	899.13	0.0000
Joint	6	3604.67	0.0000

	Contrast	Delta-method Std. Err.	[95% Conf. Interval]	
Race@Sex_F				
(Black vs White) male	−.0513345	.0030097	−.0572335	−.0454355
(Black vs White) female	−.1073373	.0027528	−.1127327	−.1019419
(Asian vs White) male	−.094281	.0040865	−.1022905	−.0862715
(Asian vs White) female	−.1561927	.0051772	−.1663399	−.1460455
(Hispanic vs White) male	−.0469885	.0027887	−.0524543	−.0415228
(Hispanic vs White) female	−.0890903	.0029711	−.0949135	−.083267

As discussed previously, the predicted margins or predicted probabilities are important to understanding the interaction effect but not sufficient to make meaningful cross-racial (cultural) comparison across all possible combinations of race and sex variables. If we want to compare

Black men and Asian men or compare Asian men and Hispanic men, we
need to perform further multigroup comparisons as below.

```
. margins Race#Sex_F,pwcompare(effect) mcompare(bon)

Pairwise comparisons of predictive margins
Model VCE    : OIM

Expression   : Pr(depression), predict()
```

	Number of Comparisons
Race#Sex_F	28

	Contrast	Delta-method Std. Err.	Bonferroni z	Bonferroni P>|z|	Bonferroni [95% Conf. Interval]	
Race#Sex_F						
(White#female) vs (White#male)	.1003129	.0015325	65.46	0.000	.0955258	.1051
(Black#male) vs (White#male)	−.0513345	.0030097	−17.06	0.000	−.0607361	−.0419329
(Black#female) vs (White#male)	−.0070244	.0027467	−2.56	0.295	−.0156042	.0015555
(Asian#male) vs (White#male)	−.094281	.0040865	−23.07	0.000	−.1070463	−.0815157
(Asian#female) vs (White#male)	−.0558798	.0051681	−10.81	0.000	−.0720235	−.0397361
(Hispanic#male) vs (White#male)	−.0469885	.0027887	−16.85	0.000	−.0556996	−.0382774
(Hispanic#female) vs (White#male)	.0112226	.0029646	3.79	0.004	.001962	.0204833
(Black#male) vs (White#female)	−.1516474	.003024	−50.15	0.000	−.1610936	−.1422012
(Black#female) vs (White#female)	−.1073373	.0027528	−38.99	0.000	−.1159363	−.0987382
(Asian#male) vs (White#female)	−.1945939	.0040999	−47.46	0.000	−.2074008	−.181787
(Asian#female) vs (White#female)	−.1561927	.0051772	−30.17	0.000	−.172365	−.1400203
(Hispanic#male) vs (White#female)	−.1473014	.002808	−52.46	0.000	−.1560728	−.13853
(Hispanic#female) vs (White#female)	−.0890903	.0029711	−29.99	0.000	−.0983712	−.0798093
(Black#female) vs (Black#male)	.0443101	.0037613	11.78	0.000	.0325609	.0560594
(Asian#male) vs (Black#male)	−.0429465	.00485	−8.85	0.000	−.0580965	−.0277965
(Asian#female) vs (Black#male)	−.0045453	.0057904	−0.78	1.000	−.0226329	.0135423
(Hispanic#male) vs (Black#male)	.004346	.0037959	1.14	1.000	−.0075115	.0162035
(Hispanic#female) vs (Black#male)	.0625571	.0039094	16.00	0.000	.0503453	.074769
(Asian#male) vs (Black#female)	−.0872566	.0046858	−18.62	0.000	−.1018939	−.0726194
(Asian#female) vs (Black#female)	−.0488554	.005652	−8.64	0.000	−.0665109	−.0312
(Hispanic#male) vs (Black#female)	−.0399642	.0035848	−11.15	0.000	−.0511622	−.0287661
(Hispanic#female) vs (Black#female)	.018247	.0036937	4.94	0.000	.0067089	.0297852
(Asian#female) vs (Asian#male)	.0384012	.0064146	5.99	0.000	.0183638	.0584386
(Hispanic#male) vs (Asian#male)	.0472925	.0047204	10.02	0.000	.0325472	.0620377
(Hispanic#female) vs (Asian#male)	.1055036	.0048205	21.89	0.000	.0904457	.1205616
(Hispanic#male) vs (Asian#female)	.0088913	.0056843	1.56	1.000	−.0088649	.0266474
(Hispanic#female) vs (Asian#female)	.0671024	.0057664	11.64	0.000	.0490899	.085115
(Hispanic#female) vs (Hispanic#male)	.0582112	.0037261	15.62	0.000	.0465719	.0698505

Interaction Effect After Controlling for Education and Income

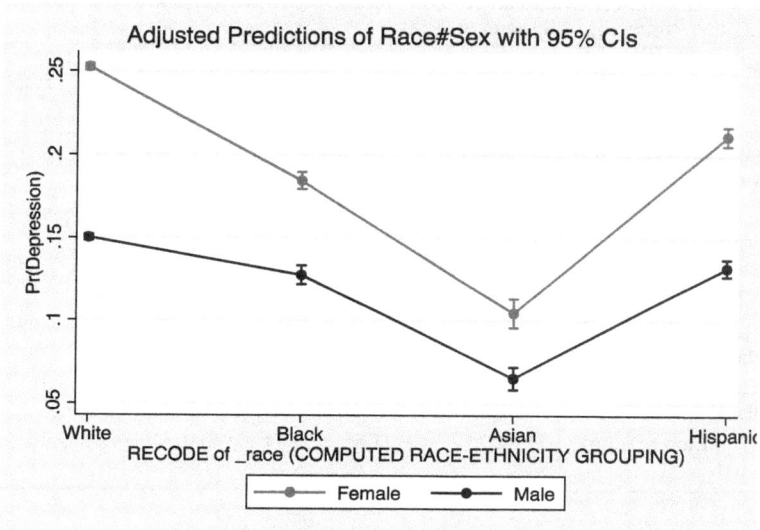

The Prob. column presents the differences of the predicted probabilities of depressive disorder, The Z column presents the Bonferroni Z test of significance for pairwise comparisons. The 95% CI presents the 95% confidence intervals for the differences of the predicted probabilities. Table 5.1 shows that racial differences are greater among females than among males. Black, Asian, and Hispanic females all had lower predicted probabilities of depressive disorder than White women. Asian females had lower probability of depressive disorder than Black females. Hispanic females had a greater probability of depressive disorder than Black females and Asian females. Among males, the pattern of difference was similar to that of females. The magnitude of difference, however, was smaller than that for females. We also can compare the difference in predicted probabilities between females and males. For example, the difference in predicted probabilities of depressive disorder between Black females and White females was −.107 (95% CI = −.115, −.098) compared to −.051 (95% CI = -.060, −.041) between Black males and White males. Because there is no overlap of the confidence intervals, we can conclude

Table 5.1. Cross-Racial Comparisons of Predicted Probabilities of Depressive Disorder Among Females and Among Males Controlling for Education and Income: Bonferroni Adjustment Z Test

Pairs	Females			Males		
	Prob.	Z	95% CI	Prob.	Z	95% CI
Black vs. White	−.107	−38.99***	−.115, −.098	−.051	−17.06***	−.060, −.041
Asian vs. White	−.156	−30.17***	−.172, −.140	−.094	23.07***	−.107, −.081
Hispanic vs. White	−.089	−29.99***	−.098, −.079	−.046	−16.85***	−.055, −.038
Asian vs. Black	−.048	−8.64***	−.066, −.031	−.042	−8.85***	−.058, −.027
Hispanic vs. Black	.018	4.94***	.006, .029	−.004	1.14	−.007, .016
Hispanic vs. Asian	.067	11.64***	.049., .085	.04	10.02***	.032, .062

that the differences were statistically significant (see Cornell Statistical Consulting Unit, 2008; Knol, Pestman, & Grobbee, 2011).

This section illustrates the application of logistic regression for a binary dependent variable in cross-cultural comparison. We emphasize the importance of examining the possible statistical interaction of the cultural variable (such as race) with other variables to rule out any possible wrong assertions of the independent effect of any cultural variable on a dependent variable. In the example we presented, if we did not test for the interactive effect between race and sex, we would wrongly conclude that race has an independent effect on the likelihood of depressive disorder. The correct analysis indicates that racial differences in depressive disorder must be explained in the context of sex differences.

Cross-Cultural Comparisons via Subgroup or Stratification Analysis

We use an extracted sample from the Children of Immigrants Longitudinal Study (CILS) (Portes & Rumbaut, 2018) to illustrate the use of subgroup or stratification analysis with logistic regression. We will examine the association of country of origin and depression stratified by those who experienced discrimination and those who did not.

Dependent Variable: Depression Measured in 1992

Before we do any transformations of the selected variables, we must always examine their frequency to detect any unusual outliers and unusual values, including any missing data. The *tabl* command produces the frequencies of these variables as below.

```
. tabl v114–v117

-> tabulation of v114
```

Felt sad past week	Freq.	Percent	Cum.
Rarely	2,646	50.72	50.72
Some of the time	1,802	34.54	85.26
Occasionally	535	10.25	95.51
Most of the time	234	4.49	100.00
Total	5,217	100.00	

```
-> tabulation of v115
```

Could not get going past week	Freq.	Percent	Cum.
Rarely	2,669	51.38	51.38
Some of the time	1,738	33.46	84.83
Occasionally	591	11.38	96.21
Most of the time	197	3.79	100.00
Total	5,195	100.00	

```
-> tabulation of v116
```

Did not feel like eating past week	Freq.	Percent	Cum.
Rarely	3,180	61.22	61.22
Some of the time	1,295	24.93	86.16
Occasionally	480	9.24	95.40
Most of the time	239	4.60	100.00
Total	5,194	100.00	

```
-> tabulation of v117
```

I felt depressed past week	Freq.	Percent	Cum.
Rarely	2,888	55.55	55.55
Some of the time	1,402	26.97	82.52
Occasionally	571	10.98	93.50
Most of the time	338	6.50	100.00
Total	5,199	100.00	

Check for the Comparability of Item Reliability

We plan to use the composite scale of depression with four items in our analysis; therefore, it important to check for their internal consistency reliability by examining the scale's Cronbach's alpha coefficient.

```
. alpha v114-v117,item asis

Test scale = mean(unstandardized items)
```

Item	Obs	Sign	item-test correlation	item-rest correlation	average interitem covariance	alpha
v114	5217	+	0.7937	0.6059	.2634984	0.6262
v115	5195	+	0.7007	0.4649	.3301048	0.7070
v116	5194	+	0.6645	0.4067	.3545346	0.7391
v117	5199	+	0.8216	0.6299	.2348842	0.6075
Test scale					.2957814	0.7342

The results above show that these items have a reasonable level of reliability at 0.7342. Our goal, however, is to compare depression between those who felt discriminated against and those who did not report perceived discrimination. We need to ensure that the reliability of the four-item depression scale is similar between these two groups.

The results above indicate that we do have a sufficient number of respondents in each group. We now can do an internal consistency analysis of the depression items between those who ever felt discriminated against and those who did not. The *bysort* or *by* prefix before the *alpha* command tells Stata to perform an internal consistency analysis for the selected variables for each category of the variable listed after *bysort* or *by*. In this example Stata will execute the *alpha* command for two categories, "Yes" and "No," of variable *v85* as below. Although the results below show that there are some differences in the item–rest correlation between the two groups as evident in the difference of the "average interitem covariance," the overall alpha coefficients are somewhat similar between those who felt discriminated against (alpha = .73) and those who did not (alpha = .72). If the difference is greater than 0.05, we need to reconsider the use of the scale or if we have to use it, we must address this issue in the interpretation of the outcomes (Tran, 2009).

```
. bysort v85:alpha v114-v117,item asis
```

`-> v85 = Yes`

`Test scale = mean(unstandardized items)`

Item	Obs	Sign	item-test correlation	item-rest correlation	average interitem covariance	alpha
v114	2866	+	0.7922	0.6018	.2870222	0.6235
v115	2856	+	0.7063	0.4687	.3544309	0.7005
v116	2852	+	0.6560	0.3989	.3917568	0.7381
v117	2856	+	0.8193	0.6237	.2563334	0.6067
Test scale					.3224114	0.7319

`-> v85 = No`

`Test scale = mean(unstandardized items)`

Item	Obs	Sign	item-test correlation	item-rest correlation	average interitem covariance	alpha
v114	2318	+	0.7861	0.5941	.2190651	0.6149
v115	2306	+	0.6756	0.4339	.2849842	0.7071
v116	2309	+	0.6791	0.4125	.2829313	0.7226
v117	2310	+	0.8170	0.6227	.1934687	0.5914
Test scale					.2451403	0.7243

Create a Summative Scale for the Four Items of Depression

We use the *gen* (generate) command to add the four items (v114–v117) together to create a summative scale of "depress92." We named the depression scale "depress92" because these items were from the 1992 data wave. Of course, we can name it whatever name we wish.

. gen depress92=v114+v115+v116+v117
(99 missing values generated)

Let's look at the descriptive statistics of the newly created variable, "depress92," using the command *sum* or *summarize*.

```
. sum depress92
```

Variable	Obs	Mean	Std. Dev.	Min	Max
depress92	5,163	6.616889	2.540192	4	16

```
. summarize depress92
```

Variable	Obs	Mean	Std. Dev.	Min	Max
depress92	5,163	6.616889	2.540192	4	16

Create a Binary Depression Variable

We created a binary depression variable (DEPR92) based on the *depress92* variable to use in logistic regression. Below are the steps that can be used to transform a continuous variable into a categorical variable. One always needs to have a rationale to do so. We will assign those who had scores from 6 to 16 based on the summative four-item scale to a high-depression group and those whose scores were lower than 6 to the low-depression group.

```
. gen DEPR92=.
(5,262 missing values generated)

. replace DEPR92 =1 if depress92>=6
(3,141 real changes made)

. replace DEPR92 =0 if depress92<6
(2,121 real changes made)

.
end of do-file

. tab DEPR92
```

DEPR92	Freq.	Percent	Cum.
0	2,121	40.31	40.31
1	3,141	59.69	100.00
Total	5,262	100.00	

Note that the newly created variable *DEPR92* has no value labels. We need to add the labels to the values 0 and 1. Again, our purpose in assigning the depression scores into two groups is purely heuristic. Below are the commands that can be used for this purpose.

```
. label define dp 1 "high" 0 "low"

. label value DEPR92 dp

.
end of do-file

. tab DEPR92
```

DEPR92	Freq.	Percent	Cum.
low	2,121	40.31	40.31
high	3,141	59.69	100.00
Total	5,262	100.00	

We still have not completed the process of creating a new variable from the existing variable like the variable *DEPR92*. Without value labels, it would be difficult to understand what DEPR92 refers to. We can take care of this concern by using the following command syntax. The *label* command assigns the description "Depression 1992 coded 1 and 0" to the variable *DEPR92*.

```
. label var DEPR92 "Depression 1992 coded 1 and 0" /*Label decription */

.
end of do-file

. tab DEPR92
```

Depression 1992 coded 1 and 0	Freq.	Percent	Cum.
low	2,121	40.31	40.31
high	3,141	59.69	100.00
Total	5,262	100.00	

Let's look at the description of the discrimination variable to determine whether we have sufficient sample size for each group before doing any further analyses.

-> tabulation of v85

Respondent ever felt discriminated	Freq.	Percent	Cum.
Yes	2,884	55.23	55.23
No	2,338	44.77	100.00
Total	5,222	100.00	

The Process of Subgroup or Stratification Analysis

After the preparation of the variables as illustrated in the previous section, we can now move to the process of subgroup or stratification analysis. Let's look at the variables to be used in the analysis.

Dependent variable: Depression (DEPR92)
Independent variables: Country of origin (CNTYPRIG)
                        Discrimination (v85)
Control variables: Age, Sex

Steps in Subgroup or Stratification Analysis

1. Simple logit regression: We begin with the simple logit regression analysis of depression and country of origin and the model specification analysis.

```
. logit DEPR92 i.CNTYORIG ,base nolog
```

Logistic regression

				Number of obs	=	2,654
				LR chi2(2)	=	13.60
				Prob > chi2	=	0.0011
Log likelihood = −1788.0619				Pseudo R2	=	0.0038

DEPR92	Coef.	Std. Err.	z	P>|z|	[95% Conf. Interval]	
CNTYORIG						
Cuba	0	(base)				
Mexico	.3123529	.0947502	3.30	0.001	.1266459	.4980598
Indochina	.2654369	.0979582	2.71	0.007	.0734424	.4574313
_cons	.2161723	.0574535	3.76	0.000	.1035655	.3287792

```
. linktest,nolog
```

Logistic regression

				Number of obs	=	2,654
				LR chi2(2)	=	13.60
				Prob > chi2	=	0.0011
Log likelihood = −1788.0619				Pseudo R2	=	0.0038

DEPR92	Coef.	Std. Err.	z	P>|z|	[95% Conf. Interval]	
_hat	.9999993	5.989246	0.17	0.867	−10.73871	12.73871
_hatsq	1.11e−06	8.216119	0.00	1.000	−16.1033	16.1033
_cons	1.12e−07	.9205889	0.00	1.000	−1.804321	1.804321

SUMMARY OF THE RESULTS

We did not estimate the odds ratios for the regression coefficients to simplify the report. If we want to see the odds ratios we can run the command below.

. logistic DEPR92 i.CNTYORIG,base nolog

In the interest of brevity, we do not report the odds ratios for this example. The results above revealed that both Mexican adolescents and

Indochinese adolescents were more likely to experience high levels of depression compared to Cuban adolescents. The *linktest* confirms that this simple logit regression had no specification problem given that the *_hatsq* coefficient is not statistically significant.

LOGIT REGRESSION OF DEPRESSION WITH TWO INDEPENDENT VARIABLES: COUNTRIES OF ORIGIN AND DISCRIMINATION

The aim here is to detect any changes in the association between countries of origin and depression when discrimination is included in the model. Note that we use the command *rename* to change the v85 to DISCRIM; the results are shown below. Changing the name of the variable does not change the data. If we compare the frequency table below and the previous table of the same variable with different names, we can see that the information is the same.

```
. rename  v85 DISCRIM

. tab DISCRIM
```

Felt discriminat ed	Freq.	Percent	Cum.
no	2,338	44.77	44.77
yes	2,884	55.23	100.00
Total	5,222	100.00	

`. logit DEPR92 i.CNTYORIG i.DISCRIM,base nolog`

```
Logistic regression                          Number of obs   =      2,634
                                              LR chi2(3)      =      37.58
                                              Prob > chi2     =     0.0000
Log likelihood = -1763.3472                   Pseudo R2       =     0.0105
```

DEPR92	Coef.	Std. Err.	z	P>|z|	[95% Conf. Interval]	
CNTYORIG						
Cuba	0	(base)				
Mexico	.2002156	.0978961	2.05	0.041	.0083429	.3920884
Indochina	.1422924	.1014077	1.40	0.161	-.056463	.3410478
DISCRIM						
no	0	(base)				
yes	.4104339	.0828231	4.96	0.000	.2481035	.5727642
_cons	.0628312	.0653914	0.96	0.337	-.0653337	.190996

`. linktest,nolog`

```
Logistic regression                          Number of obs   =      2,634
                                              LR chi2(2)      =      39.61
                                              Prob > chi2     =     0.0000
Log likelihood = -1762.332                    Pseudo R2       =     0.0111
```

DEPR92	Coef.	Std. Err.	z	P>|z|	[95% Conf. Interval]	
_hat	-.144409	.8191959	-0.18	0.860	-1.750004	1.461186
_hatsq	1.596969	1.120557	1.43	0.154	-.599282	3.793221
_cons	.1105633	.1055307	1.05	0.295	-.096273	.3173996

Summary of the Results. The results above show that the variable *DISCRIM* (discrimination) was included as an independent variable in the model. The association between CNTYORIG (countries of origin, e.g., Cuba, Mexico, Indochina) changed. The difference between Indochina and Cuba is no longer statistically significant. The results also show that DISCRIM had a significant association with depression. We might want to know whether the *DISCRIM* variable is a confounder of the association between CNTYORIG or if it is a moderator. If DISCIM is the confounder of CNTYORIG and DEPR92, there would be no interaction between CNTYORIG and DISCRIM with DEPR92. The below analysis includes the interaction effect of CNTYORIG and DISCRIM.

Interaction Analyses. We tested the interaction effect of CNTOYRIG and DISCRIM and the results below confirm that there is a statistically significant effect of the two variables on depression. This indicates that the association between countries of origin and depression differed according to respondents' experience of discrimination. The predicted probabilities (adjusted predictions) provide detailed information of the interaction effects. For example, about 60% of Cuban respondents who experienced discrimination had high depression compared to 69% of Mexican respondents and 63% of Indochinese respondents.

```
. logit DEPR92 i.CNTYORIG##i.DISCRIM,base nolog
```

Logistic regression				Number of obs	=	2,634
				LR chi2(5)	=	45.17
				Prob > chi2	=	0.0000
Log likelihood = -1759.5525				Pseudo R2	=	0.0127

DEPR92	Coef.	Std. Err.	z	P>|z|	[95% Conf. Interval]	
CNTYORIG						
Cuba	0	(base)				
Mexico	-.0441983	.1434466	-0.31	0.758	-.3253484	.2369518
Indochina	.2785527	.1539159	1.81	0.070	-.0231168	.5802223
DISCRIM						
no	0	(base)				
yes	.3369635	.1195099	2.82	0.005	.1027285	.5711986
CNTYORIG#DISCRIM						
Mexico#yes	.4237028	.1979916	2.14	0.032	.0356465	.8117591
Indochina#yes	-.1788734	.2059833	-0.87	0.385	-.5825933	.2248465
_cons	.0900078	.072813	1.24	0.216	-.052703	.2327186

```
. linktest,nolog
```

Logistic regression				Number of obs	=	2,634
				LR chi2(2)	=	45.17
				Prob > chi2	=	0.0000
Log likelihood = -1759.5525				Pseudo R2	=	0.0127

DEPR92	Coef.	Std. Err.	z	P>|z|	[95% Conf. Interval]	
_hat	1	.5493719	1.82	0.069	-.0767492	2.076749
_hatsq	-3.19e-08	.6518433	-0.00	1.000	-1.277589	1.277589
_cons	7.36e-10	.0899017	0.00	1.000	-.176204	.176204

```
. margins CNTYORIG#DISCRIM

Adjusted predictions                        Number of obs     =      2,634
Model VCE    : OIM

Expression   : Pr(DEPR92), predict()
```

	Margin	Delta-method Std. Err.	z	P>|z|	[95% Conf. Interval]	
CNTYORIG#DISCRIM						
Cuba#no	.5224868	.0181664	28.76	0.000	.4868812	.5580923
Cuba#yes	.6051502	.0226441	26.72	0.000	.5607686	.6495318
Mexico#no	.5114504	.030882	16.56	0.000	.4509228	.571978
Mexico#yes	.691358	.0209537	32.99	0.000	.6502895	.7324265
Indochina#no	.5911111	.0327752	18.04	0.000	.5268728	.6553494
Indochina#yes	.6287016	.0230596	27.26	0.000	.5835056	.6738976

The graphic below further illustrates the interaction effects. The predicted probabilities of depression conditioned on discrimination are not parallel among the three groups.

```
. marginsplot
```

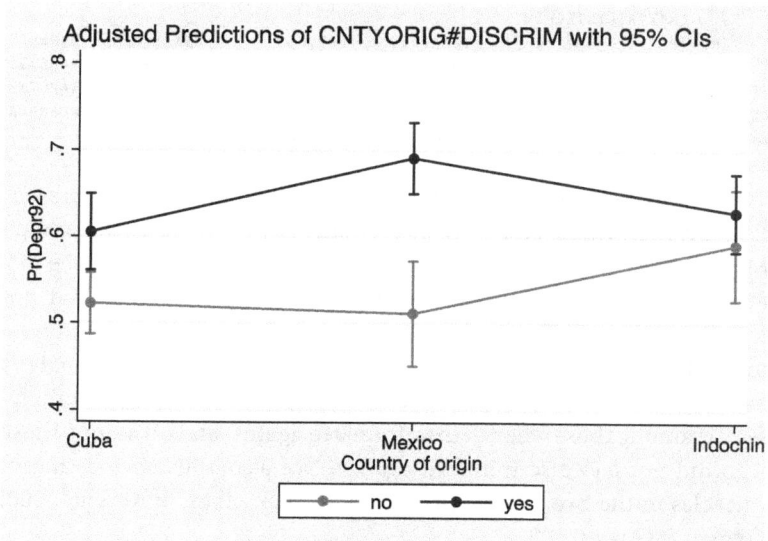

Adjusted Predictions of CNTYORIG#DISCRIM with 95% CIs

We also can compare the predicted probabilities of high depression between Mexico and Cuba and Indochina and Cuba as below.

```
. margins r.CNTYORIG,over(DISCRIM)

Contrasts of predictive margins
Model VCE     : OIM

Expression    : Pr(DEPR92), predict()
over          : DISCRIM
```

	df	chi2	P>chi2
CNTYORIG@DISCRIM			
(Mexico vs Cuba) no	1	0.09	0.7581
(Mexico vs Cuba) yes	1	7.81	0.0052
(Indochina vs Cuba) no	1	3.35	0.0671
(Indochina vs Cuba) yes	1	0.53	0.4662
Joint	4	12.46	0.0143

	Contrast	Delta-method Std. Err.	[95% Conf. Interval]	
CNTYORIG@DISCRIM				
(Mexico vs Cuba) no	−.0110364	.035829	−.0812599	.0591872
(Mexico vs Cuba) yes	.0862078	.0308515	.0257401	.1466755
(Indochina vs Cuba) no	.0686243	.0374731	−.0048217	.1420703
(Indochina vs Cuba) yes	.0235514	.0323187	−.0397921	.0868949

The results above show that only two pairs of comparison were statistically significant based on the χ^2 statistics: the difference between Mexican and Cuban among those who felt discriminated, and the difference between Indochinese and Cuban among those who did not feel discriminated. These results do not reveal the whole picture of the interaction effect. The *linktest* also confirms that the interaction analysis has no specification problem. Therefore, we can run two separate analyses: (1) among those who felt discriminated against and (2) among those who did not feel discriminated against. We also will include control variables in the two models (Assmann, Pocock, Enos, & Kasten, 2000; Oxman & Guyatt, 1992).

Analysis of Depression on Countries of Origin Among the *Yes* (Felt Discriminated Against) Group

Note that in the *logit* command syntax, we include "if DISCIMIN == 1" to tell Stata to perform the analysis for those respondents who answered "Yes = 1" to the question of discrimination. The results below show that among the respondents who answered "Yes" to the question of whether they felt discriminated against, Mexicans were more likely to say "Yes" than were Cubans. There was no statistically significant difference, however, between Indochinese and Cubans. The two control variables had statistically significant association with depression. The *linktest* revealed that the analysis has no problem with model specification.

```
. logit DEPR92 i.CNTYORIG Age i.Sex if DISCRIM==1,nolog
```

```
Logistic regression                          Number of obs   =     1,391
                                             LR chi2(4)      =     59.80
                                             Prob > chi2     =    0.0000
Log likelihood = -876.81724                  Pseudo R2       =    0.0330
```

DEPR92	Coef.	Std. Err.	z	P>|z|	[95% Conf. Interval]	
CNTYORIG						
Mexico	.3500932	.139043	2.52	0.012	.077574	.6226124
Indochina	.0488235	.1400071	0.35	0.727	-.2255855	.3232324
Age	.1778861	.0661952	2.69	0.007	.0481458	.3076263
Sex						
male	-.7867516	.1160201	-6.78	0.000	-1.014147	-.5593563
_cons	-1.65185	.9347729	-1.77	0.077	-3.483971	.1802711

```
. linktest,nolog
```

```
Logistic regression                          Number of obs   =     1,391
                                             LR chi2(2)      =     60.28
                                             Prob > chi2     =    0.0000
Log likelihood = -876.57686                  Pseudo R2       =    0.0332
```

DEPR92	Coef.	Std. Err.	z	P>|z|	[95% Conf. Interval]	
_hat	1.273607	.4160207	3.06	0.002	.4582217	2.088993
_hatsq	-.2271935	.3266631	-0.70	0.487	-.8674415	.4130545
_cons	-.0393084	.1094859	-0.36	0.720	-.2538968	.1752801

Analysis of Depression on Countries of Origin Among the *No* Group (Did Not Feel Discriminated Against)

The analysis below was with the respondents who answered "No = 0" to the question of whether they felt discriminated against. Overall, the results show no statistically significant difference between Mexicans and Cubans nor between Indochinese and Cubans. Sex was the only variable that had statistically significant association with depression, whereas male respondents were likely to report low depression.

```
. logit DEPR92 i.CNTYORIG Age i.Sex if DISCRIM==0,base nolog
```

Logistic regression	Number of obs	=	1,242
	LR chi2(4)	=	55.86
	Prob > chi2	=	0.0000
Log likelihood = -830.24979	Pseudo R2	=	0.0325

DEPR92	Coef.	Std. Err.	z	P>|z|	[95% Conf. Interval]	
CNTYORIG						
Cuba	0	(base)				
Mexico	-.0262506	.1466026	-0.18	0.858	-.3135864	.2610852
Indochina	.2051986	.1598409	1.28	0.199	-.1080839	.5184811
Age	.101851	.0671121	1.52	0.129	-.0296863	.2333884
Sex						
female	0	(base)				
male	-.8130348	.1167381	-6.96	0.000	-1.041837	-.5842323
_cons	-.9176211	.9519872	-0.96	0.335	-2.783482	.9482394

```
. linktest,nolog
```

Logistic regression	Number of obs	=	1,242
	LR chi2(2)	=	57.74
	Prob > chi2	=	0.0000
Log likelihood = -829.30814	Pseudo R2	=	0.0336

DEPR92	Coef.	Std. Err.	z	P>|z|	[95% Conf. Interval]	
_hat	1.229118	.2159547	5.69	0.000	.8058551	1.652382
_hatsq	-.7306677	.530549	-1.38	0.168	-1.770525	.3091893
_cons	.1170545	.1045696	1.12	0.263	-.0878982	.3220073

POST SUBGROUP ANALYSIS COMPARISONS

Stata offers the "seemingly unrelated estimation (SUEST)" to test intramodal and cross-model hypotheses. The *suest* procedure "combines the estimation results—parameter estimates and associated (co) variance matrices—stored under namelist into one parameter vector and simultaneous (co)variance matrix of the sandwich/robust type. This (co)variance matrix is appropriate even if the estimates were obtained on the same or on overlapping data" (https://www.stata.com/manuals/u.pdf).

In the examples above, we did two logistic regression analyses; one for those who felt discriminated against and one for those who did not feel discriminated against. We need to save the results of these two models then apply the *suest* commands to compare them and the coefficients between them.

```
. logit DEPR92 i.CNTYORIG Age i.Sex if DISCRIM==1,base nolog
```

```
Logistic regression                          Number of obs    =      1,391
                                             LR chi2(4)       =      59.80
                                             Prob > chi2      =     0.0000
Log likelihood = -876.81724                  Pseudo R2        =     0.0330
```

DEPR92	Coef.	Std. Err.	z	P>|z|	[95% Conf.	Interval]
CNTYORIG						
Cuba	0	(base)				
Mexico	.3500932	.139043	2.52	0.012	.077574	.6226124
Indochina	.0488235	.1400071	0.35	0.727	-.2255855	.3232324
Age	.1778861	.0661952	2.69	0.007	.0481458	.3076263
Sex						
female	0	(base)				
male	-.7867516	.1160201	-6.78	0.000	-1.014147	-.5593563
_cons	-1.65185	.9347729	-1.77	0.077	-3.483971	.1802711

```
. estimate store M1
```

```
. logit DEPR92 i.CNTYORIG Age i.Sex if DISCRIM==0,base nolog
```

```
Logistic regression                          Number of obs    =      1,242
                                             LR chi2(4)       =      55.86
                                             Prob > chi2      =     0.0000
Log likelihood = -830.24979                  Pseudo R2        =     0.0325
```

DEPR92	Coef.	Std. Err.	z	P>|z|	[95% Conf.	Interval]
CNTYORIG						
Cuba	0	(base)				
Mexico	-.0262506	.1466026	-0.18	0.858	-.3135864	.2610852
Indochina	.2051986	.1598409	1.28	0.199	-.1080839	.5184811
Age	.101851	.0671121	1.52	0.129	-.0296863	.2333884
Sex						
female	0	(base)				
male	-.8130348	.1167381	-6.96	0.000	-1.041837	-.5842323
_cons	-.9176211	.9519872	-0.96	0.335	-2.783482	.9482394

```
. estimate store M2
```

As shown above, the *estimate store* command saved the analyses as M1 and M2. (We can use any names that we want to save the analysis.) After we saved the results we can then use the *suest* command to test these two logistic regression models, one for male respondents and one for female respondents. The regression coefficients are the same as those in the separate analyses, but the *suest* procedure provides robust standard errors for the coefficients.

```
. suest M1 M2

Simultaneous results for M1, M2
```

| | | | | | Number of obs | = | 2,633 |

	Coef.	Robust Std. Err.	z	P>|z|	[95% Conf. Interval]	
M1_DEPR92						
CNTYORIG						
Mexico	.3500932	.1386757	2.52	0.012	.0782938	.6218926
Indochina	.0488235	.1397669	0.35	0.727	−.2251146	.3227615
Age	.1778861	.0645295	2.76	0.006	.0514105	.3043617
Sex						
male	−.7867516	.1160821	−6.78	0.000	−1.014268	−.5592348
_cons	−1.65185	.9100975	−1.82	0.070	−3.435608	.1319082
M2_DEPR92						
CNTYORIG						
Mexico	−.0262506	.147652	−0.18	0.859	−.3156431	.263142
Indochina	.2051986	.1604894	1.28	0.201	−.1093548	.519752
Age	.101851	.0672401	1.51	0.130	−.0299371	.2336392
Sex						
male	−.8130348	.1167739	−6.96	0.000	−1.041907	−.5841622
_cons	−.9176211	.952516	−0.96	0.335	−2.784518	.9492759

Following the *suest* command, we test the hypothesis that the logit regression model among females is the same as that among males. The *test* command is used for this purpose. The χ^2 test (6.10) with four degrees of freedom and the significance level of 0.192 indicates that we cannot reject the equality of the logistic regression among females and the logistic regression among males.

```
. . test [M1_DEPR92=M2_DEPR92]

( 1)   [M1_DEPR92]1b.CNTYORIG - [M2_DEPR92]1b.CNTYORIG = 0
( 2)   [M1_DEPR92]2.CNTYORIG - [M2_DEPR92]2.CNTYORIG = 0
( 3)   [M1_DEPR92]3.CNTYORIG - [M2_DEPR92]3.CNTYORIG = 0
( 4)   [M1_DEPR92]Age - [M2_DEPR92]Age = 0
( 5)   [M1_DEPR92]0b.Sex - [M2_DEPR92]0b.Sex = 0
( 6)   [M1_DEPR92]1.Sex - [M2_DEPR92]1.Sex = 0
       Constraint 1 dropped
       Constraint 5 dropped

          chi2(  4) =     6.10
        Prob > chi2 =     0.1920
```

In the previous results, we did not estimate the odds ratios and if we want to see the odds ratios of the two models simultaneously, we can use the option *eform(Odds Ratio)* with the *suest* command as below. The results below are the same as above.

```
. suest M1 M2, eform(Odds Ratio)

Simultaneous results for M1, M2

                                                 Number of obs    =      2,633
```

	Odds Ratio	Robust Std. Err.	z	P>|z|	[95% Conf. Interval]	
M1_DEPR92						
CNTYORIG						
Mexico	1.4192	.1968086	2.52	0.012	1.08144	1.86245
Indochina	1.050035	.1467601	0.35	0.727	.7984247	1.380936
Age	1.194689	.0770928	2.76	0.006	1.052755	1.355759
Sex						
male	.4553215	.0528547	-6.78	0.000	.3626677	.5716463
_cons	.1916949	.1744611	-1.82	0.070	.0322058	1.141004
M2_DEPR92						
CNTYORIG						
Mexico	.974091	.1438265	-0.18	0.859	.7293197	1.301011
Indochina	1.227769	.1970439	1.28	0.201	.8964123	1.681611
Age	1.107219	.0744495	1.51	0.130	.9705065	1.263189
Sex						
male	.4435101	.0517904	-6.96	0.000	.3527811	.5575728
_cons	.3994682	.3804998	-0.96	0.335	.0617588	2.583838

```
. . test [M1_DEPR92=M2_DEPR92]

 ( 1)  [M1_DEPR92]1b.CNTYORIG - [M2_DEPR92]1b.CNTYORIG = 0
 ( 2)  [M1_DEPR92]2.CNTYORIG - [M2_DEPR92]2.CNTYORIG = 0
 ( 3)  [M1_DEPR92]3.CNTYORIG - [M2_DEPR92]3.CNTYORIG = 0
 ( 4)  [M1_DEPR92]Age - [M2_DEPR92]Age = 0
 ( 5)  [M1_DEPR92]0b.Sex - [M2_DEPR92]0b.Sex = 0
 ( 6)  [M1_DEPR92]1.Sex - [M2_DEPR92]1.Sex = 0
        Constraint 1 dropped
        Constraint 5 dropped

           chi2(  4) =      6.10
         Prob > chi2 =      0.1920
```

The standard errors of the estimates from the *suest* procedure are different than those in the separated analyses because the *suest procedure* produces robust standard errors accounted for the clustering problems in the data. Given the example above, there is no need to undertake any further analysis. We can conclude that the hypothetical logistic regression model of depression and countries of origin controlling for age and sex is the same for those who felt discriminated against and those who did not. If the models were statistically significantly different between the two groups, we could continue the test for the equality of each regression coefficient between the two models. We will use the following example to further demonstrate the use of "seemingly unrelated estimation" in cross-cultural comparisons. We use to data from the 2017 BRFSS data set to illustrate a situation where the comparison between the 2 groups is statistically significant. We will compare the association between race and depression while controlling for education and income between females and males by running two separate logistic regression models, one for females and one for males. Please note that the results of the regression analysis for each group must be saved in order for subsequent comparisons.

ANALYSIS OF DEPRESSION AMONG FEMALES

The following is the logistic regression analysis results among female respondents. We saved the result in the file named M_Female.

```
. logit depression i.Race edu income if Sex_F==1, base nolog
```

Logistic regression

					Number of obs	=	190,965
					LR chi2(5)	=	6126.38
					Prob > chi2	=	0.0000
Log likelihood = -104356.91

| | | | | | Pseudo R2 | = | 0.0285 |

depression	Coef.	Std. Err.	z	P>|z|	[95% Conf. Interval]	
Race						
White	0	(base)				
Black	-.6530809	.0204757	-31.90	0.000	-.6932126	-.6129492
Asian	-1.109405	.0535342	-20.72	0.000	-1.21433	-1.00448
Hispanic	-.5148358	.0206436	-24.94	0.000	-.5552965	-.4743751
edu	.042653	.0061111	6.98	0.000	.0306754	.0546306
income	-.182639	.0027636	-66.09	0.000	-.1880555	-.1772225
_cons	-.1863138	.0281153	-6.63	0.000	-.2414187	-.1312089

```
. estimate sto M_Female
```

ANALYSIS OF DEPRESSION AMONG MALES

The following is the logistic regression analysis results among male respondents. We saved the results in the file named M_Male.

```
. logit depression i.Race edu income if Sex_F==0, base nolog
```

```
Logistic regression                              Number of obs   =    158,959
                                                 LR chi2(5)      =    4711.33
                                                 Prob > chi2     =     0.0000
Log likelihood = -63756.539                      Pseudo R2       =     0.0356
```

depression	Coef.	Std. Err.	z	P>|z|	[95% Conf. Interval]	
Race						
White	0	(base)				
Black	-.4872968	.030137	-16.17	0.000	-.5463641	-.4282294
Asian	-.9928985	.062081	-15.99	0.000	-1.114575	-.8712219
Hispanic	-.4439599	.0272667	-16.28	0.000	-.4974016	-.3905183
edu	.0580442	.0076961	7.54	0.000	.0429602	.0731282
income	-.2329156	.0036331	-64.11	0.000	-.2400363	-.225795
_cons	-.5979764	.0364697	-16.40	0.000	-.6694558	-.5264971

```
. estimate sto M_Male
```

COMPARING FEMALE MODEL AND MALE MODEL

Once the separate regression analyses of females and males was completed and saved, we continued the analysis by performing a seemingly unrelated regression (SUR) analysis using the "suest" procedure.

```
. suest M_Female M_Male

Simultaneous results for M_Female, M_Male

                                           Number of obs     =     349,924
```

	Coef.	Robust Std. Err.	z	P>|z|	[95% Conf. Interval]	
M_Female_depression						
Race						
Black	−.6530809	.0203586	−32.08	0.000	−.6929831	−.6131787
Asian	−1.109405	.0541138	−20.50	0.000	−1.215466	−1.003344
Hispanic	−.5148358	.0209981	−24.52	0.000	−.5559914	−.4736802
edu	.042653	.0061335	6.95	0.000	.0306317	.0546744
income	−.182639	.0027969	−65.30	0.000	−.1881208	−.1771572
_cons	−.1863138	.0280593	−6.64	0.000	−.2413089	−.1313186
M_Male_depression						
Race						
Black	−.4872968	.0301557	−16.16	0.000	−.5464008	−.4281928
Asian	−.9928985	.062728	−15.83	0.000	−1.115843	−.8699539
Hispanic	−.4439599	.0279749	−15.87	0.000	−.4987897	−.3891302
edu	.0580442	.007674	7.56	0.000	.0430034	.073085
income	−.2329156	.0036502	−63.81	0.000	−.2400698	−.2257614
_cons	−.5979764	.0366212	−16.33	0.000	−.6697526	−.5262003

```
. . test [M_Female_depression=M_Male_depression]

( 1)  [M_Female_depression]1b.Race - [M_Male_depression]1b.Race = 0
( 2)  [M_Female_depression]2.Race - [M_Male_depression]2.Race = 0
( 3)  [M_Female_depression]3.Race - [M_Male_depression]3.Race = 0
( 4)  [M_Female_depression]4.Race - [M_Male_depression]4.Race = 0
( 5)  [M_Female_depression]edu - [M_Male_depression]edu = 0
( 6)  [M_Female_depression]income - [M_Male_depression]income = 0
      Constraint 1 dropped

         chi2( 5) =  191.84
       Prob > chi2 =   0.0000
```

The results of the seemingly unrelated regression analysis indicate that the regression model among females is statistically significantly different compared to males, given that the c2 value of 191.84 with 5 degrees of freedom and a significance level of p < 0.001. With this result, we can further test for the equality of the logit regression coefficients between the model among females and the model among males as below.

TEST THE EQUALITY OF RACE AND DEPRESSION BETWEEN THE FEMALE AND MALE EQUATIONS

We present the coding of the variables "race" and "depression" again to assist the reader in following the interpretation of comparisons presented in this section.

. **tab Race**

RECODE of _race (COMPUTED RACE-ETHNIC ITY GROUPING)	Freq.	Percent	Cum.
White	337,166	80.30	80.30
Black	35,765	8.52	88.82
Asian	9,855	2.35	91.17
Hispanic	37,078	8.83	100.00
Total	419,864	100.00	

. **tab depression**

RECODE of addepev2 (EVER TOLD YOU HAD A DEPRESSIVE DISORDER)	Freq.	Percent	Cum.
No	358,683	80.08	80.08
Yes	89,209	19.92	100.00
Total	447,892	100.00	

Although the results from the seemingly unrelated regression analysis revealed that the associations between the independent variables (race, education, and income) and depression were different when comparing females and males, further analyses were needed to pinpoint where the differences might be found. We used the **test** command to test the equality of each logistic regression coefficient that predicts depression between females and males. For example, we used the **test** command to compare the logistic regression coefficient that predicts the difference in the likelihood of being depressed between Black (coded as 2) and White (Reference or Base group). The results of the **test** procedure showed that the χ^2 value of (20.76) with one degree of freedom and the significance level of < 0.001 indicates the coefficients were not the same. Looking at the simultaneous results for M_Female model and M_Male model from earlier, we see that the coefficient between Black and White in the Female model was −.653 (SE = .020), and the coefficient between Black and White in the Male model was −.487 (SE = .030). The difference between these two coefficients is statistically significant.

```
. test _b[M_Female_depression:2.Race]      = _b[M_Male_depression :2.Race]

( 1)   [M_Female_depression]2.Race - [M_Male_depression]2.Race = 0

          chi2(  1) =    20.76
        Prob > chi2 =     0.0000
```

Note that when we compare a categorical variable between the models, we must specify the coding of the category in the command, such as in the above test command we specified the category coded as 2 (Black) before the Race variable. We do not need to do this for continuous variables such as education and income variables in this example.

We can test the equality of the remaining variables as below.

```
. test _b[M_Female_depression:3.Race]      = _b[M_Male_depression :3.Race]

( 1)  [M_Female_depression]3.Race - [M_Male_depression]3.Race = 0

         chi2(  1) =    1.98
        Prob > chi2 =    0.1596

. test _b[M_Female_depression:4.Race]      = _b[M_Male_depression :4.Race]

( 1)  [M_Female_depression]4.Race - [M_Male_depression]4.Race = 0

         chi2(  1) =    4.11
        Prob > chi2 =    0.0427

. test _b[M_Female_depression:edu]        = _b[M_Male_depression :edu]

( 1)  [M_Female_depression]edu - [M_Male_depression]edu = 0

         chi2(  1) =    2.45
        Prob > chi2 =    0.1172

. test _b[M_Female_depression:income]        = _b[M_Male_depression :income]

( 1)  [M_Female_depression]income - [M_Male_depression]income = 0

         chi2(  1) =    119.54
        Prob > chi2 =    0.0000
```

Table 5.2 and Table 5.3 present the regression coefficients and their 95% confidence intervals extracted from the results of the seemingly unrelated regression analysis. This was performed to further illustrate the interpretation of the racial comparison of depression stratified by sex between Asians and Whites.

Table 5.2. Comparison of Depression for Females and Males and Asians versus Whites

Sex	Asians vs. Whites	
	Coef.	95% Confidence Interval
Female Group	−1.109405	−1.21433 −1.00448
Male Group	−.9928985	−1.115843 −.8699539

Let's look at the comparison of depression between Asians (3.Race) and Whites (Reference, Base). The χ^2 (1.98) with one degree of freedom and the probability (level of significance) at 0.156 indicates that there was no statistically significant difference between the two groups. We also can look at the 95% confidence intervals and draw the same conclusion. Table 5.2 shows an overlap between the confidence intervals of the female group and those of the male group.

The association between education and depression is the same between the female group and male group. This conclusion is based on the results of the χ^2 test (2.45) with one degree of freedom and the level of significance of 0.1172. Note that unlike the categorical variables that require us to identify the coding of the category that we want to compare (i.e., the variable Race), education and income were treated as continuous variables. Therefore, we do not need to identity the values of these two variables. The association between income and depression was statistically different between the female group and the male group as revealed by the χ^2 (119.54) with one degree of freedom and the level of significance of < 0.001. Let us look at the 95% confidence intervals of the coefficient of education between the two groups in Table 5.3.

Given the magnitude of the logistic regression coefficient of income above we can say that income had a stronger association with depression among the male group than among the female group. We already know that the difference was statistically significant based on the chi2 test discussed earlier, but in the absence of the χ^2 test, we can still conclude that the difference was statistically significant due to the fact that there is no overlap between the 95% confidence intervals of the coefficients as illustrated in the table.

Table 5.3. Comparison of Income for Females and Males and Asians versus Whites

Sex	Income	
	Coef.	95% Confidence Interval
Female Group	−.182639	−.1881208 −.1771572
Male Group	−.2329156	−.2400698 −.2257614

Multiplicative and Additive Interaction

Earlier we addressed the multiplicative or statistical interaction and how we could apply it in cross-cultural analysis. Our position is that we should not conclude any cultural effect of an independent variable on a dependent variable until we could rule out that its effect is not modified or varied according to another independent variable or a covariate. Therefore, in doing cross-cultural analysis we should always check for the possibility of an interaction effect between our cultural variable and another cultural variable or any relevant variable. Previous literature and clinical experiences should guide our selection of a possible moderator variable.

We conclude this chapter by an introduction of the concept of additive or biological interaction, which is still largely unrecognized in social work research. In multiplicative interaction, we multiply two variables to estimate their interaction effect on a particular dependent variable. In an additive or biological interaction we combine or add the effects of two variables to estimate their interaction. Epidemiologists have emphasized that additive interaction carries great public health importance (VanderWeele, 2009; Rothman, 2012). We will use Stata codes provided by Bruun, Fenger, Gron, and Prior (2017) to illustrate the computing of the additive interaction. We will look at the additive interaction effect between diabetes (no/yes) and arthritis (no/yes) on depression (no/yes) using the 2017 BRFSS data set.

Let us examine the association among depression, diabetes, and arthritis. We assume that diabetes and arthritis are risk factors for depression. The joint effect of these two risk factors would increase the likelihood of depression more than each risk factor individually.

Crosstabulation Analysis of Depression and Diabetes by Arthritis

We begin our analysis with a crosstabulation analysis and the results are presented below.

```
. bysort arthritis: tab depression Diabetes, col chi
```

```
-> arthritis = No
```

Key
frequency
column percentage

RECODE of addepev2 (EVER TOLD YOU HAD A DEPRESSIVE DISORDER)	RECODE of diabete3 ((EVER TOLD) YOU HAVE DIABETES)		Total
	No	Yes	
No	225,602	22,776	248,378
	85.54	81.19	85.12
Yes	38,150	5,275	43,425
	14.46	18.81	14.88
Total	263,752	28,051	291,803
	100.00	100.00	100.00

Pearson chi2(1) = 377.1361   Pr = **0.000**

```
-> arthritis = Yes
```

Key
frequency
column percentage

RECODE of addepev2 (EVER TOLD YOU HAD A DEPRESSIVE DISORDER)	RECODE of diabete3 ((EVER TOLD) YOU HAVE DIABETES)		Total
	No	Yes	
No	78,967	20,707	99,674
	71.84	65.31	70.37
Yes	30,959	11,001	41,960
	28.16	34.69	29.63
Total	109,926	31,708	141,634
	100.00	100.00	100.00

Pearson chi2(1) = 503.5103   Pr = **0.000**

The results show that 18.81% of respondents did not have arthritis but had diabetes as well as a depressive disorder. Of respondents who had arthritis and also had diabetes, 34.69% had a depressive disorder. These results suggest a likelihood of a joint effect of diabetes and arthritis on depressive disorder. We will illustrate the difference between multiplicative (statistical) interaction and additive interaction in this section.

Multiplicative Interaction. The multiplicative interaction between two independent variables on their respective dependent variable is estimated by their product. If we want to examine the multiplicative interaction between diabetes and arthritis, we will multiply them to generate a new variable that would capture their joint effect.

$$logit\left(\frac{P\,Yes_{Depression}}{1 - P\,NoDepreesion}\right) = \beta 0 + \beta 1 Diabetes + \beta 2 Arthritis + \beta 3\left(\beta 1^* \beta 2\right)$$

As explained earlier, we use the hashtag symbol to indicate multiplicative interaction effect in OLS or logistic regression analyses.

```
. logistic depression Diabetes##arthritis,base nolog

Logistic regression                    Number of obs   =    433,437
                                       LR chi2(3)      =   13374.67
                                       Prob > chi2     =     0.0000
Log likelihood =  -208387.8            Pseudo R2       =     0.0311
```

depression	Odds Ratio	Std. Err.	z	P>|z|	[95% Conf. Interval]	
Diabetes						
No	1	(base)				
Yes	1.369599	.0222586	19.35	0.000	1.32666	1.413927
arthritis						
No	1	(base)				
Yes	2.318407	.0201594	96.70	0.000	2.27923	2.358257
Diabetes#arthritis						
Yes#Yes	.9894191	.0209486	-0.50	0.615	.9492007	1.031342
_cons	.1691031	.0009361	-321.05	0.000	.1672783	.1709479

Note: _cons estimates baseline odds.

Given the above results, we would conclude that the multiplicative interaction effect between diabetes and arthritis on depression is not statistically significant (Diabetes*Arthritis = .9894190, p = 0.615). To further explain the concept of multiplicative interaction, we will demonstrate the computing of the odds ratios of Diabetes and Arthritis on Depression and show the readers how to estimate the multiplicative or statistical interaction effects manually using the odds ratios presented in Table 5.5.

We can manually compute the multiplicative interaction effect of diabetes and arthritis on depression as reported in the results of the previous logistic regression of depression on diabetes and arthritis. To illustrate the computing process, we organized the odds ratios in Table 5.4, and use the formula provided by VanderWeele & Knol (2014) as described in the next section. https://cdn1.sph.harvard.edu/wp-content/uploads/sites/603/2018/04/InteractionTutorial_EM.pdf

STEPS TO COMPUTE MULTIPLICATIVE INTERACTION MANUALLY

We used the formula provided by (VanderWeele, 2012, VanderWeele & Knoll, 2014) to estimate the multiplicative interaction effect.

1. After running the logistic regression, we use the "margins" command to generate the predictive probabilities of the association of diabetes and arthritis with depression.

```
. margins Diabetes#arthritis
```

```
Adjusted predictions                          Number of obs    =    433,437
Model VCE      : OIM

Expression    : Pr(depression), predict()
```

	Margin	Delta-method Std. Err.	z	P>|z|	[95% Conf. Interval]	
Diabetes#arthritis						
No#No	.1446435	.0006849	211.19	0.000	.1433011	.1459858
No#Yes	.2816349	.0013566	207.60	0.000	.2789759	.2842939
Yes#No	.1880503	.0023331	80.60	0.000	.1834776	.1926231
Yes#Yes	.3469471	.0026731	129.79	0.000	.3417079	.3521864

2. We used the predictive probabilities from the "margins" procedure to estimate the odds ratios. To help the computing process, we organized the predictive probabilities from the "margins" analysis in Table 5.4.

Table 5.4 Predicted Probabilities of Depression Estimated by Diabetes and Arthritis

		Diabetes	
		No (0)	Yes (1)
Arthritis	No (0)	.1446435	.1880503
		P00 (Reference)	P01
	Yes (1)	.2816349	.3469471
		P10	P11

3. Given the predicted probabilities in Table 5.4, we computed the odds ratios for the cells as the followings.

Odds Ratio of the No Arthritis and No Diabetes

$$OR = \frac{\left(\dfrac{0.1446435}{1-0.1446435}\right)}{\left(\dfrac{0.1446435}{1-0.1446435}\right)} = 1.00$$

Note: The odds ratio of the reference group is always 1.00
Odds Ratio of No Arthritis and Yes Diabetes

$$OR = \frac{\left(\dfrac{0.2816349}{1-0.2816349}\right)}{\left(\dfrac{0.1446435}{1-0.1446435}\right)} = 2.318406$$

Odds Ratio of No Arthritis and Yes Diabetes

$$OR = \frac{\left(\dfrac{0.188053}{1-0.188053}\right)}{\left(\dfrac{0.1446435}{1-0.1446435}\right)} = 1.3696223$$

Odds Ratio of Yes Arthritis and Yes Diabetes

$$OR = \frac{\left(\dfrac{0.3469741}{1-0.3469741}\right)}{\left(\dfrac{0.1446435}{1-0.1446435}\right)} = 3.1416886$$

4. We present the odds ratios in a 2 x 2 Table and estimate the multiplicative interaction.

Using the information in Table 5.5 and the formula below, we estimated the multiplicative interaction between Diabetes and Arthritis on Depression as follows:

$$Multiplicative\ Interaction = \frac{OR11}{(OR10 * OR01)}$$

$$Multiplicative\ Interaction = \frac{3.1416905}{(2.318407 * 1.369599)} = .9894191$$

The multiplicative term of .9894191 is the same as the one previously estimated by STATA. Although this multiplicative interaction estimate is not statistically significant, the joint probabilities (.3469471) and the joint odds ratio of Diabetes and Arthritis (3.1416905) are greater than the remaining probabilities and odds ratios presented in Table 5.4 and Table 5.5. This suggests that we should estimate the additive interaction or biological interaction of Diabetes and Arthritis on Depression.

COMPUTE ADDITIVE INTERACTION MANUALLY

Unlike the multiplicative interaction estimated by the product of the two independent variables or the multiplicative scale, the additive

Table 5.5. Odds Ratio (OR) of Diabetes and Arthritis on Depression

Arthritis	Diabetes	
Odds Ratio	No (0)	Yes (1)
No (0)	1.00 (OR 00)	1.369599 (OR 01)
Yes (1)	2.318407 (OR 10)	3.1416905 (OR 11)

interaction estimated by adding two independent variables or the additive scale. We will use the odds ratios presented in Table 5.5 to estimate the additive interaction od Diabetes and Arthritis on Depression. Rothman (1986) provided the formulas to estimate three measures of additive interaction.

Measure of "relative excess risk due to interaction (RERI):

$$RERI = (OR11) - (OR10) - (OR01) + 1$$

$$RERI = 3.1416886 - 2.318406 - 1.3696223 + 1 = .4536602$$

Additive interaction occurs when the value of RERI is different from zero.

Measure of the Proportion of Outcome Attributable to Interaction (AP):

$$AP = \frac{\big((OR11) - (OR10) - (OR01) + (OR00)\big)}{(OR11)}$$

$$AP = \frac{(3.1417 - 2.3184 - 1.3696 + 1)}{3.1417} = .14441226$$

Measure of Interaction Synergy. This synergy index is not 1 when there is an interaction effect between two independent variables:

$$S = \frac{\big((OR11) - (OR00)\big)}{\big((OR10 - (OR00) + (OR01 - (OR00)\big)}$$

$$S = \frac{(3.1417 - 1)}{\big((2.3184 - 1) + (1.3696 - 1)\big)} = 1.2687796$$

Now let us compare the values of RERI. AP and S are the same as those presented in the Table below. There were minor differences due to the rounding of the decimals. All three measures of additive interaction suggest that the joint effect of diabetes and arthritis on depressive disorder is greater than the sum of the effects of diabetes and arthritis. Thus, an important implication is to have interventions that are targeted for this at-risk population.

```
. ic depression Diabetes arthritis,rrby(or) show
```

```
Logistic regression                          Number of obs    =    433,437
                                             LR chi2(3)       =   13374.67
                                             Prob > chi2      =     0.0000
Log likelihood =  -208387.8                  Pseudo R2        =     0.0311
```

depression	Coef.	Std. Err.	z	P>|z|	[95% Conf. Interval]	
_Diabetes_NOT_arthritis	.314518	.0162519	19.35	0.000	.2826648	.3463711
_arthritis_NOT_Diabetes	.8408803	.0086954	96.70	0.000	.8238377	.8579229
_Diabetes_AND_arthritis	1.144761	.0130322	87.84	0.000	1.119218	1.170304
_cons	-1.777247	.0055358	-321.05	0.000	-1.788097	-1.766397

Summary measures	Estimates	P-value	Lower bound	Upper bound
Diabetes_NOT_arthritis	1.3696	0.0000	1.3267	1.4139
arthritis_NOT_Diabetes	2.3184	0.0000	2.2792	2.3583
Diabetes_AND_arthritis	3.1417	0.0000	3.0625	3.2230
RERI	0.4537	0.0000	0.3647	0.5427
AP	0.1444	0.0000	0.1186	0.1703
S	1.2688	0.0000	1.2116	1.3287

Interaction exists if RERI != 0 or AP != 0 or S != 1

NEGATIVE ADDITIVE INTERACTION

The above examples illustrate the positive additive interaction of two risk factors or two independent variables that could have a negative impact on the outcome. Positive additive interaction could be used to evaluate the double jeopardy of the comorbidity of two risk factors on physical or mental health status. This is a situation when the negative impact of a risk factor on the outcome could be reduced by the occurrence of another variable. For example, older adults who have arthritis could experience poor mental health such as depression. However, if they are motivated to participate in daily physical activities such as exercises, they may have a lower likelihood of depression than those who did not exercise. We will illustrate the negative additive interaction using a sample of respondents aged 65 and older from the 2017 BRFSS data set.

Before running an additive interaction analysis, we ran a multiplicative interaction of arthritis and physical activities on depressive disorder. The logistic regression below revealed that the multiplicative interaction is not statistically significant. If we concluded arthritis and physical activities had independent effects on depressive disorder among older adult respondents, we could make a serious mistake. Let us assume that a health care social worker used this result to advise her older adult clients who suffered from arthritis by saying that engaging in daily physical activities would not help them with respect to mental health problem. Although her advice was based on the statistical evidence, she would not be accurate because she did take into account the additive interaction between arthritis and physical activities.

```
. logistic depression i.arthritis##i.PhyActive,base nolog
```

Logistic regression

	Number of obs = 145,783
	LR chi2(3) = 4128.56
	Prob > chi2 = 0.0000
Log likelihood = -62725.27	Pseudo R2 = 0.0319

depression	Odds Ratio	Std. Err.	z	P>|z|	[95% Conf. Interval]	
arthritis						
No	1	(base)				
Yes	2.24035	.0566849	31.88	0.000	2.131959	2.354251
PhyActive						
No	1	(base)				
Yes	.6644016	.0171533	-15.84	0.000	.6316183	.6988866
arthritis#PhyActive						
Yes#Yes	1.041802	.0328928	1.30	0.195	.9792872	1.108307
_cons	.1567204	.0032974	-88.08	0.000	.1503891	.1633183

Note: _cons estimates baseline odds.

All three measures of additive interaction indicated a significant negative interaction.

```
. ic depression arthritis PhyActive,rrby(or) show
```

Logistic regression

	Number of obs = 145,783
	LR chi2(3) = 4128.56
	Prob > chi2 = 0.0000
Log likelihood = -62725.27	Pseudo R2 = 0.0319

depression	Coef.	Std. Err.	z	P>|z|	[95% Conf. Interval]	
_arthritis_NOT_PhyActive	.806632	.0253018	31.88	0.000	.7570414	.8562226
_PhyActive_NOT_arthritis	-.4088684	.0258176	-15.84	0.000	-.45947	-.3582669
_arthritis_AND_PhyActive	.4387151	.0239892	18.29	0.000	.3916972	.4857331
_cons	-1.853292	.0210399	-88.08	0.000	-1.894529	-1.812054

Summary measures	Estimates	P-value	Lower bound	Upper bound
arthritis_NOT_PhyActive	2.2403	0.0000	2.1320	2.3543
PhyActive_NOT_arthritis	0.6644	0.0000	0.6316	0.6989
arthritis_AND_PhyActive	1.5507	0.0000	1.4795	1.6254
RERI	-0.3540	0.0000	-0.4464	-0.2617
AP	-0.2283	0.0000	-0.2850	-0.1716
S	0.6087	0.0000	0.5524	0.6707

Interaction exists if RERI != 0 or AP != 0 or S != 1

CONCURRENT MULTIPLICATIVE AND ADDITIVE INTERACTIONS

It is possible for multiplicative and additive interaction to occur concurrently. The interpretation of the outcome depends on the purpose of the study. For example, if you test the model of stress and social support on depression, it would be more meaningful to look at the multiplicative interaction as we would expect that social support could reduce the impact of stress on depression. However, if we look the impact of two separate health chronic conditions on depression, we would want to look at their additive interaction. The following analyses illustrate the situation when both multiplicative and additive interaction are statistically significant.

We will examine the multiplicative interaction effect between diabetes and arthritis while controlling for age and sex.

```
. logistic depression c.age i.Sex_ c.educ i.Diabetes## i.arthritis,base nolog
```

Logistic regression			Number of obs	=	433,175
			LR chi2(6)	=	27687.76
			Prob > chi2	=	0.0000
Log likelihood = -201088.06			Pseudo R2	=	0.0644

depression	Odds Ratio	Std. Err.	z	P>|z|	[95% Conf. Interval]	
age	.9753155	.0002555	-95.41	0.000	.9748148	.9758164
Sex_F						
male	1	(base)				
female	1.815839	.0150767	71.85	0.000	1.786529	1.845631
educa	.9304948	.0034899	-19.21	0.000	.9236798	.9373602
Diabetes						
No	1	(base)				
Yes	1.948877	.0332434	39.12	0.000	1.884799	2.015135
arthritis						
No	1	(base)				
Yes	3.207282	.0320562	116.60	0.000	3.145064	3.27073
Diabetes#arthritis						
Yes#Yes	.7591333	.0165177	-12.67	0.000	.7274398	.7922076
_cons	.5568917	.0126787	-25.71	0.000	.5325882	.5823043

Note: _cons estimates baseline odds.

The results above showed that the multiplicative interaction between diabetes and arthritis is statistically significant (Odds Ratio: 0.7591333, p < .001). To understand the interaction effect, we need to look at the predictive probabilities below:

```
. margins Diabetes#arthritis

Predictive margins                              Number of obs    =    433,175
Model VCE    : OIM

Expression   : Pr(depression), predict()
```

	Margin	Delta-method Std. Err.	z	P>|z|	[95% Conf. Interval]	
Diabetes#arthritis						
No#No	.1310436	.0006431	203.78	0.000	.1297833	.132304
No#Yes	.3152792	.0014865	212.10	0.000	.3123658	.3181926
Yes#No	.2227957	.0026031	85.59	0.000	.2176938	.2278976
Yes#Yes	.3999863	.0028215	141.77	0.000	.3944563	.4055163

The results of the predictive margins indicated that those who had both diabetes and arthritis had the greatest probability of depressive disorder compared to those who only had one of the chronic condition or none. Thus, the probability of having a depressiive disorder among those with diabetes increased if they also had arthritis.

Now let's find out if there is an additive interaction between these two chronic conditions on the likelihood of having a depressive disorder after controlling for age and sex. We constructed a 2X2 Table to present the predictive probabilities, in order to make it easier for computing odds ratios.

Table 5.6. Predicted Probabilities of Depression

Arthritis	Diabetes	
	No (0)	Yes (1)
No (0)	.1310436 P00	.3152792 P01
Yes (1)	.2227957 P10	.3999863 P11

We use the "*display*" command to calculate the odds ratios using the predictive probabilities in Table 5.5 above.

```
. display (.1310436/(1-.1310436)))/(.1310436/(1-.1310436))
1

. display (.3152792 /(1-.3152792 ))/(.1310436/(1-.1310436))
3.0532613

. display (.2227957   /(1-.2227957   ))/(.1310436/(1-.1310436))
1.900876

. display (.3999863 /(1-.3999863 ))/(.1310436/(1-.1310436))
4.4204463
```

Now let put these odds ratio in a 2X2 table as follows in Table 5.6 to make it easier to calculate the additive interaction.

MEASURES OF ADDITIVE INTERACTION

$$RERI = (OR11) - (OR10) - (OR01) + 1$$

```
. display 4.42044630-1.900876-3.0532613+1
.466309
```

$$AP = \frac{\left((OR11) - (OR10) - (OR01) + (OR00)\right)}{(OR11)}$$

```
. display (4.4204463-1.900876+1)/4.4204463
.79620248
```

$$S = \frac{\left((OR11) - (OR00)\right)}{\left((OR10 - (OR00) + (OR01 - (OR00))\right)}$$

```
. display (4.4204463-1)/(1.900876-1)+(3.0532613-1)
5.8500616
```

All three measures of additive interaction of Diabetes and Arthritis on Depression after controlling for age, sex and education indicated that there is an additive interaction. How do we interpret the multiplicative and additive interaction when they are both significant? The answer depends on the purpose of the analysis. There are situations where multiplicative interaction is more meaningful than additive interaction. For example, when we examine whether the association between cultural identity and well-being depends on a person's education, then multiplicative interaction makes sense. However, if we consider minority cultural identity and the experience of being discriminated as risk factors of depression, then we should estimate their additive interaction on depression and not multiplicative interaction. Our purpose is to show social wok researchers the basic mechanism to estimate additive interaction that could be useful in social work research and evaluation.

CONCLUSION

In this chapter, we have examined the theoretical foundation of logistic regression and provided different examples of interaction effects. Specifically, we discussed biological interaction and additive interaction, and demonstrated how to interpret the results from these analyses. We hope this can be useful for analysts for examining cross-cultural research with their populations.

REFERENCES

The Abdul Latif Jameel Poverty Action Lab (J-PAL) (2020). *Six rules of thumb for determining sample size and statistical power.* Retrieved from https://www.povertyactionlab.org/blog/5-21-18/six-rules-thumb-understanding-statistical-power, 2-21-2020.

Assmann SF, Pocock SJ, Enos LE, Kasten LE. Subgroup analysis and other (mis) uses of baseline data in clinical trials. *Lancet.* 2000;*355*(9209):1064–1069. doi:10.1016/S0140-6736(00)02039-0

Brunn Niels Henrik Bruun & Morten Fenger-Gron & Anders Prior, 2015. "IC: Stata module to compute measures of interaction contrast (biological interaction)," Statistical Software Components S457975, Boston College Department of Economics, revised 22 Apr 2017.

Cornell Statistical Consulting Unit (2008). StatNews # 73: Overlapping Confidence Intervals and Statistical Significance. https://www.cscu.cornell.edu/news/statnews/stnews73.pdf

Knol, M. J., Pestman, W. R., & Grobbee, D. E. (2011). The (mis)use of overlap of confidence intervals to assess effect modification. *European journal of epidemiology, 26*(4), 253–254. https://doi.org/10.1007/s10654-011-9563-8.

Lewinsohn, P.M., Seeley, J.R., Roberts, R.E., & Allen, N.B. (1997). Center for Epidemiological Studies-Depression Scale (CES-D) as a screening instrument for depression among community-residing older adults. *Psychology and Aging, 12,* 277–287.

Long, J. S., & Freese, J, (2017). *Regression Models for Categorical Dependent Variables Using Stata (Third Edition).* College Station, TX: Stata Press.

Mackinnon D. P. (2011). Integrating Mediators and Moderators in Research Design. *Research on social work practice, 21*(6), 675–681. https://doi.org/10.1177/1049731511414148

Oxman AD, Guyatt GH. A consumer's guide to subgroup analyses. *Ann Intern Med.* 1992;*116*(1):78-84. doi:10.7326/0003-4819-116-1-78

Portes, Alejandro, and Rumbaut, Rubén G. *Children of Immigrants Longitudinal Study (CILS),* San Diego, California, Ft. Lauderdale and Miami, Florida, 1991-2006. Ann Arbor, MI: Inter-university Consortium for Political and Social Research [distributor], 2018-12-12. https://doi.org/10.3886/ICPSR20520.v3

Radloff, L. S. (1977). The CES-D scale: A self report depression scale for research in the general population. *Applied Psychological Measurements, 1,* 385–401.

Roth, D.L., Ackerman, M. L., Okonkwo, O. C., & Burgio, L. D. (2008). The four-factor model of depressive symptoms in dementia caregivers: A structural equation model of ethnic differences. *Psychology and Aging, 23,* 567–576.

Rothman, K.J. (2012). *Epidemiology: An Introduction* (2nd Edition). Oxford University Press.

Skelly, A. C., Dettori, J. R., & Brodt, E. D. (2012). Assessing bias: the importance of considering confounding. *Evidence-based spine-care journal, 3*(1), 9–12. https://doi.org/10.1055/s-0031-1298595

StataCorp. 2017. *Stata Statistical Software: Release 15.* College Station, TX: StataCorp LLC.

Tabatabai, M. A., Li, H., Eby, W. M., Kengwoung-Keumo, J. J., Manne, U., Bae, S., Fouad, M., & Singh, K. P. (2014). Robust Logistic and Probit Methods for Binary and Multinomial Regression. *Journal of biometrics & biostatistics, 5*(4), 202. https://doi.org/10.4172/2155-6180.1000202

VanderWeele, T.J. (2009). On the distinction between interaction and effect modification, *Epidemiology, 20*:863–871.

VanderWeele, T.J. & Knol, M.J. (2014). A tutorial on Interaction. Epidemiologic. *Methods, 3*(1), 33–72. https://catalyst.harvard.edu/docs/biostatsseminar/VanderWeele2012.pdf

VanVoorhis, C. R. W, & Morgan B.L (2007). Understanding the power and rules of thumb for determining sample sizes. *Tutorials in Quantitavie Methods for Psychology, 3*(2), 43–50.

6

Applied Structural Equation Modeling for Cross-Cultural Comparison

In this chapter, we focus on the use of Structural Equation Modeling (SEM) to compare path models across two or more cultural groups. SEM can be used to test the goodness of fit of a causal model, as well as to test equivalence of causal relationships among variables of interest across various cultural groups. We will demonstrate SEM through the use of Stata for these purposes.

INTRODUCTION TO STRUCTURAL EQUATION MODELING FOR CROSS-CULTURAL RESEARCH

Since its introduction, Structural Equation Modeling (SEM) has been used widely by social work researchers for the purposes of measurement validation and causal modeling. Published works in the *Pocket Guide for Social Work Research* series (Bowen & Guo, 2012; Harrington, 2008; Orme &

Applied Cross-Cultural Data Analysis for Social Work. Thanh V. Tran and Keith T. Chan,
Oxford University Press. © Oxford University Press 2021. DOI: 10.1093/oso/9780190888510.003.0006

Combs-Orme, 2009; Randolph & Myers, 2013) have explored topics such as multivariate statistics, multiple regression, and confirmatory factor analysis. A previous book in the series provided a framework for measurement validation with different cultural groups (Tran, Nguyen, & Chan, 2017), which provided a foundation for understanding and applying cross-cultural causal modeling analysis. The current chapter focuses on the use of SEM to test causal relationships across different cultural groups using path analysis models with cross culturally validated instruments.

RATIONALE FOR PATH MODEL ANALYSIS

Path analysis is used in social and behavioral sciences for examining relationships across social phenomena, and has been referred to as structural modeling, or more commonly, causal modeling. Despite its name, causal modeling is not used by researchers to discover causes. Rather, it is used to test hypothesized pathways that provide evidence of cause and effect. Path model analysis is important in cross-cultural research for two reasons. First, the pathways to outcomes of interest to social workers (such as psychological well-being) would likely vary among populations from different racial, ethnic, linguistic, or national backgrounds. Second, identifying the pathways of health and mental health outcomes across cultures will help to improve psychosocial interventions for vulnerable populations.

Social, psychological, and biological phenomena are complex and operate along causal pathways. Quantitative analysis is most commonly used to test hypothesized relationships between two variables, controlling for possible confounders. Path analysis is necessary to fully explicate the underlying pathways between independent and dependent variables. Intermediate variables, whether obvious or hidden, are always present, and they may be the critical point of intervention for social work policy and practice.

CAUSAL MODELING

Social scientists are often reluctant to describe their research in terms of cause and effect. Despite this, social work researchers study social science phenomena precisely to examine causal relationships in order to help improve outcomes through evidence on how to intervene for their populations of interest. The aims of causal modeling for cross-cultural social work research are to (1) test the causal pathways to outcomes for specific cultural groups, and (2) determine if these casual pathways operate in similar or different ways. Structural Equation Modeling (SEM) is a class of techniques that can be used to test causal hypotheses across cultural groups in order to satisfy these two aims. Specifically, using SEM, social work researchers can determine whether (1) the structural relationships of variables are statistically similar or different across cultural groups, and (2) if the magnitude of these relationships is the same across cultural groups among variables of interest. Statistically determining cross-cultural similarities in structural relationships entails examining the evidence of direct and indirect associations among variables.

CROSS-CULTURAL RESEARCH DESIGN FOR PATH MODELING

Thoughtfulness in research design is important for setting the stage for testing hypothesized causal pathways among social phenomena of interest. A hypothetical study on early childhood trauma and its effects across the lifespan can be examined through path analysis, ideally with data collection conducted at different developmental stages in the life course. Assuming that the data collection techniques are culturally valid and scientifically robust, this type of *longitudinal* or *panel* research design provides the strongest evidence of causality. Longitudinal studies provide clear evidence of temporal causality, by virtue of having data that was collected at an earlier timepoint. However, the financial and research labor costs of implementing large-scale longitudinal research are high. In addition, limited longitudinal surveys exist with adequate sample power for underresearched cultural groups such as minorities, immigrants, and other vulnerable populations. Most often, cross-sectional studies are used for path analysis, and can sometimes account for temporal causality by asking questions related to past major life events in one's lifecourse. For example, questions such as, "When you first experienced trauma, how old were you?"

can be used to gather data on past childhood trauma. Responses to retrospective data can be highly problematic and considerably less reliable, however, compared to data that were collected longitudinally at different time points. In addition, a major challenge is that psychometric instruments, in general, are not designed for retrospective data collection. Psychometric instruments, or *measurements*, tend to capture how respondents feel in the moment or the recent past. For example, a commonly used instrument for capturing nonspecific psychological distress is the Kessler Psychological Distress Scale (K6; Kessler et al., 2002). The scale was designed to capture distress experienced by respondents over the most recent two-week to one-month period. Therefore, the K6 cannot be reliably used by researchers to capture how adult respondents experienced psychological distress at an earlier life stage. Using the scale to retrospectively capture psychological distress at a point in time in the distant past can be biased by how respondents are experiencing psychological distress in the present, potentially leading to untrustworthy data and inaccurate conclusions. The scale can and should be used, however, to capture *recent* psychological distress among participants.

Despite these challenges, establishing a convincing argument for causal inference among social phenomena in applied data analysis is possible through theory, evidence from past research, and methodological considerations. Theory can provide a conceptual framework for understanding evidence. Evidence from past research can validate theory, refine conceptual frameworks, or in some cases, refute past theories and frameworks that are empirically unsupported. It is through this iterative process that cross-cultural social work researchers can refine and hone theory through new evidence and a new lens. New knowledge from this process can inform how future research designs can be implemented to further explicate causal pathways. Through theory and evidence, researchers can include known causes for a social phenomenon of interest as variables in the design phase of the study. The most important reason that variables are included in a study is hypothesis testing—the variable or variables are hypothesized to have a causal effect on outcomes for populations of interest. The secondary reason for the inclusion of variables is to rule out potential confounding factors.

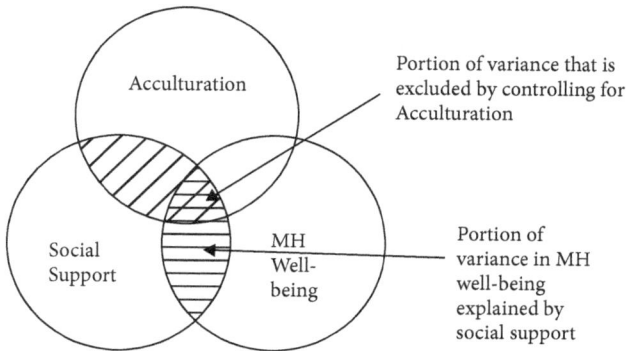

Figure 6.1. Controlling for the effect of acculturation.

For example, acculturation can be examined as a variable in a multivariate regression to rule out its potential confounding effect on the hypothesized relationship of social support and mental health well-being. Cross-cultural researchers more accurately can identify the significance and magnitude in the effect of social support on mental health well-being by including acculturation as a control variable (see Figure 6.1).

THEORY CONSTRUCTION IN PATH MODELS FOR CULTURAL GROUPS IN STRUCTURAL EQUATION MODELING

Path analysis is an extension of multiple regression in that it is concerned with statistically testing the hypothesized linkages of three or more variables, in addition to controlling for potential confounding effects. In the earlier example, acculturation was used as a variable to control for the effect of social support on mental health well-being. Acculturation also can be used as an *exogenous* variable, to examine its effect on mental health well-being indirectly through social support. Acculturation in this case is hypothesized as causally prior to social support. Past research has highlighted the impact of acculturation on a number of social indicators such as social support and perceived discrimination among immigrant and Asian American populations

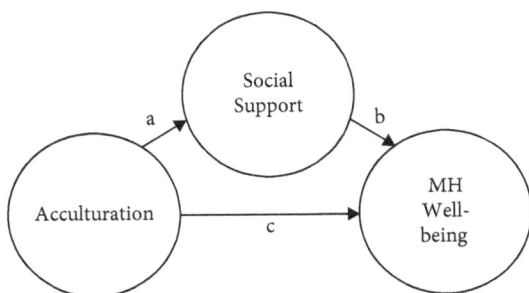

Figure 6.2. Path model of acculturation, social support, and mental health well-being.

(Chan, 2020; Chan, Tran, & Nguyen, 2012). The following (Figure 6.2) is an example of a path analysis model for acculturation, social support, and mental health well-being:

In Figure 6.2, acculturation has a direct effect on mental health well-being, expressed by *path c*. Acculturation also has an indirect effect on mental health well-being through social support, through *path a* to social support and *path b* from social support to mental health well-being. Acculturation is hypothesized in this example as temporally and causally prior to both social support and mental health well-being. Theoretically, this is plausible for a number of reasons. A substantial body of research has suggested that acculturation is associated with the social support experienced by persons in different cultures. Similarly, a robust body of research indicates that social support has an effect on mental health well-being. From a lifecourse perspective, acculturation can directly and indirectly affect social support and mental health well-being, which fluctuate based on the occurrence of major life events and life-stage changes. As noted earlier and from a methodological standpoint, psychometric measurements used to collect data on constructs such as social support and mental health well-being tend to work best for how respondents feel in the moment or the recent past. Based on theoretical, empirical, and methodological considerations, it is reasonable to assert that acculturation is temporally and causally prior to social support or mental health well-being in modeling path analysis.

IDENTIFYING CONSTRUCTS FOR CULTURAL POPULATIONS

The formulation of path models is informed by past scholarship and research, and involves the construction of theorized pathways that can be statistically tested through empirical data analysis. Cross-cultural researchers wishing to examine linkages among social phenomena can draw on past theory and evidence to identify relevant variables for inclusion in their research designs. This will allow for robust applications in examining causal pathways from *exogenous*, or predictor variables, to *endogenous*, or mediator and final outcome variables.

Identifying constructs for cultural populations for path modeling requires finding the appropriate variables for data analysis. This requires an understanding of the theoretical and practical psychosocial issues involved with cross-cultural populations. For example, the path model shown in Figure 6.2 hypothesizes that there are direct and indirect relationships from acculturation to mental health well-being.

In Figure 6.2, acculturation is an *exogenous* variable and not predicted by any other variable or variables. Social support and mental health well-being are both *endogenous* variables and predicted by acculturation. Although social support is used to predict mental health well-being, it is also preceded by acculturation. As such, as a mediator variable, social support is an *endogenous* variable.

HYPOTHESIZING PATHWAYS AND COMPARING EFFECT SIZES ACROSS CULTURAL GROUPS

Preliminary analysis can provide useful information on through multivariate analysis, with the final outcome variable as the dependent variable and all other endogenous and exogenous variables as independent variables. In Figure 6.2, a preliminary multivariate regression model can be conducted with mental health well-being as the dependent variable, and results from this initial analysis can be useful in determining whether mediation analysis can lead to meaningful results. From Figure 6.2, if neither acculturation variables or social support are statistically significantly associated with mental health well-being when controlling for all other variables, goodness-of-fit results will indicate a poor model and no direct or indirect effects will be found. If an *exogenous* variable is not significantly associated with the final outcome, it is still possible that there is an indirect effect through a *mediating* variable. Based on the above example, acculturation is hypothesized to have an indirect effect on mental health well-being through social support, which may be present even when no direct effect with mental health well-being is found.

Barron and Kenny (1983) described steps to establish mediation, and since that time, the theory of causal modeling has evolved and been elaborated upon, particularly regarding defensible analysis strategies for evaluating results on direct and indirect effect in SEM models (Bowen & Guo, 2011). In cross-cultural analysis, it is important to evaluate mediation models across cultural groups based on (1) the presence of the same pathways and (2) differences in effect sizes in these relationships. In SEM, this involves comparing the *structural form* and *beta or gamma coefficients* in the mediation model. Based on Figure 6.2, cross-culturation comparisons across groups should first consider the structural form, in the presence of significant direct and indirect effects of acculturation with social support as the mediating variable on mental health well-being. Once the direct and indirect effects are established, comparisons can be made in the directionality and strengths in association based on beta or gamma coefficients with *path a, path b, and path c*. Assuming that *path a, path b, and path c* are statistically significant and in the same direction, cross-cultural researchers then can determine if the magnitude in direct and indirect effects is statistically similar across cultural groups.

EXAMPLE FROM THE CHILDREN OF IMMIGRANTS LONGITUDINAL SURVEY

The following example is from the Children of Immigrants Longitudinal Survey (CILS), which sampled children with at least one foreign-born parent or children born abroad but brought to the United States at an early age. The sample was drawn from Wave 2 of the CILS and included 149 Vietnamese and Vietnamese Americans and 578 Cubans and Cuban Americans. Vietnamese and Cubans were chosen for this example because both are immigrant, refugee populations. Although they are racially distinct from one another, both groups share important similarities in their circumstances of involuntary migration. Vietnamese and Cubans both left their countries of origin in order to escape political persecution and have established substantial ethnic enclaves in the United States. Members of both ethnic groups occupy varying levels of socioeconomic status, and have cultural traditions and practices that differ from those of other ethnic groups in their respective race categories.

FINAL OUTCOME VARIABLE

The final outcome variable in this analysis example measured depressive symptoms, and was summed from three items from the Center on Epidemiological Studies—Depression (CESD) depression scale (1. Felt sad in the past week; 2. Couldn't get going in the past week; and 3. Felt depressed in the past week). Initial reliability analysis conducted with the study sample indicated good internal consistency of the three items as a scale (Cronbach's α = 0.77).

MEDIATING VARIABLES

Mediating variables include acculturation, measured by US-born versus years in United States, English ability, ethnic identification, and other language spoken at home. Self-esteem was measured by four items from the Rosenberg Self-Esteem Scale: (1) I am able to do things as well as most other people; (2) I feel I do not have much to be proud of; (3) I wish I could have more respect for myself; and (4) At times I think I am no good at all. Reliability analysis with these four items indicated a reasonable level of internal consistency for use in research (Cronbach's α = 0.60). More importantly, these four items from the Rosenberg Self-Esteem Scale in this data set were previously cross-culturally validated for use with the same sample of Vietnamese and Cuban youth using cross-cultural measurement development techniques illustrated in an earlier book in the *Pocket Guide to Social Work Research* series (Tran, Nguyen, & Chan, 2017).

Perceived discrimination as a construct has been measured by different scales in the past and validated for cross-cultural use with Asian populations (Chan, Tran, & Nguyen, 2012). In this example, we used four items to measure perceived discrimination as it related to children of immigrants in this study; the items asked respondents their agreement or disagreement with the following: (1) There is racial discrimination in economic opportunity in the United States; (2) The American way of life weakens the family; (3) There is much conflict between different racial and ethnic groups in the United States; and (4) Americans generally feel superior to foreigners. These items together had reasonably good internal consistency for use with the study sample of Vietnamese and Cuban youth (Cronbach's $\alpha = 0.59$).

EXOGENOUS VARIABLES

From Table 6.1, exogenous variables include sociodemographic variables such as age, gender, and income and were treated as control variables in this analysis. Family dynamics (cohesion, parental issues) and household composition also were included as control variables for analysis in this example.

STRUCTURAL EQUATION MODELING WITH LATENT VARIABLES

The following is a simple example of SEM with latent variables, which includes measurement items in the overall model. Depression as a latent variable (measured by three items) was examined as the final outcome variable. Self-esteem (measured by four items) and discrimination (measured by three items) were independent variables in this SEM analysis with latent variable. The following Stata code was used for this example:

Table 6.1. Exogenous, Mediating, and Final Outcome Variables

Exogenous Variables	Mediating Variables	Final Outcome Variable
Age	Self-Esteem	Depression
Gender	Perceived Discrimination	
Family Income		
Immigration Status		
Acculturation Factors		
Family Factors		

- sem (wellother notproud moreresp nogood <- SE4) (racedisc amwayfam raceconf
  amsupe <- DISCRIM) (sad couldntgo dep1 <- DEPRESSION) (SE4 DISCRIM ->
  DEPRESSION) if nomisscuba==1, stand
- estat gof, stats (all)
- estat teffects

The following is the Stata output:

```
. sem ( wellother notproud moreresp nogood <- SE4) (racedisc amwayfam raceconf amsupe
<- DISCRIM) (sad couldntgo dep1 <- DEPRESSION) (SE4 DISCRIM -> DEPRESSION) if
nomisscuba
> ==1, stand

Endogenous variables

Measurement:   wellother notproud moreresp nogood racedisc amwayfam raceconf amsupe sad
couldntgo dep1
Latent:        DEPRESSION

Exogenous variables

Latent:        SE4 DISCRIM

Fitting target model:

Iteration 0:   log likelihood = -28846.838
Iteration 1:   log likelihood =  -28840.54
Iteration 2:   log likelihood = -28840.143
Iteration 3:   log likelihood = -28840.136
Iteration 4:   log likelihood = -28840.136

Structural equation model                    Number of obs      =      2,253
Estimation method  = ml
Log likelihood     = -28840.136

 ( 1)  [sad]DEPRESSION = 1
 ( 2)  [wellother]SE4 = 1
 ( 3)  [racedisc]DISCRIM = 1
```

Standardized	Coef.	OIM Std. Err.	z	P>|z|	[95% Conf. Interval]	
Structural						
DEPRESSION						
SE4	-.3004382	.026533	-11.32	0.000	-.352442	-.2484345
DISCRIM	.1543503	.0278105	5.55	0.000	.0998426	.2088579
Measurement						
wellother						
SE4	.3666856	.0241502	15.18	0.000	.319352	.4140191
_cons	5.372884	.0827671	64.92	0.000	5.210664	5.535105
notproud						
SE4	.4831782	.0234378	20.62	0.000	.437241	.5291154
_cons	3.864998	.061311	63.04	0.000	3.744831	3.985165
moreresp						
SE4	.5232407	.022037	23.74	0.000	.480049	.5664323
_cons	2.307254	.0403145	57.23	0.000	2.228239	2.386269
nogood						
SE4	.7182659	.0234111	30.68	0.000	.672381	.7641508
_cons	2.969542	.0489984	60.60	0.000	2.873507	3.065577

```
racedisc    |
     DISCRIM |  .6274318   .0231123   27.15   0.000   .5821326   .672731
       _cons |  4.522699   .0705926   64.07   0.000   4.38434    4.661057
------------+------------------------------------------------------------
amwayfam    |
     DISCRIM |  .3773891   .0246505   15.31   0.000   .329075    .4257032
       _cons |  3.003761   .0494591   60.73   0.000   2.906823   3.100699
------------+------------------------------------------------------------
raceconf    |
     DISCRIM |  .6593484   .0235825   27.96   0.000   .6131274   .7055693
       _cons |  4.625663   .072058    64.19   0.000   4.484432   4.766895
------------+------------------------------------------------------------
amsupe      |
     DISCRIM |  .3913307   .0244863   15.98   0.000   .3433383   .439323
       _cons |  4.067037   .0641458   63.40   0.000   3.941313   4.192761
------------+------------------------------------------------------------
sad         |
  DEPRESSION |  .8537006   .0139518   61.19   0.000   .8263556   .8810456
       _cons |  2.040028   .036979    55.17   0.000   1.96755    2.112505
------------+------------------------------------------------------------
couldntgo   |
  DEPRESSION |  .5005541   .0178031   28.12   0.000   .4656607   .5354474
       _cons |  2.155378   .0384037   56.12   0.000   2.080108   2.230647
------------+------------------------------------------------------------
dep1        |
  DEPRESSION |  .8431703   .0139752   60.33   0.000   .8157794   .8705612
       _cons |  1.871162   .034941    53.55   0.000   1.802679   1.939645
------------+------------------------------------------------------------
 var(e.wellother)| .8655417  .0177111              .8315155   .9009603
  var(e.notproud)| .7665388  .0226492              .7234081   .8122411
 var(e.moreresp)| .7262192  .0230613              .6823978   .7728548
   var(e.nogood)| .4840941  .0336308              .4224696   .5547075
  var(e.racedisc)| .6063293  .0290027              .5520683   .6659235
  var(e.amwayfam)| .8575775  .0186057              .8218755   .8948303
  var(e.raceconf)| .5652597  .0310982              .5074795   .6296187
    var(e.amsupe)| .8468603  .0191645              .8101194   .8852675
       var(e.sad)| .2711953  .0238213              .2283043   .322144
  var(e.couldntgo)| .7494456 .0178228              .7153152   .7852046
      var(e.dep1)| .2890639  .023567               .2463749   .3391494
 var(e.DEPRESSION)| .8824018 .0178551              .8480913   .9181003
        var(SE4)|  1          .                     .          .
     var(DISCRIM)|  1          .                     .          .
------------+------------------------------------------------------------
cov(SE4,DISCRIM)| -.0378577  .0328039  -1.15  0.248  -.1021521  .0264367
------------------------------------------------------------------------
LR test of model vs. saturated: chi2(41)  =   117.24, Prob > chi2 = 0.0000
```

```
. estat gof, stats (all)

-----------------------------------------------------------------------
Fit statistic           |   Value   Description
------------------------+----------------------------------------------
Likelihood ratio        |
         chi2_ms(41)    |   117.236   model vs. saturated
             p > chi2   |     0.000
         chi2_bs(55)    |  4166.918   baseline vs. saturated
             p > chi2   |     0.000
------------------------+----------------------------------------------
Population error        |
               RMSEA    |     0.029   Root mean squared error of approximation
  90% CI, lower bound   |     0.023
         upper bound    |     0.035
```

```
              pclose |     1.000   Probability RMSEA <= 0.05
-------------------+-----------------------------------------------------------
Information criteria |
                 AIC |  57752.272  Akaike's information criterion
                 BIC |  57958.192  Bayesian information criterion
-------------------+-----------------------------------------------------------
Baseline comparison  |
                 CFI |     0.981   Comparative fit index
                 TLI |     0.975   Tucker-Lewis index
-------------------+-----------------------------------------------------------
Size of residuals    |
                SRMR |     0.026   Standardized root mean squared residual
                  CD |     0.881   Coefficient of determination
-------------------------------------------------------------------------------
.
. estat teffects


Direct effects
-------------------------------------------------------------------------------
                   |              OIM
                   |   Coef.   Std. Err.     z    P>|z|    [95% Conf. Interval]
-------------+-----------------------------------------------------------------
Measurement  |
  wellother  |
         SE4 |        1  (constrained)
-------------+-----------------------------------------------------------------
notproud     |
         SE4 | 1.766645   .1447484   12.20   0.000    1.482943    2.050346
-------------+-----------------------------------------------------------------
moreresp     |
         SE4 |  2.43785   .2034411   11.98   0.000    2.039113    2.836588
-------------+-----------------------------------------------------------------
nogood       |
         SE4 | 3.069061   .2553621   12.02   0.000     2.56856    3.569561
-------------+-----------------------------------------------------------------
racedisc     |
      DISCRIM |       1  (constrained)
-------------+-----------------------------------------------------------------
amwayfam     |
      DISCRIM |  .741355    .061113   12.13   0.000    .6215757    .8611344
-------------+-----------------------------------------------------------------
raceconf     |
      DISCRIM |  1.05847   .0671034   15.77   0.000    .9269493     1.18999
-------------+-----------------------------------------------------------------
amsupe       |
      DISCRIM | .6952195   .0551366   12.61   0.000    .5871537    .8032852
-------------+-----------------------------------------------------------------
sad          |
  DEPRESSION |        1  (constrained)
         SE4 |        0  (no path)
      DISCRIM |        0  (no path)
-------------+-----------------------------------------------------------------
couldntgo    |
  DEPRESSION | .5677752   .0255101   22.26   0.000    .5177764    .6177741
         SE4 |        0  (no path)
      DISCRIM |        0  (no path)
-------------+-----------------------------------------------------------------
dep1         |
  DEPRESSION | 1.017652    .034783   29.26   0.000    .9494783    1.085825
         SE4 |        0  (no path)
      DISCRIM |        0  (no path)
```

```
-------------+-------------------------------------------------------------
Structural   |
DEPRESSION   |
       SE4   |  -.8891523   .1014813   -8.76   0.000   -1.088052   -.6902526
    DISCRIM  |   .2521486   .0472797    5.33   0.000    .159482     .3448151
-------------+-------------------------------------------------------------


Indirect effects
-----------------------------------------------------------------------------
             |                OIM
             |   Coef.    Std. Err.     z     P>|z|    [95% Conf. Interval]
-------------+-------------------------------------------------------------
Measurement  |
  wellother  |
       SE4   |      0   (no path)
-----------+-------------------------------------------------------------
  notproud   |
       SE4   |      0   (no path)
-----------+-------------------------------------------------------------
  moreresp   |
       SE4   |      0   (no path)
-----------+-------------------------------------------------------------
  nogood     |
       SE4   |      0   (no path)
-----------+-------------------------------------------------------------
  racedisc   |
    DISCRIM  |      0   (no path)
-----------+-------------------------------------------------------------
  amwayfam   |
    DISCRIM  |      0   (no path)
-----------+-------------------------------------------------------------
  raceconf   |
    DISCRIM  |      0   (no path)
-----------+-------------------------------------------------------------
  amsupe     |
    DISCRIM  |      0   (no path)
-----------+-------------------------------------------------------------
  sad        |
 DEPRESSION  |      0   (no path)
       SE4   |  -.8891523   .1014813   -8.76   0.000   -1.088052   -.6902526
    DISCRIM  |   .2521486   .0472797    5.33   0.000    .159482     .3448151
-----------+-------------------------------------------------------------
  couldntgo  |
 DEPRESSION  |      0   (no path)
       SE4   |  -.5048387   .060326    -8.37   0.000   -.6230754   -.3866019
    DISCRIM  |   .1431637   .0274528    5.21   0.000    .0893571    .1969703
-----------+-------------------------------------------------------------
  dep1       |
 DEPRESSION  |      0   (no path)
       SE4   |  -.9048475   .1033656   -8.75   0.000   -1.10744    -.7022546
    DISCRIM  |   .2565994   .0485715    5.28   0.000    .1614011    .3517978
-------------+-------------------------------------------------------------
Structural   |
DEPRESSION   |
       SE4   |      0   (no path)
    DISCRIM  |      0   (no path)
-------------------------------------------------------------------------
```

```
Total effects
-----------------------------------------------------------------------------
             |                    OIM
             |     Coef.    Std. Err.      z     P>|z|    [95% Conf. Interval]
-------------+---------------------------------------------------------------
Measurement  |
 wellother   |
      SE4    |        1     (constrained)
-------------+---------------------------------------------------------------
 notproud    |
      SE4    | 1.766645    .1447484    12.20    0.000    1.482943    2.050346
-------------+---------------------------------------------------------------
 moreresp    |
      SE4    |  2.43785    .2034411    11.98    0.000    2.039113    2.836588
-------------+---------------------------------------------------------------
 nogood      |
      SE4    | 3.069061    .2553621    12.02    0.000     2.56856    3.569561
-------------+---------------------------------------------------------------
 racedisc    |
   DISCRIM   |        1     (constrained)
-------------+---------------------------------------------------------------
 amwayfam    |
   DISCRIM   |  .741355    .061113     12.13    0.000    .6215757    .8611344
-------------+---------------------------------------------------------------
 raceconf    |
   DISCRIM   | 1.05847     .0671034    15.77    0.000    .9269493    1.18999
-------------+---------------------------------------------------------------
 amsupe      |
   DISCRIM   | .6952195    .0551366    12.61    0.000    .5871537    .8032852
-------------+---------------------------------------------------------------
 sad         |
DEPRESSION   |        1     (constrained)
      SE4    | -.8891523   .1014813    -8.76    0.000    -1.088052   -.6902526
   DISCRIM   | .2521486    .0472797     5.33    0.000    .159482     .3448151
-------------+---------------------------------------------------------------
 couldntgo   |
DEPRESSION   | .5677752    .0255101    22.26    0.000    .5177764    .6177741
      SE4    | -.5048387   .060326     -8.37    0.000    -.6230754   -.3866019
   DISCRIM   | .1431637    .0274528     5.21    0.000    .0893571    .1969703
-------------+---------------------------------------------------------------
 dep1        |
DEPRESSION   | 1.017652    .034783     29.26    0.000    .9494783    1.085825
      SE4    | -.9048475   .1033656    -8.75    0.000    -1.10744    -.7022546
   DISCRIM   | .2565994    .0485715     5.28    0.000    .1614011    .3517978
-------------+---------------------------------------------------------------
Structural   |
DEPRESSION   |
      SE4    | -.8891523   .1014813    -8.76    0.000    -1.088052   -.6902526
   DISCRIM   | .2521486    .0472797     5.33    0.000    .159482     .3448151
-----------------------------------------------------------------------------
```

The output shown here indicated that self-esteem was negatively associated with depression ($\gamma = -0.30$, $p < 0.001$) in this latent variable analysis. Discrimination was associated with higher levels of depression ($\gamma = -0.15$, $p < 0.001$). Results from the measurement portion of the analysis indicate that all factor loadings were statistically significant, and the latent variables (self-esteem, discrimination, and depression) accounted for an acceptable level of variability from observed indicators. Goodness-of-fit statistics indicated that the model was statistically different from the saturated model, which suggested some modification can be made to improve overall fit (χ^2 = 117.236, df = 41, p < 0.001, RMSEA = 0.029).

PRELIMINARY ANALYSIS FOR SETTING UP MEDIATION MODEL USING ORDINARY LEAST SQUARES REGRESSION

For the purposes of testing structural pathways, all measurement items were summed up for use in subsequent analyses. Separate analyses were conducted for Vietnamese and Cuban youth to examine cross-cultural differences in sociodemographic variables, acculturation, and family factors with depressive symptoms. It was hypothesized that the relationship of acculturation and social factors on mental depression will be structurally different for Vietnamese compared to Cuban youth.

Preliminary multivariate regression analyses were conducted separately for Vietnamese and Cuban youth, with depression as the dependent variable. As a first step, all exogenous and mediating variables were included simultaneously as independent variables in subgroup analysis (see Table 6.2).

The following Stata codes were used for analysis with Vietnamese youth:

```
• regress depress female v19 income eng ethID otherlangf discrimr
  selfesteem4 famcohesion familism parentclash parentdislike
  parentnointerest caregive if viet1==1 & nomisscuba==1, beta
```

The following Stata codes were used for analysis with Cuban youth:

```
• regress depress female v19 income eng ethID otherlangf discrimr
  selfesteem4 famcohesion familism parentclash parentdislike
  parentnointerest caregive if cuba1==1 & nomisscuba==1, beta
```

Results from these multivariate regression models are presented in Table 6.2 as follows, comparing the effect of independent variables on depression for Vietnamese and Cuban youth.

Table 6.2. Multivariate Regression on Depression Comparing Vietnamese and Cuban Youth

Variables	Vietnamese (n = 149) B (SE)	β	Cuban (n = 578) B (SE)	β
Gender	.57 (.37)	.13	.39 (.15)	.10*
Age	.14 (.19)	.06	−.02 (.10)	−.01
Household Income	−.04 (.07)	.05	−.06 (.03)	−.08*
Acculturation				
US-Born (ref)	–	–	–	–
10 years or more	.11 (.47)	.02	−.10 (.19)	−.02
5 to 9 years	.45 (.58)	.08	−.57 (.26)	−.09*
less than 5 years	1.00 (.83)	.15	–	
English Ability	.001 (.10)	.001	−.04 (.07)	−.03
Ethnic Identification	.02 (.25)	.01	−.01 (.12)	.005
Other Language at Home	−.34 (.26)	−.11	−.21 (.10)	−.08*
Perceived Discrimination	.31 (.10)	.28**	.03 (.04)	.04
Self-Esteem	.01 (.08)	.03	−.14 (.03)	−.19***
Family Cohesion	−.13 (.06)	−.17*	−.11 (.03)	−.18***
Familism	−.02 (.11)	−.02	.03 (.05)	.03
Clash with Parents	.06 (.22)	.02	.06 (.09)	.03
Parents Dislike Me	.82 (.28)	.26**	.10 (.17)	.02
Parents Not Interested	−.32 (.22)	−.14	.16 (.09)	.07
Is a Caregiver	.03 (.50)	.005	.49 (.24)	.08*
R^2	.20		.17	
Adj. R^2	.10		.15	

*$p < .05$, **$p < .01$, *** $p < .001$

Household Composition variables excluded here due to non-significance.

Findings from this initial analysis indicate differences in associations of socioeconomic variables (gender, age, household income) and mediating variables (acculturation, perceived discrimination, self-esteem, family-related variables) with depression among Vietnamese and Cuban youth. Among Cuban youth, those who lived in the United States for five to nine years were less depressed ($\beta = -.09$, $p < .05$), but this effect became nonsignificant at ten or more years. No associations with Years in the United States were observed for Vietnamese, and no associations with English ability were observed for Cuban or Vietnamese subgroups. Higher self-esteem was associated with less depressive symptoms for Cuban ($\beta = -.19$, p < .001) but not for Vietnamese. Higher perceived discrimination was associated with more depression for Vietnamese ($\beta = .28$, p < .01) but not for Cubans.

In terms of family variables, Family Cohesion was associated with less depression for both Vietnamese ($\beta = .13$, p < .05) and Cuban ($\beta = -.18$, p < .001). Reporting that parents dislike me was associated with higher depression for Vietnamese youth ($\beta = .26$, p < .01) but not Cubans. Female gender associated with higher depression for Cubans ($\beta = .10$, p < .05) but not Vietnamese. Results from preliminary analysis suggest that the proposed mediation model for Vietnamese is *structurally different* from the proposed model for Cubans, and the *strength of associations* for exogeneous and mediating variables with the final outcome are different when comparing Cuban and Vietnamese youth.

MEDIATION ANALYSIS USING STRUCTURAL EQUATION MODELING FOR VIETNAMESE YOUTH

For Vietnamese youth, the following mediation model (Figure 6.3) should be tested:

Self-esteem → Perceived Discrimination → Depression

The following is the Stata syntax for SEM analysis specifically for Vietnamese youth:

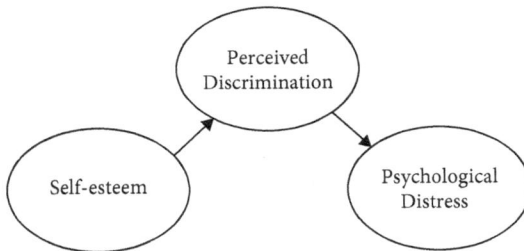

Figure 6.3. Perceived discrimination as mediator model.

- sem (discrimr<-selfesteem4 female v19 income eng famcohesion

  familism parentclash parentdislike parentnointerest ethID

  otherlangf caregive) (depress<-female v19 income eng discrimr

  selfesteem4 famcohesion familism parentclash parentdislike

  parentnointerest ethID otherlangf caregive) if viet1==1 &

  nomisscuba==1, stand

The following is the Stata output for the full model, with (1) depression regressed on all independent variables and (2) discrimination regressed on self-esteem.

```
. sem (discrimr<-selfesteem4) (depress<-female v19 income eng discrimr selfesteem4
famcohesion familism parentclash parentdislike parentnointerest ethID otherlangf
caregive) if viet1==1 & nomi
> sscuba==1, stand

Endogenous variables

Observed:  discrimr depress

Exogenous variables

Observed:  selfesteem4 female v19 income eng famcohesion familism parentclash
parentdislike parentnointerest ethID otherlangf caregive

Fitting target model:

Iteration 0:   log likelihood = -3502.4243
Iteration 1:   log likelihood = -3502.4243

Structural equation model                       Number of obs     =        149
Estimation method  = ml
Log likelihood     = -3502.4243

-------------------------------------------------------------------------------
                  |                 OIM
     Standardized |    Coef.   Std. Err.      z    P>|z|    [95% Conf. Interval]
------------------+------------------------------------------------------------
Structural        |
  discrimr        |
    selfesteem4   | -.133151   .0801133   -1.66   0.097   -.2901701    .0238682
          _cons   | 6.854335   .5074174   13.51   0.000    5.859815    7.848855
------------------+------------------------------------------------------------
  depress         |
       discrimr   | .2579764   .0769449    3.35   0.001    .1071673    .4087856
    selfesteem4   | -.0045685  .0857812   -0.05   0.958   -.1726965    .1635595
         female   |    .1365   .0771507    1.77   0.077   -.0147127    .2877126
            v19   | .0696151   .0787834    0.88   0.377   -.0847976    .2240277
         income   | -.0508315  .0774913   -0.66   0.512   -.2027116    .1010486
            eng   | -.0817747  .0863095   -0.95   0.343   -.2509347    .0873923
     famcohesion  | -.1574605   .078823   -2.00   0.046   -.3119508   -.0029702
       familism   | .0130069   .0837797    0.16   0.877   -.1511983     .177212
     parentclash  |  .022853     .08376    0.27   0.785   -.1413136    .1870197
   parentdislike  | .2617114   .0828069    3.16   0.002    .0994129    .4240098
 parentnointerest | -.1379852  .0856967   -1.61   0.107   -.3059475    .0299772
          ethID   | -.0033587  .0762684   -0.04   0.965    -.152842    .1461246
      otherlangf  | -.0990141  .0774654   -1.28   0.201   -.2508436    .0528154
        caregive  | .0024937   .0764698    0.03   0.974   -.1473844    .1523717
          _cons   | 1.162874   1.730826    0.67   0.502   -2.229483    4.555231
------------------+------------------------------------------------------------
  var(e.discrimr) | .9822708   .0213343                    .9413338    1.024988
   var(e.depress) | .7932427    .060226                    .6835648    .9205184
-------------------------------------------------------------------------------
LR test of model vs. saturated: chi2(12)   =     26.01, Prob > chi2 = 0.0107
```

Results indicate there were many nonsignificant variables, which should be dropped to ensure better goodness-of-fit results.

Stata allows for a number of different methods of estimation. By default, maximum likelihood is used as the estimation procedure for SEM commands. Analysts can change this approach, however, by selecting a different method as an option. These include **ml** (maximum likelihood, which is the default), **mlmv** (maximum likelihood with missing values), or **adf** (asymptotic distribution free function). The option for an asymptotic distribution-free (ADF) method of estimation was chosen with *method(adf)* to better account for nonnormality in the data through justifiable point estimates and standard errors (StataCorp, 2017).

```
. . sem (discrimr<-selfesteem4) (depress<-female discrimr parentdislike) if viet1==1 &
nomisscuba==1, stand method (adf)

Endogenous variables

Observed:  discrimr depress

Exogenous variables

Observed:  selfesteem4 female parentdislike

Fitting baseline model:

Iteration 0:   discrepancy =  .34126551
Iteration 1:   discrepancy =  .15477013
Iteration 2:   discrepancy =  .15477013

Fitting target model:

Iteration 0:   discrepancy =  .01416616
Iteration 1:   discrepancy =  .01360542
Iteration 2:   discrepancy =  .01360538

Structural equation model                    Number of obs     =        149
Estimation method  = adf
Discrepancy        = .01360538

---------------------------------------------------------------------------
    Standardized |    Coef.   Std. Err.     z    P>|z|    [95% Conf. Interval]
-----------------+---------------------------------------------------------
Structural       |
  discrimr       |
   selfesteem4   |  -.1469555  .0726304   -2.02  0.043   -.2893085   -.0046025
         _cons   |   6.959047  .5025963   13.85  0.000    5.973977    7.944118
-----------------+---------------------------------------------------------
  depress        |
      discrimr   |   .2212153  .0711243    3.11  0.002    .0818143    .3606164
        female   |   .1559069  .068452     2.28  0.023    .0217435    .2900703
 parentdislike   |   .2595595  .061223     4.24  0.000    .1395646    .3795544
         _cons   |   .7291637  .4509039    1.62  0.106   -.1545917    1.612919
-----------------+---------------------------------------------------------
  var(e.discrimr)|   .9784041  .0213469                   .9374469    1.021151
  var(e.depress) |   .8558623  .0463093                   .7697448    .9516144
---------------------------------------------------------------------------
Discr. test of model vs. saturated: chi2(3)   =       2.03, Prob > chi2 = 0.5668

. estat gof, stats (all)
```

```
--------------------------------------------------------------------------
Fit statistic           |    Value   Description
------------------------+-------------------------------------------------
Discrepancy             |
          chi2_ms(3)    |    2.027   model vs. saturated
          p > chi2      |    0.567
          chi2_bs(7)    |   23.061   baseline vs. saturated
          p > chi2      |    0.002
------------------------+-------------------------------------------------
Population error        |
                RMSEA   |    0.000   Root mean squared error of approximation
90% CI, lower bound     |    0.000
         upper bound    |    0.119
              pclose    |    0.699   Probability RMSEA <= 0.05
------------------------+-------------------------------------------------
Baseline comparison     |
                  CFI   |    1.000   Comparative fit index
                  TLI   |    1.141   Tucker-Lewis index
------------------------+-------------------------------------------------
Size of residuals       |
                 SRMR   |    0.026   Standardized root mean squared residual
                   CD   |    0.116   Coefficient of determination
--------------------------------------------------------------------------

. estat teffects


Direct effects
--------------------------------------------------------------------------
              |    Coef.    Std. Err.     z     P>|z|   [95% Conf. Interval]
--------------+-----------------------------------------------------------
Structural    |
  discrimr    |
  selfesteem4 |  -.1171107   .0578608   -2.02   0.043   -.2305157   -.0037056
--------------+-----------------------------------------------------------
  depress     |
    discrimr  |   .243123    .0782705    3.11   0.002    .0897155    .3965304
  selfesteem4 |      0      (no path)
      female  |   .6820565   .3116122    2.19   0.029    .0713077   1.292805
  parentdislike| .7959878   .1927559    4.13   0.000    .4181932   1.173782
--------------------------------------------------------------------------


Indirect effects
--------------------------------------------------------------------------
              |    Coef.    Std. Err.     z     P>|z|   [95% Conf. Interval]
--------------+-----------------------------------------------------------
Structural    |
  discrimr    |
  selfesteem4 |      0      (no path)
--------------+-----------------------------------------------------------
  depress     |
    discrimr  |      0      (no path)
  selfesteem4 |  -.0284723   .0147124   -1.94   0.053   -.057308    .0003634
      female  |      0      (no path)
  parentdislike|     0      (no path)
--------------------------------------------------------------------------


Total effects
--------------------------------------------------------------------------
              |    Coef.    Std. Err.     z     P>|z|   [95% Conf. Interval]
--------------+-----------------------------------------------------------
Structural    |
  discrimr    |
  selfesteem4 |  -.1171107   .0578608   -2.02   0.043   -.2305157   -.0037056
--------------+-----------------------------------------------------------
  depress     |
    discrimr  |   .243123    .0782705    3.11   0.002    .0897155    .3965304
  selfesteem4 |  -.0284723   .0147124   -1.94   0.053   -.057308    .0003634
      female  |   .6820565   .3116122    2.19   0.029    .0713077   1.292805
  parentdislike| .7959878   .1927559    4.13   0.000    .4181932   1.173782
--------------------------------------------------------------------------
```

Findings from this mediation analysis indicate that self-esteem had a negative association to perceived discrimination (gamma = −0.12, p < 0.05), and a negative indirect effect for depression. Using the Stata command *estat gof, stats (all)*, the results indicated that based on a LR Likelihood test, the model was not statistically different from the saturated model (χ^2 = 2.027, df = 3, p = .567) indicating a good fit. The RMSEA was < .001, which further supports this interpretation. The indirect effect of self-esteem on depression was negative and approached statistical significance (indirect effect = −0.03, p = 0.05), which suggests that self-esteem can buffer against the negative effect of perceived discrimination on depression for Vietnamese youth.

MEDIATION ANALYSIS USING STRUCTURAL EQUATION MODELING FOR CUBAN YOUTH

For Cuban youth, the following mediation model (Figure 6.4) should be tested:

Perceived Discrimination → Self-Esteem → Depression

The following is the Stata syntax for this analysis:

- ```
  sem (selfesteem4<-discrimr) (depress<-female v19 income eng
  discrimr selfesteem4 famcohesion familism parentclash
  parentdislike parentnointerest ethID otherlangf caregive) if
  cuba1==1 & nomisscuba==1, stand
  ```

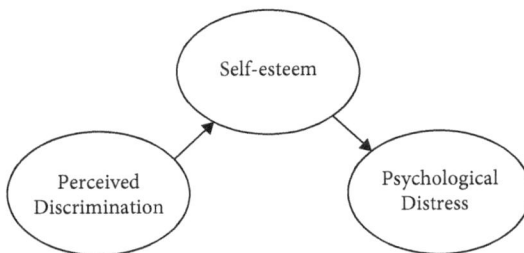

Figure 6.4. Self-Esteem as mediator model.
  ```

The following is the Stata output for this fully saturated model, with (1) depression regressed on all independent variables and (2) self-esteem regressed on discrimination.

```
. sem (selfesteem4<-discrimr) (depress<-female v19 income eng discrimr selfesteem4
famcohesion familism parentclash parentdislike parentnointerest ethID otherlangf
caregive) if cuba1==1 & nomi
> sscuba==1, stand

Endogenous variables

Observed:  selfesteem4 depress

Exogenous variables

Observed:  discrimr female v19 income eng famcohesion familism parentclash
parentdislike parentnointerest ethID otherlangf caregive

Fitting target model:

Iteration 0:   log likelihood = -12821.181
Iteration 1:   log likelihood = -12821.181

Structural equation model                      Number of obs      =        578
Estimation method  = ml
Log likelihood     = -12821.181
```

Standardized	Coef.	OIM Std. Err.	z	P>|z|	[95% Conf. Interval]	
Structural						
selfesteem4						
discrimr	-.0824945	.0412411	-2.00	0.045	-.1633256	-.0016634
_cons	5.602284	.2875522	19.48	0.000	5.038692	6.165876
depress						
selfesteem4	-.1957419	.0417784	-4.69	0.000	-.2776261	-.1138578
discrimr	.0366535	.0396238	0.93	0.355	-.0410078	.1143148
female	.0935881	.0396341	2.36	0.018	.0159067	.1712695
v19	-.015971	.0393607	-0.41	0.685	-.0931166	.0611745
income	-.0779257	.0392214	-1.99	0.047	-.1547981	-.0010532
eng	-.0158507	.0403459	-0.39	0.694	-.0949273	.0632258
famcohesion	-.1832291	.0411076	-4.46	0.000	-.2637985	-.1026596
familism	.0199328	.0402598	0.50	0.621	-.058975	.0988406
parentclash	.0289014	.0413452	0.70	0.485	-.0521337	.1099365
parentdislike	.0231711	.0423257	0.55	0.584	-.0597858	.106128
parentnointerest	.0765609	.0436351	1.75	0.079	-.0089623	.1620841
ethID	-.0045233	.0397201	-0.11	0.909	-.0823732	.0733266
otherlangf	-.0978229	.0395843	-2.47	0.013	-.1754067	-.0202391
caregive	.0779894	.0391646	1.99	0.046	.0012283	.1547505
_cons	4.869585	1.028028	4.74	0.000	2.854687	6.884483
var(e.selfesteem4)	.9931947	.0068043			.9799476	1.006621
var(e.depress)	.8622619	.0236804			.8170763	.9099464

```
LR test of model vs. saturated: chi2(12) =      91.73, Prob > chi2 = 0.0000
```

Similar to before with the Vietnamese model, nonsignificant variables should be dropped to ensure better goodness-of-fit results. Similarly, the option for an asymptotic distribution free (ADF) method of estimation was chosen with *method(adf)* due to nonnormality in the data.

```
. sem (selfesteem4<-discrimr) (depress<-female selfesteem4 famcohesion otherlangf
caregive) if cuba1==1 & nomisscuba==1, stand method (adf)

Endogenous variables

Observed:  selfesteem4 depress

Exogenous variables

Observed:  discrimr female famcohesion otherlangf caregive

Fitting baseline model:

Iteration 0:   discrepancy =  .22778012
Iteration 1:   discrepancy =  .11590772
Iteration 2:   discrepancy =  .11590772

Fitting target model:

Iteration 0:   discrepancy =  .05302503
Iteration 1:   discrepancy =  .04550979
Iteration 2:   discrepancy =  .04549111
Iteration 3:   discrepancy =  .04549111

Structural equation model              Number of obs     =        578
Estimation method  = adf
Discrepancy        = .04549111
```

Standardized	Coef.	Std. Err.	z	P>|z|	[95% Conf. Interval]	
Structural						
selfesteem4						
discrimr	-.0881432	.0388694	-2.27	0.023	-.1643259	-.0119605
_cons	5.966699	.3010485	19.82	0.000	5.376655	6.556743
depress						
selfesteem4	-.1884979	.0454335	-4.15	0.000	-.277546	-.0994498
female	.1146081	.0391178	2.93	0.003	.0379386	.1912776
famcohesion	-.219868	.037105	-5.93	0.000	-.2925925	-.1471435
otherlangf	-.1159545	.0413323	-2.81	0.005	-.1969643	-.0349448
caregive	.0538399	.0463183	1.16	0.245	-.0369422	.1446221
_cons	4.801301	.3148252	15.25	0.000	4.184255	5.418347
var(e.selfesteem4)	.9922308	.0068522			.9788913	1.005752
var(e.depress)	.8814168	.0276781			.8288044	.9373691

```
Discr. test of model vs. saturated: chi2(5)   =    26.29, Prob > chi2 = 0.0001

. estat gof, stats (all)
```

Fit statistic	Value	Description
Discrepancy		
chi2_ms(5)	26.294	model vs. saturated
p > chi2	0.000	
chi2_bs(11)	66.995	baseline vs. saturated
p > chi2	0.000	

```
Population error       |
                 RMSEA |    0.086    Root mean squared error of approximation
 90% CI, lower bound   |    0.055
          upper bound  |    0.119
               pclose  |    0.028    Probability RMSEA <= 0.05
-----------------------+-------------------------------------------------------
Baseline comparison    |
                   CFI |    0.620    Comparative fit index
                   TLI |    0.163    Tucker-Lewis index
-----------------------+-------------------------------------------------------
Size of residuals      |
                  SRMR |    0.053    Standardized root mean squared residual
                    CD |    0.092    Coefficient of determination
-----------------------+-------------------------------------------------------

. estat teffects


Direct effects
------------------------------------------------------------------------------
               |    Coef.   Std. Err.     z    P>|z|    [95% Conf. Interval]
---------------+--------------------------------------------------------------
Structural     |
 selfesteem4   |
     discrimr  |  -.1071191  .0476961   -2.25  0.025   -.2006018   -.0136364
---------------+--------------------------------------------------------------
 depress       |
 selfesteem4   |  -.1440214  .0354761   -4.06  0.000   -.2135532   -.0744895
     discrimr  |      0      (no path)
       female  |   .4289703  .1475484    2.91  0.004    .1397807    .7181599
  famcohesion  |  -.1356875  .0238963   -5.68  0.000   -.1825235   -.0888516
    otherlangf |  -.2884234  .1043996   -2.76  0.006   -.4930428   -.0838041
     caregive  |   .3183802  .2763504    1.15  0.249   -.2232565    .8600169
------------------------------------------------------------------------------


Indirect effects
------------------------------------------------------------------------------
               |    Coef.   Std. Err.     z    P>|z|    [95% Conf. Interval]
---------------+--------------------------------------------------------------
Structural     |
 selfesteem4   |
     discrimr  |      0      (no path)
---------------+--------------------------------------------------------------
 depress       |
 selfesteem4   |      0      (no path)
     discrimr  |   .0154274  .0080951    1.91  0.057   -.0004387    .0312936
       female  |      0      (no path)
  famcohesion  |      0      (no path)
    otherlangf |      0      (no path)
     caregive  |      0      (no path)
------------------------------------------------------------------------------


Total effects
------------------------------------------------------------------------------
               |    Coef.   Std. Err.     z    P>|z|    [95% Conf. Interval]
---------------+--------------------------------------------------------------
Structural     |
 selfesteem4   |
     discrimr  |  -.1071191  .0476961   -2.25  0.025   -.2006018   -.0136364
---------------+--------------------------------------------------------------

 depress       |
 selfesteem4   |  -.1440214  .0354761   -4.06  0.000   -.2135532   -.0744895
     discrimr  |   .0154274  .0080951    1.91  0.057   -.0004387    .0312936
       female  |   .4289703  .1475484    2.91  0.004    .1397807    .7181599
  famcohesion  |  -.1356875  .0238963   -5.68  0.000   -.1825235   -.0888516
    otherlangf |  -.2884234  .1043996   -2.76  0.006   -.4930428   -.0838041
     caregive  |   .3183802  .2763504    1.15  0.249   -.2232565    .8600169
------------------------------------------------------------------------------
```

For the Cuban youth subgroup, it appears that the final trimmed model's overall fit, comparatively, is not as good compared to the model for Vietnamese. Despite having all significant direct effects pathways, results indicated that based on a LR Likelihood test, the model was statistically different from the saturated model ($\chi^2 = 26.294$, df = 5, p < .001) indicating a less than ideal fit. The RMSEA was < 0.10, which further supports that this is a marginally acceptable fit. Perceived discrimination had a negative association with self-esteem (gamma = −0.11, p < 0.05), and a positive indirect relationship on depression (indirect effect = 0.02, p = 0.06). This suggests that higher perceived discrimination is associated with lower self-esteem, which increases depression for Cuban youth.

TESTING THE INVARIANCE OF STRUCTURAL COEFFICIENTS

Although the evidence presented indicated that the two models have different structural forms, it is important to statistically determine (1) whether the mediation models from Figure 6.3 and Figure 6.4 can be applied to Cuban youths and Vietnamese youth and (2) whether the structural coefficients are statistically similar across the two cultural groups. The Stata command option *group* and *ginvariant* can be used to test for invariance of two models. In order to accurately use the *group* command, a categorical variable must be created that includes the relevant cultural groups of interest. In this example, Vietnamese was coded "0" and Cuban was coded "1" and was used with the *group* command. The Stata command *ginvariant* can be used to test structural coefficients (scoef), structural intercepts (scons), measurement coefficients (mcoef), measurement intercepts (mcons), covariances of structural errors (serrvar), covariances of measurement errors (merrvar), covariances between structural and measurement errors (smerrcov), means of exogenous variables (meanex), and covariances of exogenous variables (covex), as well as all of the above (all) or none of the above (none) coefficients (StataCorp, 2017).

For the sake of clarity, a redacted model wherein *perceived discrimination was used as a mediator* was first tested for invariance among Cubans compared to Vietnamese (Figure 6.3). The *ginvariant* option was used for "all" coefficients in this model. The following Stata commands were used for this example:

- sem (discrimr<-selfesteem4) (depress<-discrimr) if nomisscuba==1, group

  (cubavietnew) ginvariant (all) stand method (adf)

- estat gof, stats (all)

- estat teffects

The following is the Stata output for this analysis:

```
. . sem (discrimr<-selfesteem4) (depress<- discrimr) if nomisscuba==1, group
(cubavietnew) ginvariant (all) stand method (adf)

Endogenous variables

Observed:  discrimr depress

Exogenous variables

Observed:  selfesteem4

Fitting baseline model for group 1:

Iteration 0:   discrepancy =  .02124022
Iteration 1:   discrepancy =  .0164868
Iteration 2:   discrepancy =  .0164868

Fitting baseline model for group 2:

Iteration 0:   discrepancy =  .06689913
Iteration 1:   discrepancy =  .04256005
Iteration 2:   discrepancy =  .04256005

Fitting target model:

Iteration 0:   discrepancy =  .08262626
Iteration 1:   discrepancy =  .06454151
Iteration 2:   discrepancy =  .06449513
Iteration 3:   discrepancy =  .06449512

Structural equation model                Number of obs     =        727
Grouping variable  = cubavietnew         Number of groups  =          2
Estimation method  = adf
Discrepancy        = .06449512

( 1)  [depress]0bn.cubavietnew#c.discrimr - [depress]1.cubavietnew#c.discrimr = 0
( 2)  [discrimr]0bn.cubavietnew#c.selfesteem4 - [discrimr]1.cubavietnew#c.selfesteem4
= 0
( 3)  [/]var(e.discrimr)#0bn.cubavietnew - [/]var(e.discrimr)#1.cubavietnew = 0
( 4)  [/]var(e.depress)#0bn.cubavietnew - [/]var(e.depress)#1.cubavietnew = 0
( 5)  [discrimr]0bn.cubavietnew - [discrimr]1.cubavietnew = 0
( 6)  [depress]0bn.cubavietnew - [depress]1.cubavietnew = 0
```

| Group | : Vietnamese | | | Number of obs | = | 149 | |

	Coef.	Std. Err.	z	P>|z|	[95% Conf. Interval]	
Structural						
discrimr						
selfesteem4	-.1198196	.0349518	-3.43	0.001	-.188324	-.0513153
_cons	6.760062	.2353548	28.72	0.000	6.298775	7.221349
depress						
discrimr	.1263925	.0413877	3.05	0.002	.0452741	.207511
_cons	1.870205	.2729122	6.85	0.000	1.335307	2.405103
var(e.discrimr)|	.9856433	.0083758			.9693629	1.002197
var(e.depress)|	.9840249	.0104622			.9637316	1.004746

```
--------------------------------------------------------------------------------
Group                : Cuban                    Number of obs     =      578
--------------------------------------------------------------------------------
                 |    Coef.   Std. Err.     z    P>|z|    [95% Conf. Interval]
-----------------+--------------------------------------------------------------
Structural       |
  discrimr       |
    selfesteem4  |  -.1242912  .0362161   -3.43  0.001   -.1952734   -.053309
         _cons   |  6.756317   .2336288   28.92  0.000    6.298413   7.214221
-----------------+--------------------------------------------------------------
  depress        |
    discrimr     |  .1264615   .0414238    3.05  0.002    .0452722   .2076507
         _cons   |  1.870189   .2729237    6.85  0.000    1.335268   2.405109
-----------------+--------------------------------------------------------------
var(e.discrimr)  |  .9845517   .0090027                   .9670639   1.002356
var(e.depress)   |  .9840075   .010477                    .9636857   1.004758
--------------------------------------------------------------------------------
Discr. test of model vs. saturated: chi2(8)   =    46.89, Prob > chi2 = 0.0000

. estat gof, stats (all)

---------------------------------------------------------------------------
Fit statistic           |   Value   Description
------------------------+--------------------------------------------------
Discrepancy             |
            chi2_ms(8)  |   46.888  model vs. saturated
             p > chi2   |    0.000
            chi2_bs(6)  |   42.927  baseline vs. saturated
             p > chi2   |    0.000
------------------------+--------------------------------------------------
Population error        |
                 RMSEA  |    0.116  Root mean squared error of approximation
  90% CI, lower bound   |    0.085
          upper bound   |    0.149
------------------------+--------------------------------------------------
Baseline comparison     |
                   CFI  |    0.000  Comparative fit index
                   TLI  |    0.210  Tucker-Lewis index
------------------------+--------------------------------------------------
Size of residuals       |
                  SRMR  |    0.123  Standardized root mean squared residual
                    CD  |    0.015  Coefficient of determination
---------------------------------------------------------------------------
Note: pclose is not reported because of multiple groups.

. estat teffects

Direct effects
-------------------------------------------------------------------------------
                 |    Coef.   Std. Err.     z    P>|z|    [95% Conf. Interval]
-----------------+-------------------------------------------------------------
Structural       |
  discrimr       |
    selfesteem4  |
      Vietnamese |  -.0959692  .0282036   -3.40  0.001   -.1512473  -.0406912
          Cuban  |  -.0959692  .0282036   -3.40  0.001   -.1512473  -.0406912
-----------------+-------------------------------------------------------------
  depress        |
    discrimr     |
      Vietnamese |  .1166716   .0387671    3.01  0.003    .0406895   .1926537
```

```
        Cuban |   .1166716    .0387671     3.01   0.003     .0406895    .1926537
  selfesteem4 |
          [*] |          0  (no path)
------------------------------------------------------------------------------
Note: [*] identifies parameter estimates constrained to be equal across groups.


Indirect effects
------------------------------------------------------------------------------
              |     Coef.    Std. Err.      z    P>|z|     [95% Conf. Interval]
--------------+---------------------------------------------------------------
Structural    |
  discrimr    |
  selfesteem4 |
          [*] |          0  (no path)
--------------+---------------------------------------------------------------
depress       |
  discrimr    |
          [*] |          0  (no path)
  selfesteem4 |
   Vietnamese | -.0111969    .0057758    -1.94   0.053    -.0225172    .0001234
        Cuban | -.0111969    .0057758    -1.94   0.053    -.0225172    .0001234
------------------------------------------------------------------------------
Note: [*] identifies parameter estimates constrained to be equal across groups.


Total effects
------------------------------------------------------------------------------
              |     Coef.    Std. Err.      z    P>|z|     [95% Conf. Interval]
--------------+---------------------------------------------------------------
Structural    |
  discrimr    |
  selfesteem4 |
   Vietnamese | -.0959692    .0282036    -3.40   0.001    -.1512473   -.0406912
        Cuban | -.0959692    .0282036    -3.40   0.001    -.1512473   -.0406912
--------------+---------------------------------------------------------------
depress       |
  discrimr    |
   Vietnamese |   .1166716    .0387671     3.01   0.003     .0406895    .1926537
        Cuban |   .1166716    .0387671     3.01   0.003     .0406895    .1926537
  selfesteem4 |
   Vietnamese | -.0111969    .0057758    -1.94   0.053    -.0225172    .0001234
        Cuban | -.0111969    .0057758    -1.94   0.053    -.0225172    .0001234
------------------------------------------------------------------------------
```

The test of invariance constrained the two models to have the same parameters for both the Vietnamese and Cuban models. In this example, six structural invariance hypotheses were tested for the *discrimination as mediator model*: (1) the structural coefficients for discrimination as a predictor of self-esteem are statistically the same for Vietnamese compared to Cuban; (2) the structural intercepts for discrimination as a predictor of self-esteem are statistically the same for Vietnamese compared to Cuban; (3) the structural coefficients for self-esteem as a predictor of depression are statistically the same for Vietnamese compared to Cuban; (4) the structural intercepts for self-esteem as a predictor of depression are statistically the same for Vietnamese compared to Cuban; (5) the covariance of structural errors for discrimination are statistically the same for Vietnamese compared to Cuban; and (6) the covariance of structural errors for depression are statistically the same for Vietnamese compared to Cuban. The χ^2 test of invariance indicated a poor fit, which indicated that two models were statistically significantly different from one another ($\chi^2 = 46.89$, df = 8, p < 0.0001).

A similar redacted model where *self-esteem was used as a mediator* (Figure 6.4) was tested for invariance among Cubans compared to Vietnamese and is presented below. The following Stata commands were used for this example:

- sem (selfesteem4<-discrimr) (depress<-selfesteem4) if nomisscuba==1, group

  (cubavietnew) ginvariant (all) stand method (adf)

- estat gof, stats (all)

- estat teffects

The following is the Stata output for this analysis:

```
. sem (selfesteem4<-discrimr) (depress<-selfesteem4) if nomisscuba==1, group
(cubavietnew) ginvariant (all) stand method (adf)

Endogenous variables

Observed:  selfesteem4 depress

Exogenous variables

Observed:  discrimr

Fitting baseline model for group 1:

Iteration 0:   discrepancy =  .02124022
Iteration 1:   discrepancy =   .0164868
Iteration 2:   discrepancy =   .0164868

Fitting baseline model for group 2:

Iteration 0:   discrepancy =  .06689913
Iteration 1:   discrepancy =  .04256005
Iteration 2:   discrepancy =  .04256005

Fitting target model:

Iteration 0:   discrepancy =  .13031375
Iteration 1:   discrepancy =  .08606636
Iteration 2:   discrepancy =   .0858349
Iteration 3:   discrepancy =  .08583481

Structural equation model              Number of obs       =        727
Grouping variable   = cubavietnew      Number of groups    =          2
Estimation method   = adf
Discrepancy         = .08583481

 ( 1)  [depress]0bn.cubavietnew#c.selfesteem4 - [depress]1.cubavietnew#c.selfesteem4 =
0
 ( 2)  [selfesteem4]0bn.cubavietnew#c.discrimr - [selfesteem4]1.cubavietnew#c.discrimr
= 0
 ( 3)  [/]var(e.selfesteem4)#0bn.cubavietnew - [/]var(e.selfesteem4)#1.cubavietnew = 0
 ( 4)  [/]var(e.depress)#0bn.cubavietnew - [/]var(e.depress)#1.cubavietnew = 0
 ( 5)  [selfesteem4]0bn.cubavietnew - [selfesteem4]1.cubavietnew = 0
 ( 6)  [depress]0bn.cubavietnew - [depress]1.cubavietnew = 0

Group          : Vietnamese        Number of obs       =        149
```

	Coef.	Std. Err.	z	P>|z|	[95% Conf. Interval]
Structural						
selfesteem4						
discrimr	-.1159741	.0339796	-3.41	0.001	-.1825729	-.0493753
_cons	5.646105	.2520067	22.40	0.000	5.152181	6.14003

```
depress         |
     selfesteem4 |  -.2295628    .0409477    -5.61   0.000    -.3098188   -.1493069
           _cons |   3.692498    .1892222    19.51   0.000     3.321629    4.063367
-----------------+---------------------------------------------------------------
  var(e.selfesteem4)|    .98655    .0078815                     .9712228    1.002119
   var(e.depress)|   .9473009    .0188001                     .9111608    .9848745
-----------------+---------------------------------------------------------------

Group                : Cuban                    Number of obs      =       578

-----------------------------------------------------------------------------------
                   |     Coef.    Std. Err.      z    P>|z|    [95% Conf. Interval]
-------------------+---------------------------------------------------------------
Structural         |
  selfesteem4      |
        discrimr   |  -.1168352    .034225    -3.41   0.001    -.1839149   -.0497556
           _cons   |   5.645532   .2517107    22.43   0.000     5.152188    6.138876
-------------------+---------------------------------------------------------------
  depress          |
     selfesteem4   |  -.2295849   .0409533    -5.61   0.000    -.3098519   -.1493179
           _cons   |   3.692478   .1892132    19.51   0.000     3.321627    4.06333
-------------------+---------------------------------------------------------------
  var(e.selfesteem4)|  .9863495   .0079974                     .9707989    1.002149
     var(e.depress)|   .9472908   .0188045                     .9111424    .9848733
-------------------+---------------------------------------------------------------
Discr. test of model vs. saturated: chi2(8)   =    62.40, Prob > chi2 = 0.0000

.
. estat gof, stats (all)

---------------------------------------------------------------------------
Fit statistic       |    Value   Description
--------------------+------------------------------------------------------
Discrepancy         |
        chi2_ms(8)  |   62.402   model vs. saturated
          p > chi2  |    0.000
        chi2_bs(6)  |   42.927   baseline vs. saturated
          p > chi2  |    0.000
--------------------+------------------------------------------------------
Population error    |
             RMSEA  |    0.137   Root mean squared error of approximation
 90% CI, lower bound|    0.106
         upper bound|    0.169
--------------------+------------------------------------------------------
Baseline comparison |
                CFI |    0.000   Comparative fit index
                TLI |   -0.105   Tucker-Lewis index
--------------------+------------------------------------------------------
Size of residuals   |
               SRMR |    0.100   Standardized root mean squared residual
                 CD |    0.014   Coefficient of determination
---------------------------------------------------------------------------
Note: pclose is not reported because of multiple groups.

.
. estat teffects
```

```
Direct effects
------------------------------------------------------------------------------
              |     Coef.   Std. Err.      z     P>|z|     [95% Conf. Interval]
--------------+---------------------------------------------------------------
Structural    |
 selfesteem4  |
    discrimr  |
  Vietnamese  |  -.1521929   .0449244    -3.39   0.001    -.240243    -.0641428
       Cuban  |  -.1521929   .0449244    -3.39   0.001    -.240243    -.0641428
--------------+---------------------------------------------------------------
depress       |
 selfesteem4  |
  Vietnamese  |  -.1705783    .031022    -5.50   0.000   -.2313804    -.1097763
       Cuban  |  -.1705783    .031022    -5.50   0.000   -.2313804    -.1097763
    discrimr  |
         [*]  |         0   (no path)
------------------------------------------------------------------------------
Note: [*] identifies parameter estimates constrained to be equal across groups.


Indirect effects
------------------------------------------------------------------------------
              |     Coef.   Std. Err.      z     P>|z|     [95% Conf. Interval]
--------------+---------------------------------------------------------------
Structural    |
 selfesteem4  |
    discrimr  |
         [*]  |         0   (no path)
--------------+---------------------------------------------------------------
depress       |
 selfesteem4  |
         [*]  |         0   (no path)
    discrimr  |
  Vietnamese  |   .0259608   .0097375     2.67   0.008    .0068758     .0450459
       Cuban  |   .0259608   .0097375     2.67   0.008    .0068758     .0450459
------------------------------------------------------------------------------
Note: [*] identifies parameter estimates constrained to be equal across groups.


Total effects
------------------------------------------------------------------------------
              |     Coef.   Std. Err.      z     P>|z|     [95% Conf. Interval]
--------------+---------------------------------------------------------------
Structural    |
 selfesteem4  |
    discrimr  |
  Vietnamese  |  -.1521929   .0449244    -3.39   0.001    -.240243    -.0641428
       Cuban  |  -.1521929   .0449244    -3.39   0.001    -.240243    -.0641428
--------------+---------------------------------------------------------------
depress       |
 selfesteem4  |
  Vietnamese  |  -.1705783    .031022    -5.50   0.000   -.2313804    -.1097763
       Cuban  |  -.1705783    .031022    -5.50   0.000   -.2313804    -.1097763
    discrimr  |
  Vietnamese  |   .0259608   .0097375     2.67   0.008    .0068758     .0450459
       Cuban  |   .0259608   .0097375     2.67   0.008    .0068758     .0450459
------------------------------------------------------------------------------
```

Similar to the previous analysis, the test of invariance constrained the two models to have the same parameters for both the Vietnamese and Cuban models. In this example, six structural invariance hypotheses were tested for the *self-esteem as mediator model*: (1) the structural coefficients for self-esteem as a predictor of discrimination are statistically the same for Vietnamese compared to Cubans; (2) the structural intercepts for self-esteem as a predictor of discrimination are statistically the same for Vietnamese compared to Cubans; (3) the structural coefficients for discrimination as a predictor of depression are statistically the same for Vietnamese compared to Cubans; (4) the structural intercepts for discrimination as a predictor of depression are statistically the same for Vietnamese compared to Cubans; (5) the covariance of structural errors for self-esteem are statistically the same for Vietnamese compared to Cubans; and (6) the covariance of structural errors for depression are statistically the same for Vietnamese compared to Cubans. The χ^2 test of invariance indicated a poor fit, which indicated that two models were statistically significantly different from one another ($\chi^2 = 62.40$, df = 8, p < 0.0001).

INTERPRETATION OF RESULTS

Once controlling for sociodemographics, family, and other relevant variables, the direct relationship of self-esteem to depression was observed for Cuban but not Vietnamese youth. Perceived discrimination had a direct relationship to depression for Vietnamese youth but not Cuban youth. Cuban youth have a more established Cuban American identity, whereas Vietnamese youth were a more recent refugee group in the year that the data was collected (1995). In addition, Vietnamese youth as a cultural group were less assimilated overall compared to Cubans, as suggested by English ability, years in the United States, and overall income. Acculturation variables such as English ability, other language spoken at home, and ethnic identification were nonsignificant with depression, but significant for perceived discrimination and self-esteem. It is likely that immigrant status (years in the United States), usually protective against poor mental health, diminishes for Cuban youth the longer they live in the United States. Family was important for both groups, though the mechanisms in which they are protective against depression seemed to differ based on culture.

Discrimination had a negative effect for Vietnamese youth, and this may be explained due to political circumstances and the reception of this group after an unpopular war in the 1970s during an economic recession. As persons who had escaped a communist regime, Cubans were mostly welcomed as a group to the United States, and their arrival in the late 1950s to 1960s coincided with a period of economic prosperity in the united States. Based on this cross-cultural analysis, it can be determined that the mediating relationships of acculturation, perceived discrimination, and self-esteem are structurally different when comparing Vietnamese and Cuban youth. In this example, the direct relationships on psychological distress would include: (1) perceived discrimination → psychological distress for Vietnamese youth, and (2) social support → psychological distress for Cuban youth. Indirect relationships in this example would include (1) social support → perceived discrimination → psychological distress for Vietnamese youth and (2) perceived discrimination → social support → psychological distress for Cuban youth. Because the mediating relationships are structurally different for the two groups, it is not useful to compare strength of associations in pathways.

CONCLUSION

Structural equation modeling (SEM) is a powerful class of techniques that can elucidate the structural pathways, described as direct, indirect, and total effects of variables with outcomes of interest. In cross-cultural analysis, these techniques can be used to examine the invariance of groups, in regard to predictors of interest for health and social outcomes. In this chapter, we discussed the conceptual framework for SEM as it related to cross-cultural data analysis using a real-world example from population data. We demonstrated the procedures that are used in Stata to examine a latent variable model, determine statistical significance of exogenous and mediator variables with an outcome of interest, and generate and interpret relevant goodness-of-fit statistics and direct, indirect, and total effects. We concluded by presenting procedures to test for structural invariance of two mediator models using an example for comparing Vietnamese and Cuban youth. It is our hope that these hands-on examples can be useful for cross-cultural researchers who wish to apply these principles and techniques to their own cross-cultural analysis and research.

REFERENCES

Baron, R. M., & Kenny, D. A. (1986). The moderator–mediator variable distinction in social psychological research: Conceptual, strategic, and statistical considerations. *Journal of Personality and Social Psychology, 51*(6), 1173–1182. https://doi.org/10.1037/0022-3514.51.6.1173

Bowen, N., & Guo, S. (2012). *Structural Equation Modeling.* Oxford University Press, New York.

Chan, K. (2020). The association of acculturation with overt and covert perceived discrimination for older Asian Americans. *Social Work Research, 44*(1), 59–71. https://doi.org/10.1093/swr/svz023

Chan, K., Tran, T. V., & Nguyen, T. N. (2012). Cross-cultural equivalence of a measure of perceived discrimination between Chinese and Vietnamese Americans. *Journal of Ethnic and Cultural Diversity in Social Work, 21*(1), 20–36. https://doi.org/10.1080/15313204.2011.647348

Harrington, D. (2008). *Confirmatory Factor Analysis.* Oxford University Press, New York.

Orme, J. & Combs-Orme, T. (2009). *Multiple Regression with Discrete Dependent Variables.* Oxford University Press, New York.

Randolph, K. & Myers, L. (2013). *Basic Statistics in Multivariate Analysis.* Oxford University Press, New York.

StataCorp. (2017). *Stata Statistical Software: Release 15.* College Station, TX: StataCorp.

StataCorp. (2017). *Stata Structural Equation Modeling Reference Manual: Release 15.* Stata Press Publication. College Station, TX: StataCorp.

Tran, T. V., Nguyen, T., & Chan, K. T. (2017). *Developing cross-cultural measurement for social work research and evaluation* (2nd ed.). New York: Oxford University Press.

7

Applied Hierarchical Linear Modeling for Cross-Cultural Comparison

We will explain and demonstrate the application of hierarchical linear modeling (HLM) in cross-cultural research. This method of analysis has not been sufficiently explored in social work research, and it can be a highly useful and appropriate statistical approach for making cross-cultural comparisons.

HIERARCHICAL LINEAR MODELING IN CROSS-CULTURAL RESEARCH

Hierarchical linear modeling (HLM), also known as multilevel modeling or mixed modeling, is a "class of statistical models developed (a) to analyze 'nested' or clustered data; (b) to address multilevel influences on outcomes; and (c) to seek important predictors of change trajectories in a longitudinal study" (Chan, 2020; Guo, 2013, p. 4). Although it has

Applied Cross-Cultural Data Analysis for Social Work. Thanh V. Tran and Keith T. Chan,
Oxford University Press. © Oxford University Press 2021. DOI: 10.1093/oso/9780190888510.003.0007

not been widely used in social work research, HLM or mixed modeling has been applied extensively in education research and demographic analysis. The techniques of HLM are rooted in understanding meaningful grouping structures, such as persons who belong to the same geographic neighborhood where there is a shared experience based on location. For example, immigrants who live in a specific ethnic enclave will have shared experiences in their interactions with others who have similar language, culture, or practices, which will have an influence on their sense of social connectedness. Past research has examined the "neighborhood effects" (Diez Roux, 2001) that contribute to racial disparities in health outcomes such as low birthweight due to residential segregation (Grady, 2006) and maternal and infant health (Cubbin et al., 2008). HLM as a class of statistical models is also useful in education research to understand classroom effects wherein students may have a shared experience that affects the acquisition of learning (Kaya & Rice, 2010). A hypothetical example is the shared learning that can happen in a cohort of PhD students of color in a social work program, which can take place year after year.

RATIONALE FOR HIERARCHICAL LINEAR MODELING IN CROSS-CULTURAL RESEARCH

Multilevel analysis has an intuitive fit to cross-cultural research because this approach takes into account the heterogeneity of different cultural populations. For social science researchers, this can be understood as the *context* under which the likelihood of outcomes such as depression can be influenced by social and environmental stressors (Luke, 2004). The variance of the error term is allowed to vary, but it is specific to the grouping structure. For example, each ethnic enclave may have its own variation in social connectedness. Similarly, each cohort of PhD social work students will have its own unique group dynamic, which can contribute to learning. HLM is different from other approaches that allow error variance to be completely random (such as using *robust* estimations in OLS regression), which does not take into account the specific variations within groups. In cross-cultural research, wherein grouping is the central focus of any analysis, HLM can be a useful approach in examining the importance of heterogeneity in cultural groups of interest.

HIERARCHICAL LINEAR MODELING AS A METHOD OF ANALYSIS

Hierarchical linear modeling as a method of analysis can be used to examine data structures in which persons are nested in *groups* or *over multiple observations*. The analytical motivation for HLM or mixed modeling is the same as panel analysis in terms of controlling for *error variance*, or σ^2 (sigma square), where there are multiple waves of data that were collected for the same people. HLM is used for controlling for the unique variance of specific groups, when making comparisons from one group to another. Analytic techniques in HLM or mixed modeling were designed to examine relationships from independent variables to a dependent variable while taking into account the interaction of group-level effects. Similar to panel analysis, HLM is best used for analysis where there is a sizeable n, or sample size, and a small number of groups. Using the earlier example on ethnic enclaves, HLM can best be applied to data in cases where a limited number of ethnic enclaves are being considered and a sizeable number of persons are being sampled in each enclave.

HLM when used with a continuous outcome or dependent variable can be considered as an extension of ordinary least squares (OLS) linear regression. In OLS regression, the variance of the error is *finite*. It means the following:

- Var (ε) = σ^2
- Assumption of i.i.d. (identically and independently distributed errors), or homoscedasticity
- Although we don't know what ε and σ^2 are, we assume that the variance of residuals from our estimations is held constant for all values.

In HLM, we assume that the error variance within the group (Race, Schools, Classrooms, Job Categories) is the same. This makes sense because we expect the variation of outcomes to be similar for certain groups of interest. The heteroscedasticity, or variance in error, is accounted for by the grouping structure where individual-level error variance is the same for individuals within a group. The group-level variance is accounted for separately, and can be understood as the variation of any given group from the group average. Due to the nature of estimations in HLM, the analysis uses *Restricted Maximum Likelihood (REML)* to arrive at estimates for specified models (Raudenbush, 2004). In Stata, there is an additional step using a gradient-based method (Newton-Raphson) to generate more robust and efficient estimations (StataCorp, 2017).

ESTIMATIONS IN HIERARCHICAL LINEAR MODELING FOR CROSS-CULTURAL RESEARCH

When building HLM models in cross-cultural research, the first step is to examine whether the outcome of interest varies across the grouping structure in a *null model*, which for all intents and purposes is analogous to the F-ANOVA (Luke, 2004).

- Building a null model (Full model is analogous to F-ANOVA)
  Level 1: $Y_{ij} = \beta_{0j} + r_{ij}$
  Level 2: $\beta_{0j} = \gamma_{00} + \upsilon_{0j}$
  $r_{ij} \sim N\,(0,\,\sigma^2)$
  $\upsilon_{0j} \sim N\,(0,\,\tau_{00})$

The above indicate that the outcome variable, Y_{ij}, can be expressed as the average for each group, β_{0j}, added to r_{ij}, which represents the variation of each person from that group. The average of each group, β_{0j}, is, in turn, estimated by the average of all groups, γ_{00}, added to υ_{0j}, which represents the variation of each group from the average of all other groups.

- $ICC = \tau_{00} / (\tau_{00} + \sigma^2)$

The ICC (Intraclass Correlation Coefficient) is the proportion of the variability explained by the grouping structure, and indicates whether

HLM is justified. In cross-cultural analysis, this is an important step in determining whether the grouping structure that is specified is meaningful for analysis using HLM techniques. If the grouping structure does not yield statistically significant effects, or if the ICC is very low, HLM would not be justified for use in examining cross-cultural differences among groups of interest.

The following are commands used in Stata for HLM for mixed modeling analysis:

- xtset *group*
- xtreg *dv iv1 iv2 iv3 iv4 . . .*
- xtlogit *dv iv1 iv2 iv3 iv4 . . .*

EXAMPLE FROM THE CENTER FOR ECONOMIC OPPORTUNITY DATA FROM NEW YORK CITY

The following example is from the 2014 Center for Economic Opportunity (CEO), which is a subset of the American Community Survey based on New York City. The sample included 52,608 respondents (18 years of age and older) of White, African American, Latino, or Asian descent. New York City was chosen for this example because of its high population density and important geographical differences that impact the effect of race and disability on poverty across each of its five boroughs (Manhattan, Brooklyn, Queens, Bronx, and Staten Island). Immigrant groups such as Asians and Latinos represent both extremes of socioeconomic and health indices. Asians in particular are the most economically divided race group in the United States (Pew Research Center, 2018) and have the highest poverty rate in New York City (Mayor's Office of Operations, The City of New York, 2017).

This example analysis examined: (1) racial/ethnic differences in poverty for New York City and (2) when controlling for sociodemographics, disability, and foreign-born status, do these differences persist? In addition, the HLM portion of the analysis examined (3) whether the effects are fixed, or vary according to geography (borough).

DEPENDENT VARIABLE

The dependent variable in this analysis is poverty, which was scaled for use in New York City based on cost of living specifically associated with higher rent and property costs.

INDEPENDENT VARIABLES

The independent variables of interest were race and disability. Race was captured with non-Hispanic White as the reference group, and African American, Asian, and non-White Hispanic as cultural groups of interest. Disability was measured by the Washington Measure of Functional Disability, which is commonly used in population health surveys. It is captured using six questions, which ask if a respondent has difficulty with the following: (1) seeing, (2) hearing, (3) dressing or bathing, (4) remembering, (5) performing physical activities, and (6) going out and running errands. A response of "Yes" to one of these questions was coded as "1," and a response of "No" to all questions was coded as "0."

Other demographic variables included gender, age categories, being a college graduate, marital status, and foreign-born status, which were used as covariates in the analysis.

Residence in borough was used both as an independent variable and as a group structure. Manhattan was used as the reference group, to compare with Brooklyn, Bronx, Queens, and Staten Island. Multivariate logistic regression analysis using stratified survey weights was conducted for this example. The first example did not account for borough-level differences using HLM. The second example used HLM techniques to illustrate differences in results when conducting cross-cultural analysis.

DESCRIPTIVE RESULTS

Initial analysis indicated that the highest rates of poverty were among Asians (27.2%), followed by Hispanics (24.0%), Blacks (19.3%), and Whites (14.0%), and this was statistically significant ($p < 0.001$). Highest rates of disability were found among Hispanics (27.2%), then Blacks (23.3%), Whites (22.4%), and Asians (16.3%).

In terms of borough of residence, more Whites (28.7%) and Blacks (43%) live in Brooklyn, while Asians tended to live in Queens (51.4%), and Hispanics live in the Bronx (28.7%). The following Stata code was used to produce a preliminary model examining the effect of race and disability on poverty.

- ```
  svy: logit ceo_poverty i.ethdum i.age4cat disabledum fgender
  ```

  ```
  ib1.married ib1.collegegradplus ib3.boro foreign if nomissm1==1,
  ```

  ```
  or
  ```

The following is the output from Stata:

```
. svy, subpop(region): logit ceo_poverty i.ethdum i.age4cat disabledum fgender
ib1.married ib1.collegegradplus ib3.boro foreign if nomissm1==1, or
(running logit on estimation sample)

SDR replications (80)
----+--- 1 ---+--- 2 ---+--- 3 ---+--- 4 ---+--- 5
..................................................   50
............................

Survey: Logistic regression           Number of obs     =      52,608
                                       Population size    =   6,018,512
                                       Subpop. no. obs    =      52,608
                                       Subpop. size       =   6,018,512
                                       Replications       =          80
                                       Wald chi2(14)      =     2605.47
                                       Prob > chi2        =      0.0000
```

		SDR				
ceo_poverty	Odds Ratio	Std. Err.	z	P>|z|	[95% Conf. Interval]	
ethdum						
black	.9908827	.0563288	-0.16	0.872	.8864085	1.107671
asian	1.780752	.1169019	8.79	0.000	1.565757	2.025269
hispanic	1.085091	.0610545	1.45	0.147	.9717892	1.211604
age4cat						
35 to 54	.8042615	.0284802	-6.15	0.000	.7503344	.8620643
55 and older	.7543961	.0293686	-7.24	0.000	.6989758	.8142105
disabledum	1.617461	.0618187	12.58	0.000	1.500725	1.743277
fgender	1.12228	.0270134	4.79	0.000	1.070565	1.176495
0.married	1.628202	.0653496	12.15	0.000	1.505027	1.761457
0.collegegradplus	2.591515	.1022719	24.13	0.000	2.398622	2.79992
boro						
Bronx	1.444114	.110651	4.80	0.000	1.242741	1.678117
Brooklyn	1.326273	.0925836	4.05	0.000	1.156679	1.520734
Queens	1.070383	.0753973	0.97	0.334	.9323546	1.228847
Staten Island	1.123959	.1457832	0.90	0.368	.8716561	1.449291
foreign	1.441604	.0529618	9.96	0.000	1.34145	1.549236
_cons	.0587909	.0040651	-40.98	0.000	.0513398	.0673234

```
Note: _cons estimates baseline odds.
.
```

The results can be formatted as shown in Table 7.1.
```

Table 7.1. Logistic Regression Results of Race & Disability on Poverty (n = 52,608)

Variables	Odds Ratio (SE)	95% Confidence Interval
White (Ref)	1.00	–
Black, non-Hispanic	0.99 (0.06)	0.89; 1.11
Asian, non-Hispanic	1.78*** (0.12)	1.56; 2.02
Hispanic	1.09 (0.06)	0.97; 1.21
Age Categories		
18 to 34 (Ref)	1.00	–
35 to 54	0.80*** (0.03)	0.75; 0.86
55 and older	0.75*** (0.03)	0.70; 0.82
Have 1 or more disability	1.62*** (0.06)	1.50; 1.74
Female Gender	1.12*** (0.03)	1.07; 1.17
Not Married	1.63*** (0.07)	1.51; 1.76
Not College Grad	2.59*** (0.10)	2.40; 2.80
Borough		
Manhattan (Ref)	1.00	–
Bronx	1.44*** (0.11)	1.24; 1.68
Brooklyn	1.33*** (0.09)	1.16; 1.52
Queens	1.07 (0.08)	0.93, 1.23
Staten Island	1.12 (0.15)	0.87; 1.45
Foreign-born	1.44 *** (0.05)	1.34; 1.55

*p < 0.05, **p < 0.01, ***p < 0.001

RESULTS FROM LOGISTIC REGRESSION MODEL

Findings from this initial logistic regression analysis suggested that Asians in New York City have 78% higher odds for being in poverty, compared to Whites. Once controlling for all variables in the analysis, no other race group was different in regard to odds for poverty. Being female, being unmarried, having a disability, and lacking a college degree resulted in higher odds for being in poverty. Older age, counterintuitively, was associated with lower odds for being in poverty in this analysis. Living in the Bronx and Brooklyn had higher odds for being in poverty. Being foreign-born was associated with 44% higher odds for being in poverty in New York City.

To account for borough-level effects, these results were reexamined using HLM and the following Stata code.

- xtset boro

- xtlogit ceo_poverty i.ethdum i.age4cat disabledum fgender

  ib1.married ib1.collegegradplus ib3.boro foreign if nomissm1==1,

  or

The following is the output from Stata:

```
.
. xtlogit ceo_poverty i.ethdum i.age4cat disabledum fgender ib1.married
ib1.collegegradplus ib3.boro foreign if nomissm1==1, or

Fitting comparison model:

Iteration 0:    log likelihood = -25359.558
Iteration 1:    log likelihood = -23984.711
Iteration 2:    log likelihood = -23926.179
Iteration 3:    log likelihood = -23925.988
Iteration 4:    log likelihood = -23925.988

Fitting full model:

tau =  0.0     log likelihood = -23925.988
tau =  0.1     log likelihood = -24010.636

Iteration 0:    log likelihood = -23938.269
Iteration 1:    log likelihood = -23928.527    (not concave)
Iteration 2:    log likelihood = -23927.043    (not concave)
Iteration 3:    log likelihood = -23926.685    (not concave)
Iteration 4:    log likelihood = -23926.381    (not concave)
Iteration 5:    log likelihood = -23926.306    (not concave)
Iteration 6:    log likelihood = -23926.267    (not concave)
Iteration 7:    log likelihood = -23926.254    (not concave)
Iteration 8:    log likelihood = -23926.244    (not concave)
Iteration 9:    log likelihood = -23926.235    (not concave)
Iteration 10:   log likelihood = -23926.227    (not concave)
Iteration 11:   log likelihood =  -23926.22    (not concave)
Iteration 12:   log likelihood = -23926.213    (not concave)
Iteration 13:   log likelihood = -23926.206    (not concave)
Iteration 14:   log likelihood =   -23926.2    (not concave)
Iteration 15:   log likelihood = -23926.194    (not concave)
Iteration 16:   log likelihood = -23926.188    (not concave)
Iteration 17:   log likelihood = -23926.183    (not concave)
Iteration 18:   log likelihood = -23926.177    (not concave)
Iteration 19:   log likelihood = -23926.172    (not concave)
Iteration 20:   log likelihood = -23926.167    (not concave)
Iteration 21:   log likelihood = -23926.162    (not concave)
Iteration 22:   log likelihood = -23926.158    (not concave)
Iteration 23:   log likelihood = -23926.153    (not concave)
Iteration 24:   log likelihood = -23926.149    (not concave)
Iteration 25:   log likelihood = -23926.144    (not concave)
Iteration 26:   log likelihood =  -23926.14    (not concave)
Iteration 27:   log likelihood = -23926.136    (not concave)
Iteration 28:   log likelihood = -23926.132    (not concave)
Iteration 29:   log likelihood = -23926.128    (not concave)
Iteration 30:   log likelihood = -23926.124    (not concave)
Iteration 31:   log likelihood = -23926.121    (not concave)
Iteration 32:   log likelihood = -23926.117
Iteration 33:   log likelihood = -23925.988
Iteration 34:   log likelihood = -23925.988
```

```
Random-effects logistic regression              Number of obs      =      52,608
Group variable: boro                            Number of groups   =           5

Random effects u_i ~ Gaussian                   Obs per group:
                                                             min =       3,076
                                                             avg =    10,521.6
                                                             max =      18,359

Integration method: mvaghermite                 Integration pts.   =          12

                                                Wald chi2(14)      =     2523.33
Log likelihood   = -23925.988                   Prob > chi2        =      0.0000

------------------------------------------------------------------------------------
     ceo_poverty | Odds Ratio   Std. Err.       z    P>|z|     [95% Conf. Interval]
-----------------+------------------------------------------------------------------
          ethdum |
           black |   .9249633   .0313616     -2.30   0.021     .8654936    .9885193
           asian |   1.544208   .0566093     11.85   0.000     1.437148    1.659243
        hispanic |   1.082228    .036228      2.36   0.018     1.013502    1.155615
                 |
         age4cat |
        35 to 54 |    .79964     .023942      -7.47  0.000     .7540649    .8479697
     55 and older |   .727017    .0227465    -10.19  0.000     .6837741    .7729946
                 |
       disabledum |   1.576934   .0535965     13.40  0.000     1.475309    1.685559
          fgender |   1.150141   .0269581      5.97  0.000     1.098499    1.20421
        0.married |   1.683725   .0439276     19.97  0.000     1.599792    1.77206
 0.collegegradplus |  2.496423   .0739831     30.87  0.000     2.35555     2.645721
                 |
            boro |
           Bronx |   1.344341   .0616123      6.46  0.000     1.228848    1.470688
        Brooklyn |   1.197079   .0484258      4.45  0.000     1.105832    1.295856
          Queens |   .9774678   .0405607     -0.55  0.583     .9011172    1.060288
   Staten Island |   .9687344   .0612985     -0.50  0.616     .855743     1.096645
                 |
         foreign |   1.470156   .0380676     14.88  0.000     1.397407    1.546693
           _cons |   .0631482   .0031247    -55.82  0.000     .0573116    .0695793
-----------------+------------------------------------------------------------------
        /lnsig2u |  -31.52712   114003.9                     -223475      223411.9
-----------------+------------------------------------------------------------------
         sigma_u |   1.43e-07   .0081257                            0            .
             rho |   6.18e-15   7.04e-10                            0            .
------------------------------------------------------------------------------------
Note: Estimates are transformed only in the first equation.
Note: _cons estimates baseline odds (conditional on zero random effects).
```

Results from HLM can be reformatted as shown in Table 7.2.

RESULTS FROM LOGISTIC REGRESSION MODEL USING HIERARCHICAL LINEAR MODELING

Once controlling for borough-level effects, Hispanic ethnicity was associated with higher odds for poverty, which was a different result compared to the previous analysis. Having a disability was associated with over 58% higher odds for being in poverty after controlling for borough effects. The associations for other sociodemographic variables (gender, marital status, lack of a college degree) with poverty were similar to the previous analysis.

Table 7.2. Logistic Regression Results of Race, Poverty on Poverty Using HLM (n = 52,608)

Variables	Odds Ratio (SE)	95% Confidence Interval
White (Ref)	1.00	–
Black, non-Hispanic	0.92* (0.03)	0.87; 0.99
Asian, non-Hispanic	1.54*** (0.03)	1.44; 1.66
Hispanic	1.08** (0.04)	1.18; 1.48
Age Categories		
18 to 34 (Ref)	1.00	
35 to 54	0.80*** (0.02)	0.75; 0.85
55 and older	0.73*** (0.02)	0.68; 0.77
Have 1 or more disability	1.58*** (0.05)	1.48; 1.69
Female Gender	1.15*** (0.03)	1.10; 1.20
Not Married	1.68*** (0.04)	1.60; 1.77
Not College Grad	2.50*** (0.07)	2.36; 2.65
Borough		
Manhattan (Ref)	1.00	–
Bronx	1.34*** (0.06)	1.23; 1.47
Brooklyn	1.20*** (0.05)	1.11; 1.30
Queens	0.98 (0.04)	0.90; 1.06
Staten Island	0.97 (0.06)	0.86; 1.10
Foreign-born	1.47*** (0.04)	1.40; 1.55

$*p < 0.05$, $**p < 0.01$, $***p < 0.001$

Asians and Hispanics have the highest prevalence rates of poverty in New York City, and once controlling for borough-level effects, both Asian and Hispanic ethnicity were statistically significant.

TESTING FOR INVARIANCE ACROSS GROUPS

Testing for the invariance of groups in this analysis can be performed with the *test* command, which was described earlier in Chapter 4. The following postestimation command was used to test whether the odds for being in poverty were statistically similar for Asians compared to Hispanics:

- ```
  test 2.ethdum = 3.ethdum
  ```
  ```

For the purposes of this analysis, Asian was coded as "2" while Hispanic was coded as "3" in *ethdum*, which is our race/ethnicity variable. As explained in an earlier chapter, the use of the "i." in front of an independent variable informs Stata that the analysis that is specific will treat the variable as a categorical variable, where each category will be used a dummy variable (i.e., Asian will be coded as "1" and all others coded as "0"), and the reference group will by default be the category coded with the lowest value (in our example, non-Hispanic White was coded as "0" and treated as the base).

The following is the output from Stata:

```
. test 2.ethdum = 3.ethdum

 ( 1)   [ceo_poverty]2.ethdum - [ceo_poverty]3.ethdum = 0

           chi2(  1) =      92.66
         Prob > chi2 =       0.0000
```

This commands executes a Wald χ^2 test, which can be used to determine if the odds of Asian is statistically similar to the odds of Hispanic for poverty. The χ^2 value of 92.99, df = 1 with a p-value less than 0.0001 indicated that the associated odds for poverty are statistically different for Asians compared to Hispanics in this analysis. Similarly, the *test* command can be used to determine statistical significance for non-Hispanic Black compared to non-Hispanic Asian, or non-Hispanic Black compared to Hispanic.

INTERPRETATION OF HIERARCHICAL LINEAR MODELING FINDINGS

This series of analyses indicated that the association of race with poverty can vary based on borough-level effects. Once controlling for these variations, Hispanics in New York City had higher odds for poverty even when controlling for disability and other sociodemographic variables. This may be explained by the environmental conditions associated with living in a particular borough. Although New York City has experienced a long period of gentrification, there is considerable variation in geographic locations, especially in the Bronx and certain parts of Brooklyn. It is also important to note that after controlling for borough-level effects, the associations of race with poverty became weaker. This suggests that while race/ethnic difference persisted even when controlling for borough-level effects, a portion of this relationship may be accounted for by the variance found across boroughs. Analyses to examine more specificity in neighborhood and census tract levels can further tease out these neighborhood-level effects and relationships.

GEOMAP VISUALIZATIONS OF POVERTY AND DISABILITY ACROSS CENSUS TRACT LEVELS

A series of geomaps of New York City from the 2014 Center for Economic Opportunity data set are presented here to help to illustrate neighborhood differences as they relate to age, poverty, and disability. These maps were produced using QGIS (formerly known as Quantum GIS), which is a free and open-source software that can be used to handle spatial data and analysis. QGIS is developed and maintained by the QGIS Development Team and can be downloaded from the official QGIS website at (https://www.qgis.org/en/site/).

A new GIS project was created utilizing the NAD83/New York Long Island (ftUS) or ESPG:2263 Coordinate Reference System (CRS). An ESRI (Environmental Systems Research Institute) shapefile, which contained the shape and size of each Public Use MicroData Areas (PUMA) in New York City, was downloaded from the NYC Open Data website. This was added to the GIS project as a vector layer. The 2014 CEO data was *collapsed* at the PUMA level to represent the average poverty and disability at the neighborhood level, and then converted to comma separated value (CSV) format. This data was added to the project as a vector layer for each of the following maps that were produced. The layer referencing the unique shapefile was merged to the CSV files using PUMA as an unique identifier. Data for poverty and disability from the CSV file was linked to the shapefile. Each layer was assigned to a theme, which was used to create a layout in QGIS with a map and scale representative of the percentage of poverty or disability in each census tract or PUMA.

The following is a geomap visualization indicating the density of poverty among the population of 55 and older in New York City.

As shown in Figure 7.1, there are greater concentrations of older adults living in poverty in the Bronx, Queens, and Brooklyn.

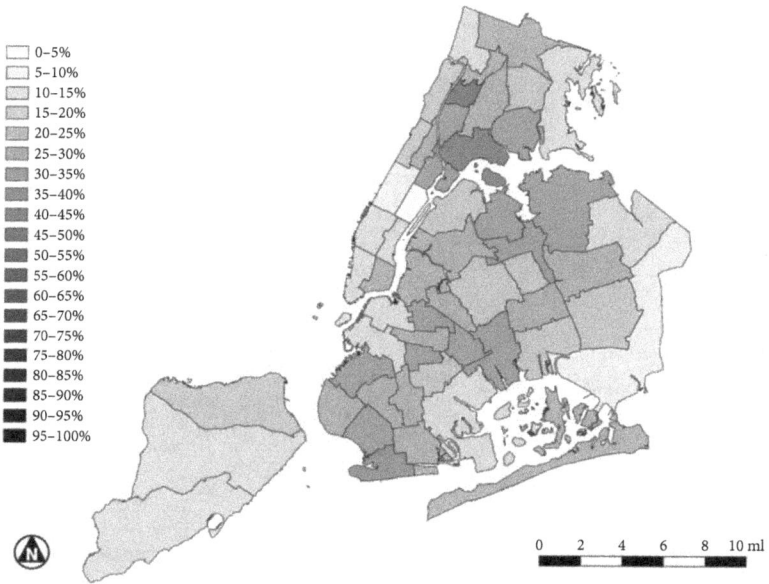

Figure 7.1. Poverty among 55 and older in New York City.

The following is a geomap visualization indicating the density of poverty among those who are 65 and older.

Similar to Figure 7.1, we can observe more clearly that the percentage of those 65 and older living in poverty is higher in the Bronx, Queens, and Brooklyn.

The following is a geomap visualization indicating the density of those with a disability among those 55 and older in New York City.

As shown in Figure 7.3, there is a higher concentration of those with a disability among those who are 55 and older in parts of the Bronx, Queens, and Brooklyn, which corresponds to areas with a higher percentage of poverty.

The following is the same geomap of disability, but for those who are 65 and older.

From Figure 7.4, it can be observed that concentrations of those with a disability are highest in the Bronx, and the pattern is similar to what was observed for poverty among those who are 65 and older.

Figure 7.2. Poverty among 65 and older in New York City.

Figure 7.3. Disability among 55 and older in New York City.

Figure 7.4. Disability among 65 and older in New York City.

GEOMAP VISUALIZATIONS OF POVERTY AND DISABILITY ACROSS RACE GROUPS

The following are geomap visualizations indicating density of poverty (Figure 7.5) and disability (Figure 7.6) for non-Hispanic Whites who are 55 and older.

As shown in Figure 7.5, the concentration of non-Hispanic Whites living in poverty is higher in the Bronx and parts of Brooklyn and Queens. From Figure 7.6, it can be observed that the areas with the highest percentages of disability also have a higher density of poverty, though they are even more concentrated in certain geographical areas.

The following are geomap visualizations indicating density of poverty (Figure 7.7) and disability (Figure 7.8) for non-Hispanic Blacks who are 55 and older.

Compared to non-Hispanic Whites, poverty is more concentrated for non-Hispanic Blacks who are 55 and older (Figure 7.7). There are also higher percentages of non-Hispanic Black older adults with a disability, and they can be found in different geographic areas as compared to non-Hispanic Whites.

Figure 7.5. Poverty among 55 and older non-Hispanic Whites in New York City.

Figure 7.6. Disability among 55 and older non-Hispanic Whites in New York City.

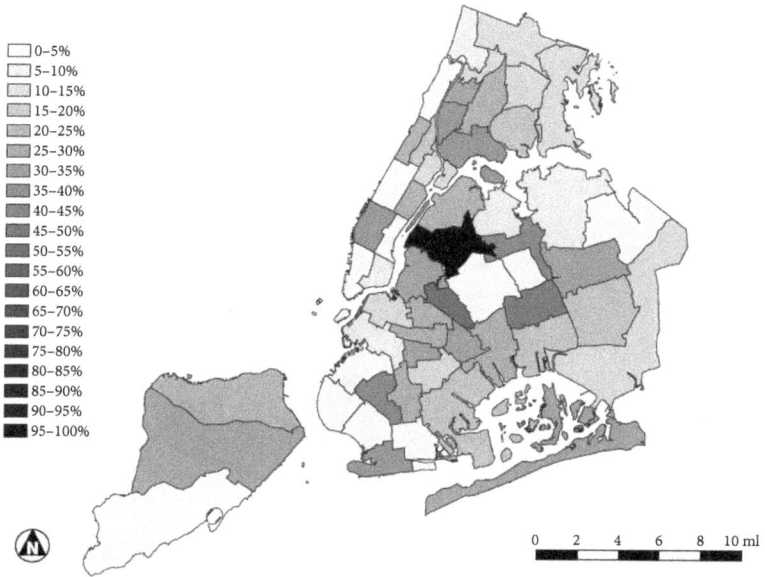

Figure 7.7. Poverty among 55 and older non-Hispanic Blacks in New York City.

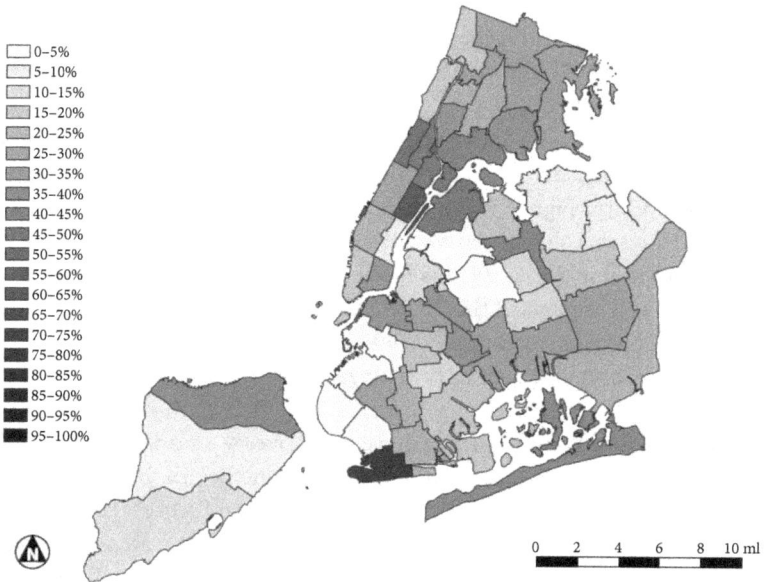

Figure 7.8. Disability among 55 and older non-Hispanic Blacks in New York City.

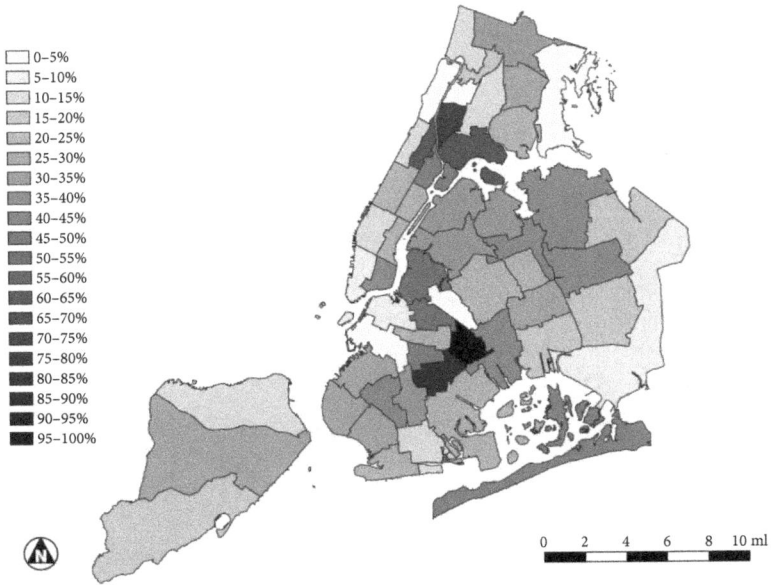

Figure 7.9. Poverty among 55 and older Asians in New York City.

The following are geomap visualizations indicating density of poverty (Figure 7.9) and disability (Figure 7.10) for Asians who are 55 and older.

As shown in Figure 7.9, the density of poverty among Asians 55 and older is similarly specific to certain census tracts as compared to non-Hispanic White (Figure 7.5) and non-Hispanic Black (Figure 7.7) race groups. However, older Asians with a disability are concentrated in different geographic areas, such as lower Manhattan where Chinatown is located as well as parts of the Bronx and Brooklyn.

The following are geomap visualizations indicating density of poverty (Figure 7.11) and disability (Figure 7.12) for Hispanics who are 55 and older.

As shown in Figure 7.11, the density of poverty among Hispanics 55 and older is similarly distributed in parts of the Bronx, Brooklyn, and Queens, but also in Upper Manhattan. As shown in Figure 7.12 and consistent with results from HLM analysis, there are higher rates of disability among older Hispanic adults across all geographic areas in New York City, with concentrated pockets in the Bronx, in parts of Brooklyn, and across areas in Manhattan.

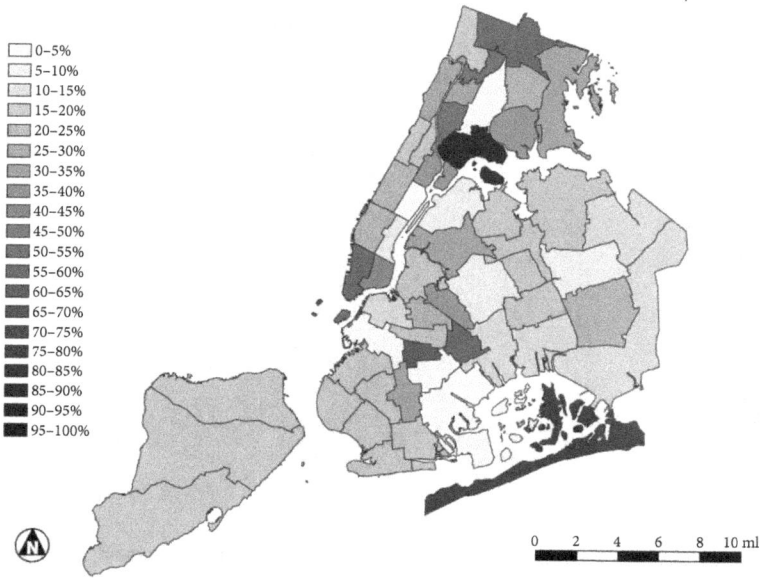

Figure 7.10. Disability among 55 and older Asians in New York City.

Figure 7.11. Poverty among 55 and older Hispanics in New York City.

Figure 7.12. Disability among 55 and older Hispanics in New York City.

CONCLUSION

In this chapter, we discussed the conceptual basis for HLM or mixed modeling for use with cross-cultural groups. We presented an example using the Center for Economic Opportunity data from the U.S. Census, which focused on poverty outcomes for residents of New York City. The analysis indicated that there was a borough-level effect when examining race and ethnic differences in the odds for poverty when controlling for all other sociodemographic variables. We demonstrated the use of the *test* command in Stata, which executed a Wald χ^2 test that can be used to statistically determine the invariance of associations between different cultural groups in HLM analysis. In addition, we included geomap visualizations of the data using QGIS to illustrate census-tract level differences in poverty and disability across various race and ethnic groups of older adults.

We hope the contents of this chapter can be useful for cross-cultural researchers who are interested in examining neighborhood effects for various cultural groups. What we presented in this chapter encompasses some broad considerations for HLM. We recommend using specific grouping variables that have a deeper level of meaning. For our example, we first used borough as a grouping variable. Initial results indicated that there was a borough-level effect. Subsequent analysis found that borough-level effects were no longer observed after accounting for neighborhood-level differences in the analysis. Further analysis is needed to drill down into specific, more meaningful grouping structures. For example, grouping variables such as ethnic enclaves or a ranking of neighborhoods with proximity to ethnic-specific formal and informal supports and services can potentially yield even more meaningful results for interpretation. The process of identifying and determining meaningful grouping structures can be complex and will require other sources of data, which can then be matched based on geocodes for more fine-tuned analyses. This can be accomplished through primary data sources collected from participants in specific neighborhoods, which can then be merged with data from the U.S. Census using unique geocode identifiers.

In conclusion, HLM or mixed modeling is a powerful method of analysis with cross-cultural populations, which can be enhanced with mapping tools such as QGIS. Most importantly, meaningful grouping structures can further disentangle the effects of social determinants on outcomes of interest, such as poverty and disability for cross-cultural populations. Findings from HLM alongside of GIS analysis can inform practice and policy to target resources and interventions for cross-cultural populations that are most in need.

REFERENCES

Chan, K. (2020). Cross-cultural measurement in social work research and evaluation. In C. Franklin (Ed.). *Encyclopedia of Social Work*. New York: NASW Press and Oxford University Press. https://doi.org/10.1093/acrefore/9780199975839.013.1345

Cubbin, C., Marchi, K., Lin, M., Bell, T., Marshall, H., Miller, C., & Braveman, P. (2008). Is neighborhood deprivation independently associated with maternal and infant health? Evidence from Florida and Washington. *Maternal and Child Health Journal, 12*(1), 61–74. https://doi.org/10.1007/s10995-007-0225-0

Diez Roux A. V. (2001). Investigating neighborhood and area effects on health. *American Journal of Public Health, 91*(11), 1783–1789. https://doi.org/10.2105/ajph.91.11.1783

Grady S. C. (2006). Racial disparities in low birthweight and the contribution of residential segregation: A multilevel analysis. *Social Science & Medicine (1982), 63*(12), 3013–3029. https://doi.org/10.1016/j.socscimed.2006.08.017

Guo, S. (2013). Advanced statistical analysis. In C. Franklin (Ed.). *Encyclopedia of Social Work*. New York: NASW Press and Oxford University Press. https://doi.org/10.1093/acrefore/9780199975839.013.840

Kaya, S., & Rice, D. C. (2010). Multilevel effects of student and classroom factors on elementary science achievement in five countries. *International Journal of Science Education, 32*(10), 1337–1363. doi:10.1080/09500690903049785

Luke, D. A. (2004). *Multilevel modeling*. Thousand Oaks, CA: Sage Publications.

Mayor's Office of Operations, The City of New York. (2017). *New York City Government Poverty Measure 2005–2015*. Retrieved fromhttp://www1.nyc.gov/assets/opportunity/pdf/NYCgovPovMeas2017-WEB.pdf

Pew Research Center. (2018). *Income inequality in the U.S. is rising most rapidly among Asians: Asians displace blacks as the most economically divided group in the U.S.* Retrieved from https://www.pewsocialtrends.org/2018/07/12/income-inequality-in-the-u-s-is-rising-most-rapidly-among-asians/

Raudenbush, S. W. (2004). *HLM 6: Hierarchical linear and nonlinear modeling*. Lincolnwood, IL: Scientific Software International.

StataCorp. (2017). *Stata 15 Base Reference Manual*. College Station, TX: Stata Press.

StataCorp. (2017). *Stata Statistical Software: Release 15*. College Station, TX: StataCorp.

8

Conclusion and
Future Directions

Defining culture in scholarship and research is a complex task. Across disciplines, there seems to be an unequivocal consensus that culture is an essential component of human nature, which includes human behavior, socialization, and social structure. Current social work education aims to promote cultural awareness and competency and to increase an understanding of diversity in practice. There is, however, insufficient training in cross-cultural analysis and cross-cultural comparison, especially regarding the potential outcomes that arise from the delivery of social services and implementation of interventions for vulnerable populations.

We made a modest attempt to provide practical guides for social work students and researchers who are interested in making cross-cultural comparisons in their research. Our view is that the field of cross-cultural research is vast and remains underdeveloped in social work. Using appropriate data analysis strategies is crucially important to providing accurate answers to program evaluation and research questions. We use the Stata statistical package to demonstrate the application of statistical approaches used by social work students and

Applied Cross-Cultural Data Analysis for Social Work. Thanh V. Tran and Keith T. Chan,
Oxford University Press. © Oxford University Press 2021. DOI: 10.1093/oso/9780190888510.003.0008

researchers. Although most techniques used in this book can be replicated with other statistical packages, we believe that, overall, Stata is more affordable and comprehensive. We recognize that most social work students and researchers are familiar with SPSS and that transitioning to another statistical package will require some amount of effort, but the transition from SPSS to Stata is fairly smooth and achievable for users. In addition, Stata has statistical applications that are not found in SPSS. Increasing numbers of social work doctoral students in many schools of social work are using large-scale data sets for their dissertation research; in addition, the volume of publications by social work faculty who used large-scale data sets has increased steadily in the past two decades. Thus, it is important for social work students and researchers to be able to handle complex survey data in their research to arrive at the appropriate answers. Stata handles complex survey designs in data analysis fairly well and easily. If readers follow the examples we provide in this book, they can replicate them in their data analysis with no problems. We realize there are some redundancies presented in the process of data analysis throughout the various chapters of the book. Our aim, however, is to help readers follow examples without having to return to the previous sections or chapters to find relevant information or guides.

SUMMARY OF THE CHAPTERS

We began this book with a discussion of culture and its relation to social work. We then guided readers through the process of data management and the use of descriptive statistic techniques to describe differences among cultural groups. After preparing and describing the data, we demonstrated and illustrated the application of linear regression analysis in cross-cultural analysis with an emphasis on interaction effect analysis and subgroup comparisons. In Chapter 5, we explained logistic regression for binary dependent variables and provided several examples to help readers apply their own statistical approach in cross-cultural analysis. In particular, we demonstrated the application of useful procedures to compare the results among cultural groups. We introduced the concept of additive interaction and showed readers how to compute and interpret additive interaction in cross-cultural research, as well as testing equivalence of causal relationships among variables of interests across different cultural groups. In Chapter 6, we demonstrated the use SEM through the use of Stata to compare causal coefficients across cultural groups. We demonstrated the analysis using Stata for SEM rather than other packages such as LISREL. In Chapter 7, we included an introduction to the application of hierarchical linear modeling (HLM) in cross-cultural research. This method of analysis has not been sufficiently explored in social work research, and it can be a highly useful and appropriate statistical approach for making cross-cultural comparisons. When paired with geomap visualizations, researchers can have greater explanatory power when examining differences based on geographic areas and distributions.

LIMITATIONS

Cross-cultural analysis and comparisons are complicated and demanding. First, we need to ask the right questions, have the appropriate data, and be able to identify comparable measurements of the research variables. We also have to apply appropriate statistical techniques and approaches to find appropriate and accurate answers to our research questions. The data and examples we present throughout the book do not capture all aspects of cultural analysis and comparison. Like other statistical methods, the statistical approaches we introduced in this book do not capture all the nuances of cross-cultural analyses. It is important to always be cautious in drawing conclusions about cross-cultural similarities or differences based on statistical results. Although no statistical method can offer definitive conclusions, cross-cultural researchers can provide convincing evidence through factual data and interpretations that can inform ways to advance the needs of vulnerable populations.

FUTURE DIRECTIONS

The field of social work needs to pay greater attention to cross-cultural analyses and comparisons. This area of practice and research should be infused in all levels of social work education. Both qualitative and quantitative approaches of cross-cultural comparison should be utilized in program development and program evaluation. We recommend the following:

1. Undergraduate social work programs should teach students basic concepts of culture and the role of culture in human development, social problems, social structures, and social services.
2. At the Master of Social Work (MSW) level, students should be taught how to apply research methods in the context of cross-cultural investigations and analyses. Students should be competent in the assessment of cross-cultural comparability of evidence-based practice and outcome measurement.
3. Finally, at the doctoral level of social work education (PhD or DSW), students should be taught how to apply advanced statistical methods and approaches in the study of cross-cultural differences in all aspects of social work.

We hope this book can make a small contribution to the field of cross-cultural social work research. It is not an exaggeration to say that all social work practice and research are cross-cultural, and examination of culture is at the center of social work research, education, and practice.

Index

Tables and figures are indicated by *t* and *f* following the page number.